PRINCETON THEOLOGICAL MONOGRAPH

Series

Dikran Y. Hadidian

General Editor

D0872134

3

TRADITION RENEWED

The Oxford Movement Conference Papers

Tradition Renewed

*The Oxford Movement
Conference Papers*

Edited by
Geoffrey Rowell

Pickwick Publications
Allison Park, Pennsylvania

First published in Great Britain in 1986 by
DARTON LONGMAN & TODD LTD

and in the USA in 1986 by
PICKWICK PUBLICATIONS
4137 Timberlane Drive
Allison Park, PA 15101

Library of Congress Cataloging-in-Publication Data

Oxford Movement Conference (1983: Oxford University)
  Tradition renewed.

  (Princeton theological monograph series; 3)
  1. Oxford movement—Congresses. 2. Anglo-
Catholicism—Congresses. 3. Anglican Communion—
Doctrines—Congresses. I. Rowell, Geoffrey. II. Title.
III. Series.
BX5100.093 1983   283′.09′034   85–32078
ISBN 0–915138–82–4

Phototypeset by Input Typesetting Ltd, London SW19 8DR
Printed in Great Britain by Anchor Brendon Ltd
Tiptree, Essex

Contents

The Contributors

A. M. Allchin is a residentiary Canon of Canterbury Cathedral and Warden of the Sisters of the Love of God, of Fairacres, Oxford. He is the author of several books of which the most recent is *The Joy of All Creation* (London 1984). He is at present working on a book on the doctrine of deification in Anglican tradition, to be called *Participation in God*.

Frederick Houk Borsch is Dean of the Chapel and Lecturer with the rank of Professor in the Department of Religion at Princeton University. He is a graduate of Princeton University (AB), Oxford University (MA), the General Theological Seminary (STB), and the University of Birmingham (Ph.D). He was formerly Dean and Professor of New Testament at the Church Divinity School of the Pacific. He is the author of a number of books, including *The Son of Man in Myth and History*, *God's Parables*, and *Power in Weakness*.

Reginald H. Fuller was until recently Professor of New Testament at the Virginia Theological Seminary. Born and educated in England, he is the author of numerous articles and books on New Testament theology, and has a long-standing interest in the Anglican Evangelical tradition.

Dr Sheridan Gilley, Senior Lecturer in the Department of Theology of the University of Durham, is the author of numerous articles on modern English and Roman Catholic religious history. He is the recent co-editor, with Dr Roger Swift, of *The Irish in the Victorian City* (London 1985), which contains a number of studies of the religion of Irish immigrants in nineteenth-century Britain.

Dr Alf Härdelin, born in 1927, is Docent at the University of Uppsala. He has published *The Tractarian Understanding of the Eucharist* (Uppsala 1965) and papers on other aspects of the nineteenth century Church renewal. His main field of research is now the spirituality, liturgy and culture of the early medieval church. Publications in this domain include *Aquae et vini mysterium* (Münster 1973) and numerous anthologies, papers and review articles. Forthcoming are a study of early medieval Christian literature and a collection of Latin office hymns in Swedish translation with commentary.

Barnabas Lindars SSF has been Rylands Professor of Biblical Criticism and Exegesis, Manchester University, since 1978. Educated at Altrincham Grammar School, St John's College, Cambridge, and Westcott House, Cambridge, he saw war service from 1943 to 1945. He was ordained deacon in 1948, priest in 1949 and was Curate of St Luke's Pallion, Sunderland, 1948–52. He has been a member of the Society of St Francis from 1952. He was appointed Assistant Lecturer in Divinity at Cambridge University 1961–6 and Lecturer 1966–78, and was Fellow and Dean of Jesus College, Cambridge, 1976–8. His publications include *New Testament Apologetic* (1961), *The Gospel of John* (New Century Bible, 1972) and *Jesus Son of Man* (1983).

Andrew Louth is Head of the Department of Religious Studies at Goldsmith's College, London, and was formerly Fellow, Chaplain and Tutor in Theology at Worcester College, Oxford. He is the author of *The Origins of the Christian Mystical Tradition* and *Discerning the Mystery: an essay on the nature of theology*.

David Nicholls is Vicar of Littlemore. Author of *The Pluralist State* and two books on Haiti, he is giving the Hulsean Lectures at Cambridge (1985–6), which he hopes to publish under the title *Deity and Domination*.

Peter Nockles studied Modern History at Worcester College, Oxford. He wrote a doctoral thesis on 'Continuity and Change in Anglican High Churchmanship in Britain, 1792–1850' and is the author of 'Pusey and the Question of Church and State' in *Pusey Rediscovered*, ed. Perry Butler (London 1983). He contributed a major chapter on 'The Oxford Movement and the University' for volume VI in *The History of the University of Oxford*, and also the nineteenth-century chapter in a *History of Canterbury Cathedral*. Since 1980 he has been Assistant Librarian in the John Rylands Library, University of Manchester.

W. S. F. Pickering is a Lecturer in Sociology in the Department of Religious Studies in the University of Newcastle upon Tyne. In 1951 he was ordained priest in the Church of England. He has written several books on the French sociologist, Emile Durkheim. He has also been involved in editing and contributing to two books concerned with issues common to sociology and theology. *A Social History of the Diocese of Newcastle* appeared in 1981. At the moment he is writing a book on Anglo-catholicism.

Geoffrey Rowell is Fellow, Chaplain and Tutor in Theology at Keble College, Oxford, and a University Lecturer. He is the author of *Hell and the Victorians*, *The Liturgy of Christian Burial* and *The Vision Glorious* (published in 1983 to mark the 150th anniversary of the Oxford Movement). He is a Canon of Chichester Cathedral and a member of the Liturgical Commission and has a long-standing interest in ecumenical relations with the Eastern churches.

Richard Sharp was born in 1953 and educated at the Royal Grammar School in Newcastle and Jesus College, Cambridge, where he read history. After working in the Northumberland County Record Office, he began research at Jesus College, Oxford, on the eighteenth-century High Church tradition. In 1980 he published an account of the Newcastle nonjuring congregation in *Archaeologia Aeliana*. He has taught at Dulwich College and Abingdon School and hopes soon to return to the north-east to work on a new biography of the First Earl of Eldon.

Stephen Whitefield Sykes is the Regius Professor of Divinity at the University of Cambridge, an Honorary Canon of Ely Cathedral and Fellow of St John's College, Cambridge. He was formerly Van Mildert Professor at the University of Durham 1974–85 and Fellow and Dean of St John's College, Cambridge, 1964–74. He was the Edward Cadbury Lecturer, University of Birmingham, 1977–8 and Hensley Henson Lecturer in the University of Oxford 1982–3. He is the author of *Friedrich Schleiermacher* (1971); *Christian Theology Today* (1971 and 1983); *The Integrity of Anglicanism* (1978); and editor of *Karl Barth, Studies of his theological methods* (1980); *New Studies in Theology* (1980); *England and Germany, Studies in Theological Diplomacy* (1982); and *The Identity of Christianity* (1984).

Gordon Wakefield is a Methodist minister and Principal of The Queen's College, Birmingham, where Anglican, Methodist and United Reformed Church students are trained ecumenically for ministry. He has written widely on spirituality, often from an historical perspective, and is editor of the SCM *Dictionary of Christian Spirituality*.

Sister Benedicta Ward SLG is a member of the Community of the sisters of the Love of God. She also holds a doctorate from Oxford for a thesis now published under the title *Miracles and the Medieval Mind* (London 1980). Her other published works include *Prayers and Meditations of St Anselm of Canterbury* (London 1973 and 1980); *Sayings of the Desert Fathers* (Oxford 1979 and 1983); *Lives of the Desert Fathers* (Oxford 1982); *Wisdom of Fathers* (Oxford 1979 and 1986). She teaches for the Centre for Medieval Studies in Oxford as well as for the University.

The Rev. Louis Weil STD (Institut Catholique, Paris). Since 1971 Professor of Liturgics and Church Music at Nashotah House (USA). The author of numerous articles and reviews, he has contributed to several books: *To be a Priest*; co-author *Liturgy for Living* in the Episcopal Church Teaching Series; *Sacraments and Liturgy* (1983). He is a graduate of Southern Methodist University, Harvard, the General Theological Seminary, and a member of the North American Academy of Liturgy.

Foreword

The Archbishop of Canterbury

There can have been few movements in the history of the Church of England which have touched so many dimensions of Christian life as the Oxford Movement. Much of what it stood for can still speak powerfully to our own secular society: the centrality of prayer and sacrament, the primacy of God in national life, the pastoral reponsibility of priesthood, the search for authentic Christian spirituality.

These anniversary essays celebrate not only the Oxford Movement, but also all those sources of energy and renewal which flow from God and from the Church, catholic and universal, at vital moments in history. If, in its early years, the Oxford Movement gave English Christianity what Pusey called 'many pearls of controversy', it also gave us, in its dedicated and disciplined quest for catholicity, the vision of a united Church. For this, perhaps above all else, we remain deeply indebted.

Lambeth Palace
May 1986

Message of Greeting to the 1983 Conference

Pope John Paul II

His Holiness Pope John Paul II has learned with interest of the Conference and other celebrations that have been arranged to mark the 150th Anniversary of the beginning of the Oxford Movement in the Church of England. As is well known, this was by no means the least of the factors that was to play a significant part in the renewed efforts for reconciliation between the Anglican Communion and the Catholic Church, which after so many years are bearing evident fruit. Many names such as those of John Keble and Edward B. Pusey will always have an honoured place in the history of our long pilgrimage of reconciliation, and if Cardinal John Henry Newman is singled out for special mention, it is because 'As a leading figure of the Oxford Movement, and later as a promoter of authentic renewal in the Catholic Church, Newman is seen to have a special ecumenical vocation not only for his own country but also for the whole Church' (Letter of Pope John Paul II to Archbishop George Patrick Dywer of Birmingham, 7 April 1979).

It is the prayer of His Holiness that the present celebrations may be richly blessed by the Holy Spirit 'who alone can lead us to the day when we will profess the fullness of our faith together' (Pope John Paul II, Homily in Canterbury Cathedral, 29 May 1982).

Acknowledgements

I am grateful to the many who helped in many different ways at the time of the conference in 1983 thus coming to the aid of one who had foolishly dreamed of an international conference and had tried to run it single-handed; and to the contributors for their patience both before and during the conference and for revising their texts for publication. In particular Mrs Pauline Valentine, the Fellows' secretary at Keble, has given cheerful and invaluable assistance in typing some of the papers, and Mr Patrick Lambe, a former pupil, has helped with the editorial chores.

Two of the papers reproduced here have been published earlier in journals: Dr Borsch's paper appeared in the *Anglican Theological Review*, lxvi:4 (1984); and a longer version of Professor Lindars' paper was published in the *Bulletin of the John Rylands Library*, 66:2 (1984).

DGR

Note on References

References to the *Tracts for the Times* give the Tract number and title only. Fuller bibliographical details are as follows:

Tracts for the Times by Members of the University of Oxford, 7 vols (London and Oxford 1835–41):

Tracts	1–46	Vol. I	for 1833–4	(1835)
	47–70	Vol. II	for 1834–5	(1836)
	71–77	Vol. III	for 1835–6	(1837)
	78–82	Vol. IV	for 1836–7	(1838)
	83–88	Vol. V	for 1838–40	(1840)
	89	–		(1840)
	90	–		(1841)

Introduction
Geoffrey Rowell

In 1933 the centenary of the Oxford Movement was celebrated with publications, a great congress and services, meetings and addresses in Oxford, London and elsewhere. A 150th anniversary does not merit the celebrations of a centenary but was marked none the less in 1983. The fifty years between 1933 and 1983 were years of great and increasing change, and the character and context of both the Church of England and the Anglican Communion are very different in the 1980s to what they had been in the 1930s. Fifty years ago there would be much talk of colonial bishops and colonial churches. Today the churches of the Anglican Communion, like the former British imperial possessions, are independent, and the fastest growing churches are not in England but in Africa. The Second World War changed society in England and elsewhere. Secularisation and a smaller world are both part of that changed context. Ecumenically relations between the churches are closer, and most significantly between the Anglican Communion and the Roman Catholic Church, yet ecumenical co-operation has also brought with it questions of identity which have posed particular problems for the Anglican inheritance.

The whole Anglican Communion is a sharer in the Oxford Movement inheritance, which has an influence beyond the consciously 'catholic' in churchmanship. Other churches in the English-speaking world and beyond have also been influenced by some of the important contributions of English catholicism. That Catholic tradition however has never existed alone. It has always understood itself in relation to the Church of the early centuries, and the great communions of the Roman Catholic Church and the Orthodox churches of the East. It was those influenced by the Oxford Movement who first sought to build ecumenical bridges to these great churches, in ways which have born rich fruit in the participation of the Orthodox in the World Council of Churches on the one hand, and in the Anglican-Roman Catholic International Commission on the other. Yet it cannot be doubted that the Second Vatican Council was something of a watershed for Anglicans (and in a special way for those in the Catholic tradition) as well as for Roman Catholics. Not only was this true in the ecumenical dimension; the liturgical reforms which were an important part of Vatican II had the effect of changing what was,

at least informally, normative for Catholic Anglicans. Moreover the
'reformed catholicism' of Vatican II laid down an implicit challenge
to the much older 'reformed catholicism' of Anglicanism. In a
different area both the 'secular' theology of the 1960s and a resurgent
conservative evangelicalism modified the character of the Church of
England. More recently feminist theology and the associated question
of the ordination of women have put questions of authority and of
Catholic identity to the Anglican Catholic tradition.

It was against this shifting background, which demonstrated, if
demonstration were needed, that Anglican catholicism even more
than its Roman Catholic counterpart is not monolithic, that the
commemoration of the 150th anniversary of the Oxford Movement
was planned. In Oxford the major public events were a sermon
preached by Bishop Trevor Huddleston, CR, in the University Church
of St Mary the Virgin on 14 July 1983, the exact anniversary date
of John Keble's 1833 Assize Sermon, and two days later a Pilgrimage
Eucharist in the University Parks, at which the Archbishop of Canterbury was the chief celebrant and preacher. During the week in which
these events took place an academic conference was held at Keble
College, which was attended by some two hundred people from
England, America and other parts of the world. At the end of the
week this congress joined forces with the Religious Communities
Conference to hear two more papers particularly concerned with the
Religious Life, whose revival in the Anglican Communion was a
notable result of the Oxford Movement. Alongside the conference
there were exhibitions of ecclesiastical art and original documents of
the time of the Oxford Movement.

The papers delivered aimed at historical reassessment and critical
appraisal of the Oxford Movement and theological renewal of its
continuing influence in the Anglican Communion. It was generally
recognised that the contributions had been of a very high standard
and that the aims of the conference would be best served by giving
them a more permanent form. This book is the result of that
endeavour and includes all the papers save that of Fr Jerome Vereb,
CP, of the Secretariat for Christian Unity in Rome, whose text was
not in the end available, through no fault of his own. The first three
contributions analyse the high church tradition in Anglicanism in
the century preceding the Oxford Movement and the reactions of
older high churchmen to the Tractarian programme. There are
important re-evaluations here of the vitality of the tradition on the
one hand and the question of continuity and innovation on the other.
The spirituality and sacramental theology of the Tractarians is then
analysed, Dr Härdelin's paper leading into the important reflections
on the nature of the theological enterprise discussed by Andrew
Louth in his comparison of Newman and Gadamer. Liturgy, episcopacy, and the tensions in Anglo-Catholic political thought receive
attention. Dr Pickering's paper looks at some of the sociological

reasons for the changing position and character of Anglo-catholicism since the heady days of the Anglo-Catholic congresses. An Evangelical and a Methodist scholar then give their evaluations of the Oxford Movement and its inheritance, followed by two contributions on the Religious Life. In the final chapter A. M. Allchin looks at the relationship of theology and spirituality in the Oxford Movement with a particular concern for unity.

This series of studies, provoked by a particular anniversary, are published with the hope that the kind of critical reflection they embody may contribute to the renewal of a great tradition within Anglicanism and indeed within the whole Church. What was first heard in Oxford during one of the hottest weeks of summer for many years is now offered to a wider public with that end in view.

1

New Perspectives on the High Church Tradition: historical background 1730–1780*

Richard Sharp

When John William Burgon, a former Fellow of Oriel College, Oxford, and a lifelong observer of the ascendant fortunes of Tractarianism, published his *Lives of Twelve Good Men* in 1888, he ventured a gentle protest against what he regarded as the corresponding and undeserved eclipse of the reputation of the old high churchmen. It was important, he claimed, not to forget that 'the cheerful blaze which followed the efforts made in 1832–4 . . . had been the residuum of the altar-fires of a long succession of holy and earnest men'.[1] The remark was timely, for although a few of Burgon's contemporaries retained a sympathy for those whom Dean Church graciously acknowledged as 'the manly school, distrustful of high-wrought feelings and professions', less favourable images were coming to prevail.[2] The social conservatism of the old high churchmen, which was usually expressed as political Toryism, with their sustained attachment to the principle of the confessional state and their consistent suspicion of Roman catholicism and Protestant dissent, engendered little sympathy in a post-Reform Bill State and a post-Tractarian Church. Criticism of the old high churchmen came both from the Church's political and ecclesiastical rivals, who depicted them as politically intolerant and spiritually apathetic: 'the Tory Party at Prayer' distinguished only by 'love of tithes and hatred of methodists'; and also from the Tractarians themselves. 'Primitive Christianity . . . had well-nigh faded out of the land, through the political changes of the last 150 years', alleged Newman characteristically; the high church tradition accordingly was thought to have lapsed either into 'high and dry' spiritual aridity, or into the self-indulgent complacency of those whom John Keble memorably castigated in 1839 as 'the old orthodox two-bottles'.[3]

A strikingly different impression of the old high churchmen emerges from a study of the 1730s, when the Church faced a crisis that remarkably resembled that of 1833. Then, as at the time of Keble's Assize Sermon, high churchmen felt threatened by ministerial indifference or even hostility. Sir Robert Walpole's dalliance with the

Quakers and the Dissenting Deputies had revived the prospect of the overthrow of the Church's defences: the Test Act, subscription to the Thirty-Nine Articles, and maintenance by tithe. Simultaneously the deistical controversy had reached its height, and countless sermons and charges testified to the extent of orthodox concern with the apparent spread of vice in all sections of the community, from the fashionable masquerade to the vulgar gin-shop. Within the Church itself, under the influence of men such as William Whiston and Samuel Clarke, it seemed that Arian heresy had gained alarming ground. The nomination of Dr Thomas Rundle, a friend of Clarke's, to be Bishop of Gloucester in 1734, provoked a powerful, and ultimately successful, clerical opposition, in a case that anticipated many features of the campaigns of 1836 and 1848 against Dr Hampden. Nor was Rundle the only threat to the integrity of an apostolic episcopate, for Benjamin Hoadly, already notorious in orthodox eyes for his part in the Bangorian controversy of 1717–19, re-entered contention in 1735 with a minimalising treatise on the Eucharist, *The Plain Account of the Sacrament of the Lord's Supper*.[4]

At the same time the Church's claim to exercise judgment in matters of faith had come under renewed attack. In 1735 a major controversy was precipitated by the decision of Dr Thomas Coney, the high church Rector of Bath, to refuse communion to a visiting minister, a Mr Jackson, who was suspected of Arian sympathies. Jackson's grievances were taken up by James Foster, a dissenting minister, who used arguments derived from John Locke and Benjamin Hoadly to deny that the Church had power to assess issues of faith, or any other matter not 'of importance to the cause of solid virtue, or the happiness of mankind'. These claims drew many orthodox retorts, notably from the high churchman Dr Henry Stebbing, who upheld the Church's claim to a divine, not human, commission, and denied that the arbitrary criteria of 'happiness', 'virtue' or 'sincerity' were appropriate measures for assessing the integrity of the faith.[5]

As this and other controversies revealed, high church principles in the 1730s, and throughout the century, were more widely diffused than is often supposed. Nor was promotion confined to men whose theological opinions resembled those of Hoadly, or whose private conduct emulated that of Archbishop Blackburne, the former buccaneer, whose early irregularities readily survived the translation to Bishopthorpe. Among bishops in the 1730s, for example, Edmund Gibson (London) was a prominent antagonist of vice and infidelity; Thomas Sherlock (Salisbury) wrote with distinction in the deistical controversy, and Richard Smalbroke (Lichfield) was a consistent defender of the spiritual and material privileges of the Church against the claims of Hoadly and the Dissenting Deputies. Moreover among archbishops of Canterbury William Wake (1716–37) was noted for his learned interest in the Gallican and Eastern churches; John Potter

(1737–47) had earned the reputation of a high churchman with his early *Discourse on Church Government* (1710); and Thomas Secker (1758–68) was a consistent friend to the claims of episcopacy, not least in Scotland and America. At York Archbishop Dawes (1714–24) shared the high church sympathies of his predecessor John Sharp (1691–1714), and even as late as 1784 it was said that Archbishop Markham's 'nonjuring principles' were his 'brightest jewel'.[6] The ranks of archdeacons likewise contained many distinguished high churchmen, among them Thomas Sharp (Northumberland 1723–58); Daniel Waterland (Middlesex 1730–40); Henry Stebbing (Wiltshire 1735–63); Edward Cobden (London 1742–64); James Ibbetson (St Albans 1754–81) and Thomas Randolph (Oxford 1767–83). Many important parishes maintained consistent high church traditions, including, in London, St Andrew's, Holborn; St Clement Dane's; St Giles, Cripplegate and St Mary-le-Bow.[7]

The strength of the continuing high church influence was also reflected in the contents of clerical libraries. Many contained works by high churchmen on ecclesiastical history and discipline, such as William Cave's *Primitive Christianity* (1673); Jeremy Collier's *Ecclesiastical History* (1708–14); John Sage's *Principles of the Cyprianick Age* (1707); Joseph Bingham's *Ecclesiastical Antiquities* (1708–22) and Nathaniel Marshall's *Penitential Discipline of the Primitive Church* (1714). Works of commentary or controversy reflected a similar orthodox strength; William Law's *Three Letters to the Bishop of Bangor* (1717–19), consolidating the foundation of works such as John Potter's *Discourse on Church-Government* (1710) or John Johnson's *Clergyman's Vade-Mecum* (6th edn, 1731). Bishop Gibson's definitive *Codex Iuris Ecclesiae Anglicani* (1713, reprinted 1761) also maintained a strong orthodox line. Popular religious publishing, similarly, was dominated throughout the century by Rivington's, a high church house which traded under the significantly loyal emblem of the Bible and Crown.[8] Classics, such as Henry Hammond's *Practical Catechism*, with its emphasis on the duty of 'obedience and submission to the Catholic Apostolick Church', retained much of their popularity; the ubiquitous *Whole Duty of Man* (28th edn, 1790) being said to enjoy a prominence second only to that of the Bible and the Book of Common Prayer. Other notably influential high church works included Robert Nelson's *Companion to the Festivals and Fasts* (36th edn, 1826); William Holmes' *Pious Country Parishioner* (32nd edn, 1819), and the anonymous *Week's Preparation for a Worthy Receiving of the Sacrament of the Lord's Supper* (38th edn, 1778).

The strength of high church continuity in the Church's controversial and devotional life throughout the eighteenth century sustains the contention that the nonjuring deprivations of 1690 and 1715 had less contemporary impact than is often supposed. Moreover it can be shown that few friendships were broken by the fact of deprivation: Edward Cobden, Archdeacon of London, for example was speaking representatively when he declared that 'the one error' of 1715 had done nothing to disrupt his lifelong friendship with the nonjuring scholar Edward Holdsworth.[9] As the example of Bishop Ken, Henry Dodwell and Francis Cherry had suggested, many nonjurors were reluctant schismatics, while even among those who persisted in separation many, including Thomas Brett, *primus* from 1726 to 1743, remained on cordial terms with the clergy of the Establishment. Care was frequently taken in cases of deprivation, particularly when private patronage was involved, to ensure that nonjurors were succeeded on easy terms: when John Griffin, for example, a later nonjuring bishop, forfeited his benefice at Sarsden in north Oxfordshire in 1715, the patron, Sir John Walter, a former Queen Anne Tory MP and enthusiastic partisan of Dr Sacheverell, took care to appoint a High Tory successor who was later to act as Griffin's executor, administering several nonjuring bequests, in 1731.

Such friendships were facilitated by the frequent and continuing theological accord that existed between conforming and nonjuring high churchmen. Many conforming churchmen, from Archbishop Sharp at the beginning of the century to Bishop Horsley at the end, freely admitted their preference for features of the English 1549 and Scottish 1637 liturgies over the existing order of the Book of Common Prayer. Notable conforming commentators, such as Charles Wheatly or John Johnson, expressed liturgical preferences that corresponded to those embodied in the advanced 'usager' nonjuring liturgy of 1718, while more general nonjuring scholarship and devotion was widely esteemed. As late as 1791 works by Charles Leslie, Henry Dodwell, Thomas Brett, Robert Nelson, Nathaniel Spinckes and William Law featured in a list of books recommended to younger clergy by the orthodox Bishop of Chester, William Cleaver; while Dr George Horne, Bishop of Norwich, regarded the *Works* of Charles Leslie as 'a library in themselves to any young student of the Church of England'.[10]

To conforming high churchmen therefore it seemed that the nonjurors' sacrifices had been made in a political rather than a religious cause. Bishop Sherlock spoke for many when he acknowledged the nonjurors' 'courage and plainness' but wished them 'what I think they well deserve, a better cause'. Even political differences were limited.[11] Both groups shared the fundamental Tory conviction memorably expressed by John Wesley, that 'God, and not the people [was] the original of all civil power',[12] with the corresponding belief that, as Dr Johnson put it, 'the first Whig was the Devil'.[13] Both also adhered to the doctrines of passive-obedience and non-resistance as necessary to the preservation of society: a fact illustrated by the continuing popularity of traditional texts inculcating the duty of submission to authority, such as Romans 13 and 1 Peter 2:17. Unlike nonjurors, however, conforming high churchmen repudiated arguments based upon notions of indefeasible hereditary succession as an innovation, which they traced to the failure of seventeenth-century theorists such as Archbishop Laud, Robert Filmer and Thomas Hobbes, to distinguish the obedience due to *executive* power, which they saw as limited and conditional, from that due to *legislative* power, which, as Archbishop Sharp had declared, must be unlimited, 'otherwise the Government would be precarious, and the Publick Peace at the Mercy of every Malcontent'.[14] Although Tories, therefore, eighteenth-century high churchmen repudiated Jacobitism and retained their benefices with a good conscience. Their assurance was strengthened by the argument, current in standard works of reference, that Christ himself had inculcated obedience to the powers actually in possession, by his answer to the Pharisees in Matthew 22:20–1.[15]

Nor were the old high churchmen, unlike some later writers, inclined to accept that the nonjurors had been 'pioneering in the attempt to save the Church from Erastianism . . . surely asserting the rights of individuals and minorities against the omnicompetence of the Hobbesian State'.[16] Even in the Hanoverian Settlement they saw little cause to abandon what they regarded, with Richard Hooker, as the positive advantages of the mutually-sustaining relationship of Church and State. Memories of the Civil War, which remained vivid for over a century, were constantly invoked to demonstrate how civil and religious disorder might again ensue upon the overthrow of the Establishment.[17] Issues that were later to provoke Tractarian sensibilities had little impact on eighteenth-century churchmen. Even the *congé d'élire*, as Bishop Gibson's *Codex* demonstrated, did not usurp the Church's ultimate and exclusive right in spirituals, while even high churchmen such as Bishop Smalbroke acknowledged that the suspension of regular sittings of convocation in 1717 had been necessary to protect 'the Peace and Tranquility of the Publick' after the 'Heats and Animosities' of previous years.[18]

Throughout the eighteenth century high churchmen retained a clear view of the true nature of their calling. 'No human laws can destroy or deprive us of . . . the spiritual authority we are intrusted with, as ministers of Christ at large', noted Thomas Sharp in his definitive work, *The Rubrick . . . consider'd* (1753).[19] Consequently when Bishop Warburton's famous work on *The Alliance of Church and State* appeared in 1736, acclamation was less extensive than some later writers supposed: rather, as John Nichols noted, 'the old orthodox phalanx was highly scandalized, that the author should . . . subject the Church to such a humiliating dependence on the State'.[20] Equally forceful was the response in 1748 when a clause in the Bill for Disarming the Highlands appeared to allow the government discretion to decree the invalidity of orders granted by Scottish bishops. The measure was opposed by every bishop in the House of Lords: it was, said Thomas Secker, later Archbishop of Canterbury, a matter that 'no true member of the Church of England will allow the civil authority to have anything to do with'.[21]

Such confidence in the Church's independent commission was sustained by the general belief that the Church of England was a branch of the Church universal, professing what Jude 3 called 'the faith once delivered to the Saints', and holding the teaching of the first general councils and the catholic creeds.[22] The Athanasian Creed in particular was jealously defended, as preserving the *depositum* of the faith in accordance with the apostolic precept to 'hold fast the form of sound words' (2 Tim. 2:13), but comparable claims were made for the liturgy as a whole, which was seen to conform more closely than any other to the customs of the primitive Church.[23] Frequent appeals to the Fathers, in particular SS Cyprian, Ignatius and Irenaeus, were made in defence of these claims, while the famous maxims of Tertullian (*Verum quodcunque primum, adulterum quodcunque posterius*) and of Vincentius (*Verum quod semper, quod ubique, quod ab omnibus*) were also widely known and approved.[24] Popular texts like Proverbs 24:21 and Jeremiah 6:16 endorsed the ensuing conservative outlook, which high churchmen such as Henry Stebbing could express in terms of emphatic brevity: 'Faith is subject to no variation.'[25]

The old high churchmen's suspicion of change was exemplified by their constant attachment to the Book of Common Prayer as 'the most primitive and compleat collection of publick Devotion in the World'.[26] Its excellence, said Charles Wheatly, was 'deservedly admired by the eastern churches, and by the most eminent Protestants beyond the seas . . . [and] in short, honoured by all but the Romanist, whose interest it opposeth, and the Dissenters, whose prejudices will not let them see its lustre'.[27] To depart from its forms was seen both as unjustifiable and as a breach of necessary Church unity, which, as a commentator of 1737 expressed it, 'should be testified by *Uniformity* and *Agreement* in publick prayer; glorifying God with *one* mind and *one* mouth'.[28] Careful adherence to the rubricks was seen, accordingly, as the most distinctive characteristic of high churchmen, but it is important to notice that it was often subject in practice to Bishop Beveridge's often-quoted reservation, that 'charity is above rubricks'.[29] The ensuing readiness to subordinate private preferences to the greater needs of unity constituted one of the greatest differences between the eighteenth-century high churchmen and their nineteenth-century successors. In his treatment of the ornaments rubrick, for example, Dr Thomas Sharp exemplified this approach when he wrote in 1753 that 'since the *use* of hoods and *disuse* of Copes and Tunicles are now so notoriously and universally allowed of by the Ordinaries . . . although neither of them could in strictness be reconciled with the letter of the Rubrick, yet we are not *bound*, at this time, to make any alteration in our practice'.[30]

A similar pragmatism was displayed by Charles Wheatly, whose *Rational Illustration of the Book of Common Prayer* (8th edn, 1759) may be claimed as the definitive liturgical commentary of the age. A study of Wheatly's career provides insights into many aspects of eighteenth-century high churchmanship. His school, Merchant Taylors', maintained a tradition of unrivalled orthodoxy from the days of Lancelot Andrewes to those of William van Mildert. It had been conspicuous for loyalty during the Civil War: Bishops Buckeridge, Juxon and Wren had numbered among its *alumni*. One headmaster had been deprived for royalism in 1644, another for converting to Rome in 1686, while a third, Ambrose Bonwicke, was ejected as a nonjuror in 1691.[31] Wheatly's years in the school coincided with those of future nonjurors, such as John Byrom, and of distinguished future high churchmen including Henry Stebbing, William Berriman and Alexander Catcott, the latter an early Hutchinsonian.[32] From Merchant Taylors' Wheatly removed in 1705 to St John's College in Oxford, the college of Archbishop Laud and of many nonjurors including Dr Richard Rawlinson, the antiquary and bishop. In 1707 he was elected Fellow, and in 1726 was presented to the united benefices of Brent and Furneaux-Pelham in Hertfordshire. On his death in 1742 he was buried in the church at Furneaux-Pelham, where a monument ventured cautiously to invite intercession for his soul.[33]

Wheatly published widely. In addition to the *Rational Illustration* there were works on the Eucharist, on the creeds, and against the perils, as he saw them, of George Whitefield's Methodists. His many sermons revealed him as no mere 'high and dry' churchman: many were concerned with mystical speculations, while others explored the nature and ministry of angels. A catholic understanding of the communion of saints was consistently developed, with the teaching that the Church was a universal society comprehending 'all God's servants from the beginning of the World ... the Patriarchs, Prophets, Apostles and Martyrs'.[34]

In the *Rational Illustration* Wheatly maintained the claims of the Church to a spiritual commission independent of any reliance on the State, although, as he noted, in normal circumstances, 'we must pray for the prosperity of both, since they mutually defend and support each other'.[35] He reminded readers that St Ambrose had refused communion to the Emperor Theodosius, and that 'there may be a Church where there is no Christian civil magistrate'.[36] The English Reformation, accordingly, had been no mere political revolution: not until the ecclesiastical settlement had been made in due form by 'the Convocations or provincial Synods of the Realm', had it been 'confirmed and ratified by the supreme Magistrate in Parliament'.[37] Just as the Church's foundations were not human but divine, so Wheatly argued, as William Law had done, that ministry could not be 'a function founded in the natural or civil rights of mankind': it was, rather, limited to those whose commission derived from the apostles by visible descent, 'being consecrated as Aaron and his sons and the Levites'.[38] Ministry not so authorised, as in the case of non-episcopal dissenting orders, was seen as an impious presumption

which invited the fate of Korah and his associates, or that of King
Uzziah, described respectively in Numbers 16 and 2 Chronicles 26.

Wheatly taught further, characteristically, that divine service
should be conducted with regularity and dignity in accordance with
the apostolic precept, 'Let all things be done decently and in order'
(1 Cor. 14:40). His insistence on the duty of daily public prayer, and
on the need for fixed places of worship formally dedicated and treated
with scrupulous reverence, was echoed throughout the century in
charges and in consecration-sermons, such as that preached in 1753
by Dr John Brown at the opening of St James, Whitehaven (the recent
wilful destruction of whose magnificent pulpit provides a depressing
reflection upon our own age).[39] With many others, Wheatly also
shared an appreciation of the value of external gestures to serve
interior devotion, a matter that found characteristic expression in his
defences of the practices of facing east for the creed and bowing at
the name of Jesus.[40] In his comments on the Ornaments Rubrick
Wheatly also revealed accurate knowledge about the nature of the
alb, cope and pastoral staff, although he accepted their obsolete
status. The tunicle however he called 'a silk sky-coloured coat, made
in the shape of a cope', and the 'vestment', or chasuble, he equated
with the cope.[41] Altar lights, which Wheatly declared should be used
'in all parish Churches and chapels', featured widely in illustrations
throughout the eighteenth century.[42]

For Wheatly, as for all high churchmen, the greatest duty of Christian people was the Eucharist, 'wherein we intercede on earth, in
conjunction with the great intercession of our high Priest in heaven,
and plead in the virtue and merits of the same sacrifice here, which
he is continually urging for us there'.[43] Although sparingly-adminis-
tered, a frequency above five or six times a year being unusual in
rural areas, later claims that infrequency of celebration reflected
indifference of attitude will bear little close examination. High churchmen throughout the eighteenth century were conspicuous for their
efforts to raise standards of eucharistic observance, by exhortation
and by the publication of popular manuals for communicants. 'It is
well for common Christians that they are so plentifully provided with
useful works of that kind,' observed Daniel Waterland in 1737,[44] not
unjustly: the anonymous *Week's Preparation for a Worthy Receiving the
Sacrament of the Lord's Supper*, for example, reached a thirty-eighth
edition in 1778, while Bishop Wilson's *Short and Plain Instruction for a
better understanding the Sacrament*, and Robert Nelson's *Great Duty of
Frequenting the Christian Sacrifice*, reached respectively a twenty-fourth
edition in 1796 and a thirteenth in 1756.

In their understanding of the Eucharist, the high churchmen of
the eighteenth century were guided by two principal schools of
thought. The first, usually regarded as definitive, derived from
Cranmer, Laud, Taylor and Cudworth, and found its ultimate
expression in Dr Daniel Waterland's *Review of the Doctrine of the*

Eucharist (1737). This found no 'proper or material sacrifice in the Eucharist', preferring to see what Waterland termed 'a symbolical feast upon a sacrifice, that is to say, upon the grand sacrifice itself, commemorated under certain symbols'. The second derived from Andrewes, Overall, Heylin, Thorndike and Mede, and from the revived awareness, in the late seventeenth century, of the liturgies of the early Eastern Church. Writers such as John Johnson of Cranbrook, author in 1714 of *The Unbloody Sacrifice*, were particularly influenced by one of these, the so-called Clementine liturgy. This second tradition emphasised the continuity of the Eucharist with the material sacrifices of the Old Testament as described in Leviticus 24, and Malachi 1:10–11, and contended that Christ was offered in every Eucharist, not hypostatically, as the Tridentine Church of Rome supposed, but representatively and really, 'in mystery and effect'. With this tradition were associated the four so-called 'usages', which the nonjurors had incorporated in their liturgy of 1718: the mixture of water with wine in the chalice; the invocation of the Holy Ghost upon the elements during the prayer of consecration; a prayer of oblation, to emphasise the sacrificial nature of the Eucharist; and prayer for the dead.[45]

Just as Johnson of Cranbrook had never scrupled to take the oaths, so by no means all of his supporters were nonjurors. At least five of the conforming high churchmen who wrote against Hoadly's *Plain Account* of 1735, for example, revealed their understanding of the Eucharist in material terms. One such writer was Wheatly, whose *Christian Exceptions to the Plain Account* (1736) endorsed the earlier teaching of the *Rational Illustration*, that a 'materialist' construction might even be placed upon the existing Prayer Book order. Invocation, for example, was to be understood by placing a suitable construction on the petition, 'Grant that we receiving'. The 'Ancient and Catholick practice' of prayer for the dead was likewise held to be implicit, in the petition in the prayer for the Church, 'that we *with them* may be made partakers . . .'; a sense further assisted by omission of the restricting term 'militant here in earth'. Oblation was to be effected by transferring the first prayer in the post-communion office ('we, thy humble servants, entirely desire thy fatherly goodness mercifully to accept this our sacrifice') to a position at the end of the prayer of consecration.[46]

This understanding was widely shared. Many popular works endorsed some or all of the features of the 'materialist' scheme. Bishop Wilson's *Short and Plain Instruction*, for example, provided prayers of invocation and prayers for 'the whole mystical Body of Christ', for optional private use, and interpreted eucharistic oblation in a material sense, an understanding shared by *The Week's Preparation.*[47] Nelson's *Great Duty of Frequenting the Christian Sacrifice* included an optional prayer of oblation, taken out of the Clementine liturgy, while the same author's *Companion to the Festivals and Fasts* conveyed a clear understanding of invocation: 'the spiritual Energy and Virtue of [Christ's] holy Flesh and Blood ... [are] communicated to the Blessed Elements by the Power and Operation of the Holy Ghost descending upon them'.[48]

High churchmen such as Wheatly, however, differed from the 'usager' nonjurors in their conviction that although the four 'usages' might be desirably primitive they did not justify the violation of the existing order of the Book of Common Prayer, and the inevitable ensuing schism. As Wheatly noted, speaking of mixture in the *Rational Illustration*, in a remark implicitly critical of the nonjurors, 'since every Church has liberty to determine for herself in things not essential, it must be an argument sure of a very indiscreet and over-hasty zeal to urge the omission of it, as a ground for separation'.[49] Moreover, he wrote in 1739 to the nonjuring primus Thomas Brett, even Waterland 'really maintains the sacrifice as we do, but expresses himself in a different manner'.[50] By then the continuing isolation of the 'usager' nonjurors had come to seem increasingly incongruous, in view of Waterland's own declaration in 1737 that the two positions were separated only by a mere 'difference of words or names, arising chiefly from the difficulty of determining what sacrifice properly means'.[51]

Just as the high churchmen's sense of the excellence of the Book of Common Prayer led them to deplore the schism of Protestant and nonjuring dissenters, so their understanding of the 'branch' theory of catholicism led them to look critically upon the Church of Rome. With earlier writers including Hooker, Laud, Mede, Taylor and Leslie, the high churchmen of the eighteenth century repudiated Roman claims to infallibility and to an exclusive 'catholic' title: the Roman system, said Charles Wheatly, was guilty of 'abominable corruptions'.[52] Equally however high churchmen remembered Richard Hooker's reminder that much was 'still due' to Rome, as 'a part of the House of God, a Limb of the visible Church of Christ'.[53] They deplored what they regarded as the excesses of popular protestantism, both in the sixteenth century, when, as Wheatly said, it had not been 'the design of our Reformers to introduce a *new* form of worship into the Church, but to correct and amend the *old* one', and also in their own age, when it seemed that much nominal 'protestantism' had degenerated into scepticism and unbelief.[54] 'There are some called *Protestants* here', noted the high church periodical, *Mitre and Crown*, in 1748, 'who have no priests, and some who have no sacraments; some who believe no creeds, and some who believe no Gospel.'[55] In short, as a correspondent of the *Gentleman's Magazine* observed in 1776, even Roman catholicism was 'better than simple Deism'.[56]

Favourable reassessment of Roman catholicism was assisted during the eighteenth century by the declining temporal influence of the papacy, the receding threat of a Stuart restoration, and the concili-

atory reputation of pontiffs such as Benedict XIII, the so-called
'protestant pope'. Interest in the Gallican church moreover – fostered
notably by Archbishop Wake's dialogues of 1717–20 – further
sustained hopes that the obstacle of papal supremacy might be
outmanoeuvred eventually by what one high churchman in 1768
termed 'a further General Council . . . the most effectual means to
unite all the Western Churches'.[57] Added encouragement was
provided by the publication in 1723 of the *Dissertation on the Validity
of English Ordinations* by the exiled French canon Pierre le Courayer,
a protégé of Archbishop Wake, who continued to live in England
until his death in 1776 at the age of ninety-five. Although never
forsaking the Roman Communion, Le Courayer regularly attended
his local church, St Mary's, Ealing, where standards reflected the
high church preferences of the patron, Dr William King, Jacobite
Principal of St Mary Hall, Oxford. King had other Roman Catholic
contacts including Cardinal Melchior de Polignac, the Archbishop
of Auch, and Sir Andrew Ramsey, convert tutor to the Pretender's
sons in Rome. Le Courayer likewise had a wide Anglican acquaintance. One friend, Charles Wheatly, helped him to obtain an honorary
DD at Oxford, while another, the high church diarist and antiquary
William 'Cardinal' Cole, had a wide acquaintance among English
recusants, clerical and lay, and delighted when abroad to be
addressed as 'Monsieur l'Abbé'.[58]

Roman Catholic devotional works were also widely valued. More
than a century before Bishop Heber declared his admiration for the
saints of the Counter-Reformation, the religious societies of London
acknowledged their debt to St Vincent de Paul.[59] Societies such as
those established by Antony Horneck also encouraged private devotion based on a form of the Hours, a custom sustained throughout
the eighteenth century by works such as *The Countess of Moreton's Daily
Exercize* (24th edn, 1760) or by Robert Nelson's *Practice of True Devotion*
(16th edn, 1769). Works by Pascal and Fénelon were admired by
many, apart from obvious high churchmen: Hannah More's devotion
to Pascal and 'other Port Royal authors' being commended by Dr
Johnson, for example, in 1781.[60] Other works, such as St Francis de
Sales, *Introduction to the Devout Life*, or Lorenzo Scupoli, *Spiritual
Combat*, were also widely available, if often only in versions 'reformed
from Romish errors'. Thomas à Kempis' *Imitation of Christ* enjoyed
unparalleled popularity and esteem: *The Pious Country Parishioner*
(32nd edn, 1819) wished that copies were available in every household 'to keep up a Sense of Religion'. George Stanhope's version of
the *Imitation*, the most popular, appeared in nineteen editions between
1698 and 1814, while John Wesley's partial translation of 1735
remained in print until 1806.[61]

With sympathy to Roman Catholic devotion went a considerable
interest in the religious life. Admiration was qualified, some high
churchmen such as Joseph Trapp fearing monastic austerity as a

form of enthusiasm, while others shared Dr Johnson's misgiving that 'it cannot be allowed, that flight is victory'.[62] Nevertheless few eighteenth-century orthodox failed to deplore the greed that had accompanied the dissolution of the monasteries, and many shared Sir Henry Spelman's misgivings expressed in his work, *De non Temerandis Ecclesiis*, that Acts of Parliament were incapable of re-appropriating gifts dedicated to religious use. Others, believing with Charles Wheatly that 'self-Denial, Abstinence and mortification are Parts of Religion', contended in defence of the regular celibate life, devoted to charity and prayer.[63] This, as William Law argued in the *Serious Call*, was an ideal that 'so far from being chargeable with any *superstition*, or *blind devotion* . . . might justly be said to restore *that piety* which was the *boast* and *glory* of the Church when the greatest Saints were alive'.[64]

Proposals for establishing religious communities in the eighteenth century were confined to sisterhoods, or to extensions of devout family life. This was in accordance with seventeenth-century practice, as outlined by Clement Barksdale (*A Letter touching a College of Maids*, 1675), Mary Astell (*A Serious Proposal to the Ladies*, 1694) and Sir George Wheler, whose intention in *The Protestant Monastery* (1698) that 'families shall be the monasteries', had recalled the spirit of Nicholas Ferrar's practice at Little Gidding during the 1630s. In 1737 an Edinburgh baronet, Sir William Cunninghame, wrote to the Archdeacon of Northumberland, Dr Thomas Sharp, with proposals for 'a nunnery of Protestant religious and virtuous persons, well-born, of the female sex, conforming themselves to the worship of the Church of England'. Thirty women were to live in community under a 'prioress', and were to observe daily offices. No vows were to be taken. Sharp's response was sympathetic, but sceptical. He feared suspicions of popery, and thought that candidates would be deterred at the prospect of being 'thought a company of discontented and desponding creatures, that are tired of the world, because they think the world is tired of them'. No action was taken.[65] In 1766 a similar, but almost certainly fanciful, scheme was described by Philip Burton, father-in-law to Bishop Horne, who envisaged a community of a dozen well-bred ladies living in 'a remote but pleasant village . . . in . . . the Northern part of England'. These sisters were to dress in a uniform white habit, observing two daily offices in a private chapel and devoting their time to charitable work. It was however emphasised that they were 'not like poor cloister'd Nuns', having 'no unnatural barbarous rules to hinder or make [their] lives unprofitable, gloomy and discontented', although many appeared to have forsaken society voluntarily, at least for the present, following unhappy 'Romantic Turns'.[66]

The vision of William Hanbury, eccentric high church rector of Church Langton, Leicestershire from 1753 to 1778, was distinctly more ambitious. His proposed 'hospital or convent for sixty poor women, and such others as may choose the like kind of devout life, will wear the habit and submit to the rules of the house' was merely one aspect of a grandiose scheme to which Hanbury devoted his entire life. It was intended that elaborate afforestation projects should produce a vast revenue (which never materialised) that was to support a 'grand Cathedral Church', built in the Gothic style and larger than York minster, in which daily choral service was to be performed with unparalleled splendour. An academic community of six professors, twelve canons and twenty-four fellows, was also to be maintained on the foundation, and a 'Printing-House' was to distribute works of orthodox piety: à Kempis, Taylor, Kettlewell, Nelson, Spinckes, Law and, with particular emphasis, 'Wells, against the Dissenters, to preserve members of the Church from falling into that dreadful sin of schism'.[67]

With his minster that was to be 'truly Gothic' with 'painted windows' to 'reflect a religious Gloom', Hanbury resembled some of those who, more than three generations later, came to share his enthusiasm for what they called, rather simplistically, 'Christian architecture'. Accordingly it is important for us to notice that not all eighteenth-century essays in Gothic were as derisory as many later writers, particularly those of a 'Camdenian' bias, made out. Ever since Richard Hooker had exhorted men to follow 'Job's observation, who giveth men to seek wisdom among the ancient', serious churchmen had been keen students of antiquity. During the eighteenth century this tradition was maintained, not only by eminent nonjurors such as Baker, Carte, Rawlinson and Hearne, but also by many conforming high churchmen whose interest in antiquity highlighted their shared distaste for the values of the age of enlightenment. Equally significantly, of the numerous laymen who dabbled with early neo-medievalism, many had links with the politics of Tory opposition. Browne-Willis of Bletchley, for instance, the friend and patron of William Cole, was a former Queen Anne Tory MP, who constructed a chapel in the Gothic style at Fenny Stratford as early as 1730. Similarly James West, FSA, MP for St Albans from 1741 to 1762, rebuilt the church at Preston-on-Stour where he was patron and Revd Joseph Greene, the antiquary, was incumbent, to the Gothic designs of Edward Woodward between 1752 and 1757. At nearby Arbury in Warwickshire Sir Roger Newdigate, MP for Oxford University 1750–80 and an indefatigable high churchman, employed four major architects, Hiorne, Keene, Couchman and Sanderson Miller, on various stages of his ambitious gothicising projects; while at Wicken, Northamptonshire, the church was rebuilt in 1758 to the Gothic designs of Thomas Prowse, Tory MP for Somerset 1740–67: a plaster fan-vault in the chancel is particularly impressive.

Eighteenth-century theoretical studies of medieval architecture were often likewise more distinguished than 'Camdenian' critics were ready to admit. Francis Price's *Observations upon Salisbury Cathedral*

(1753), for example, which Hanbury adopted as the basis for his fantasies at Church Langton, has been described by Howard Colvin as 'the first serious attempt to describe and analyse the structure of a major Gothic building'. Other important contributions were made by James Bentham's *History of the Antiquities of the Conventual and Cathedral Church at Ely* (1771), and, in practice, by James Essex, whose sympathetic Gothic restoration work at Ely (1757–62) and Lincoln (1762–5) has only recently begun to claim the credit that it deserves.[68]

Not all exercises in eighteenth-century Gothic could claim such merit. As the curious vogue for hermits in the 1760s and 1770s attested, much of the early neo-medieval impetus derived less from serious religious inspiration than from the prevailing literary fashion for the picturesque and the sentimental. The result was often insipid, as when visiting Battle Abbey in 1761 the novelist Elizabeth Carter was moved to restore, not the monks but the 'scritch-owls and ravens'.[69] On other occasions cynicism prevailed, as when in 1754 Horace Walpole's 'Strawberry Committee' took 'incense and mass-books' to 'the most heavenly chapel in the world' at the Vyne in Hampshire for 'a most Catholic enjoyment';[70] while in the case of Sir Francis Dashwood's notorious 'Monks' of Medmenham, the tone was decadent and sinister as they assembled with bogus religious rites 'in the chapel, at the tolling of a bell, when solemn plaintive music [began] to play'.[71]

More frequently however the tone of early Gothic revivalism was ambivalent. Thomas Warton's representative, and revealingly entitled poem of 1747, 'The Pleasures of Melancholy', juxtaposed conventional images of Gothic horror, such as Juliet in the tomb, with antiquarian reveries about 'sacred sounds' in 'gothic vaults' that might have been worthy of Pugin himself.[72] Similarly Dr Thomas Leland, another antiquary, in his novel of 1762, *Longsword, Earl of Salisbury*, provided a curious combination of idealism and caricature, depicting on one hand a sympathetic view of 'an Ancient Abbey . . . of the Cistercian Order', and on the other a grotesque portrayal of the 'wicked monk', Reginhald, whose involvement in coerced marriages and murder anticipated by more than a generation the sensational tone of Matthew Lewis's *Ambrosio, or The Monk* (1795). Even at William Beckford's Fonthill Abbey, the ultimate monastic fantasy, not all was theatre: a real monk, the French emigré abbé Macquin, was employed to conduct visitors round; and the subscription list to Britton's definitive volume of aquatint-views (1823) included the names of Archdeacon Nares, editor of the *British Critic*, and A. W. Pugin.[73]

To duller eyes of the Camdenian period the ambivalence of Gothic revivalism was less apparent. It was left to Sir Leslie Stephen to extend the application of eighteenth-century experience to his own day when he remarked of Horace Walpole that 'the restorers of churches, the manufacturers of stained-glass, the modern decorators

and artists of all varieties, the Ritualists and the High Church party
should think of him with kindness'.[74] It was not a flattering
comparison. Walpole's theatricality, and his avowed doctrinal indifference, were displayed not only in his friendship with the Arian
Conyers Middleton but also in a revealing letter written in 1778 to
the high church antiquary William Cole: 'I like Popery as well as
you do,' Walpole declared: 'I like it as I do chivalry and romance
. . . a Gothic Church or convent fills one with romantic dreams, but
for the mysterious, the Church in the abstract, it is a jargon that
means nothing.'[75]

Similar suspicions adhered, at least in part, to the later stages of
the nonjuring movement. The leading patron of the English nonjurors
for nearly half a century until his death in 1771 was Charles Jennens,
better known for his private literary endeavours and personal osten-
tation: contemporaries knew him as 'Soleyman the Magnificent'.
While some remembered his friendship with Edward Holdsworth the
nonjuring scholar, and his collaboration with G. F. Handel on the
libretti for many oratorios including the 'Messiah', others recalled
his household of paid sycophants and his attempt to redraft *King Lear*
with a happy ending.[76] Sir Hildebrand Jacob, patron of the last
regular nonjuring congregation at London in the 1780s, was similarly
remembered as 'a very extraordinary character', whose literary
ambitions resulted in several early plays, and a later collection of
verses, which were no more distinguished than Christian.[77]

It is important to consider these curious aspects of the early neo-
medievalists and later nonjurors because of the reflection they cast
upon their more self-conscious admirers and emulators in the mid-
nineteenth century. Whether the Oxford Movement was in fact 'a
phase of the romantic movement', as Norman Sykes once claimed,
would be of little consequence, were it not for the fact that it is
still from Tractarian sources that many of our notions of old high
churchmanship derive. Such a picture is not complete, and it is
possible that we may regret the deficiency. Just as the loss of the old
high churchmen's positive view of a national religious Establishment
may be thought to diminish us all as citizens, so as churchmen we
may deplore the damage that has been done in the last 150 years to
our doctrinal and disciplinary unity by those whose wilful pursuit of
'the quackery of affecting antiquity'[78] led them to defy the previously
current authority of episcopacy and rubric. The Church gained
many blessings by 'the movement of 1833' but we should also pause
briefly to consider whether the losses may not have been greater than
we often suppose.

1. J. W. Burgon, *Lives of Twelve Good Men* (London 1891), pp. 80–2.
2. R. W. Church, *The Oxford Movement 1833–1845* (London 1932), pp. 9–10.
3. ibid. p. 111. Tractarian relations with old high churchmen are compre-

hensively surveyed by Peter Nockles, 'Continuity and Change in Anglican High Churchmanship 1792–1850' (unpublished D. Phil. thesis, Univ. Oxford 1982). For general background on old high churchmen, see G. W. O. Addleshaw, *The High Church Tradition* (London 1941); H. R. McAdoo, *The Spirit of Anglicanism* (London 1965); W. K. Lowther Clarke, *Eighteenth-Century Piety* (London 1944); C. J. Stranks, *Anglican Devotion* (London 1961).

4. N. C. Hunt, *Two Early Political Associations: the Quakers and the Dissenting Deputies in the age of Sir Robert Walpole* (Oxford 1961); R. N. Stromberg, *Religious Liberalism in Eighteenth-Century England* (Oxford 1954); J. Redwood, *Reason, Ridicule and Religion, 1660–1750* (London 1976); J. Brown, *An Estimate of the Manners and Principles of the Times* (London 1757); J. Leland, *A View of the Principal Deistical Writers* (London 1754). On the Rundle case, see N. Sykes, *Edmund Gibson* (London 1926), pp. 155–9; *Gentleman's Magazine* (December 1734). For Parliamentary Debates on Test and Quakers' Title Bills, 1736, see *Hansard Parliamentary History of England*, 36 vols (London 1806–20), IX.

5. Anon., *A Narrative of the Case of Revd Mr Jackson being refus'd the Sacrament of the Lord's Supper . . . by Dr Coney minister of Bath* (London 1736). For the debate over Foster's sermon on Heresy, see *Gentleman's Magazine* (June 1735). For a review of the debate between Stebbing and Foster, see ibid. (April 1737).

6. E. E. Beardsley, *Life of Samuel Seabury* (London 1884), p. 137n.

7. J. P. Malcolm, *Londinium Redivivum*, 4 vols (London 1802–7); J. Wickham-Legg, *English Church Life from the Restoration to the Tractarian Movement* (London 1914), pp. 108–11.

8. S. Rivington, *The Publishing House of Rivington* (London 1894).

9. J. Nichols, *Literary Anecdotes of the Eighteenth Century*, 2nd edn, 9 vols (London 1812–15), III, p. 68n.

10. W. Jones, *Memoirs of the Life, Studies and Writings of the Rt Rev. George Horne*, DD (London 1795); W. Cleaver, *A List of Books intended for the younger Clergy . . . within the diocese of Chester* (Oxford 1791); S. Horsley, letter to Bishop Drummond, in A. Jolly, *The Christian Sacrifice in the Eucharist* (Aberdeen 1831), p. 121; T. Sharp, *Life of Archbishop Sharp*, 2 vols (London 1825), I, p. 355.

11. G. Stanhope, *Paraphrase and Comment on the Epistle and Gospels*, 3 vols (London 1705–6), I, entry for 29 May; C. Wheatly, *Rational Illustration of the Book of Common Prayer*, 7th edn (London 1741), ch. 17, sect. 2 §6.

12. Charles Wesley, in Nichols, *Literary Anecdotes*, V, p. 241.

13. James Boswell, *Life of Dr Samuel Johnson*, ed. G. Birkbeck-Hill, 6 vols (Oxford 1887), III, p. 326, entry for 28 April 1778.

14. J. Sharp, 'The Duty of Subjection to the Higher Powers', in *The Works of J. Sharp*, 7th edn, 7 vols (London 1738), III, pp. 59–62.

15. J. Swift, 'The Sentiments of a Church of England Man with Respect to Church and Government'; in *The Churchman Armed* (London 1814), II, p. 30; for sermons, cf. S. Letsome, *The Preacher's Assistant* (London 1753); contd by J. Cooke, *The Preacher's Assistant* (Oxford 1783).

16. L. M. Hawkins, *Allegiance in Church and State: the problem of the nonjurors in the English revolution* (London 1928).

17. On 30 January sermons, see H. W. Randall, 'The Rise and Fall of a Martyrology', *Huntington Library Quarterly*, 10 (1947), pp. 135ff; B. S.

Stuart, 'The Cult of the Royal Martyr', *Church History*, 38 (1969), pp. 175–87. For a late controversy over a 30 January sermon preached in 1772 by Dr Thomas Nowell, see *Hansard Parliamentary History*, XVII, pp. 312–18.

18. E. Gibson, *Codex Iuris Ecclesiastici Anglicani* (London 1713), V, sect. 2; R. Smalbroke, *Some Account of . . . Edmund Gibson* (London 1749), p. 7. On the Convocation controversy, see Sykes, *Edmund Gibson*, pp. 25–53; G. V. Bennett, *The Tory Crisis in Church and State* (Oxford 1975), pp. 44–62.

19. T. Sharp, *The Rubric in the Book of Common Prayer Considered* (London 1753), 1834 edn, p. 45.

20. Nichols, *Literary Anecdotes*, III, p. 18n.

21. Cobbett, *Parliamentary History*, XIV, pp. 269ff.

22. For 'Catholick' ideas of the Church, cf. W. Wake, *The Principles of the Christian Religion explained in a brief Commentary upon the Church-Catechism*, 7th edn (London 1757), Part 2, xvi.

23. On the Athanasian Creed, cf. C. Wheatly, 'Sum of all Orthodox Divinity', in *Rational Illustration*, ch. 3, sect. 15.

24. N. Marshall, ed., *The Genuine Works of St Cyprian*, 2 vols (London 1717); J. Sage, *Principles of the Cyprianick Age* (London 1707), used by J. Potter, *A Discourse of Church Government*, 2nd edn (London 1711), pp. 175–83; and C. Wheatly, 'Out of the Church there is no safe passage to heaven . . .', in *Rational Illustration*, ch. 2, sect. 2. On Ignatius and Irenaeus, see Potter, *Discourse*, op. cit. pp. 155–64.

25. H. Stebbing, *A Letter to Mr Foster on the Subject of Heresy* (London 1735), p. 27; T. Bisse, *The Beauty of Holiness in the Common Prayer* (London 1716).

26. John Johnson, *The Clergy-man's Vade-Mecum*, 6th edn (London 1731), p. 11.

27. C. Wheatly, 'Appendix to Introduction', in *Rational Illustration*.

28. T. Collis, *The Rubrick . . . examin'd* (London 1737), p. 5.

29. On the theme of unity, see also William Beveridge, *A Sermon concerning the Excellency and Usefulness of the Common-Prayer*, 35th edn (London 1766).

30. T. Sharp, *The Rubric . . . considered*, p. 244n.

31. H. B. Wilson, *History of Merchant Taylors' School*, 2 vols (London 1812–14).

32. C. J. Robinson, ed., *Register of Merchant Taylors' School* (London 1882).

33. R. Clutterbuck, *History and Antiquities of the County of Hertford*, 3 vols (London 1815–27), III, p. 457.

34. C. Wheatly, 'The Cloud of Witnesses', in *Fifty Sermons on several Subjects and Occasions*, 3 vols (London 1753), I, p. 329; id. *Private Devotions at the Holy Communion* (London 1723); id. *Christian Exceptions to the Plain Account* (London 1736); id. *The Nicene and Athanasian Creeds . . . explain'd and confirm'd* (London 1738); id. *St John's Test of knowing Christ and being Born of Him (London 1739)*.

35. C. Wheatly, *Rational Illustration*, ch. 3, sect. 24.

36. ibid. ch. 6, sect 1; also 'Appendix to Introduction', pp. 33–4.

37. ibid. p. 34.

38. ibid. ch. 2, sect. 3; Potter, *Discourse of Church Government*, ch. 5; William Law, *Three Letters to the Bishop of Bangor*, 3 vols (London 1717–19), II, sect. 4.

39. Wickham-Legg, *English Church Life*, pp. 77–118; J. Brown, *On the Use and Abuse of Externals in Religion* (London 1753).

40. Wheatly, *Rational Illustration*, ch. 3, sect. 14 §9; on daily service, ibid. ch. 2, sect. 1 §2.
41. ibid. ch. 2, sect. 4 §4–5.
42. ibid. ch. 2, sect. 4 §8; T. Collis, *The Rubrick . . . examin'd*, pp. 9–11; T. Sharp, *The Rubric . . . considered*, pp. 244–8. Copes were still being worn in Durham in 1764: J. B. Craven, ed., *The Journal of Bishop Robert Forbes* (London 1923), p. 31; and at the coronation in 1761: *Gentleman's Magazine* (1761), pp. 414–21. See also Wickham-Legg, *English Church Life*, pp. 139–43 (lights); pp. 369–73 (vestments); M. E. C. Walcott, *Sacred Archaeology* (London 1868), p. 183 (copes); p. 97 (lights).
43. Wheatly, *Rational Illustration*, ch. 6, 'Introduction' §1.
44. D. Waterland, *Review of the Doctrine of the Eucharist* (Cambridge 1737), ch. 13. On weekly celebration, see T. T. Carter, *Undercurrents of Church Life in the Eighteenth Century* (London 1899), p. 139n.; 'Hull', *Victoria County History: Yorkshire (East Riding)*, vols I– (London 1920–   ), I, p. 287; Wickham–Legg, *English Church Life*, pp. 30–5, 108–11. On the North-End, cf. Wheatly, *Rational Illustration*, ch. 6, sect. 22 §6. On incense, cf. C. J. Abbey and J. Overton, *The English Church in the Eighteenth Century*, 2 vols (London 1878), II, p. 481; at the coronation in 1761, *Notes and Queries*, 2nd series, 3, 8 (1857), p. 11. On reservation, cf. S. Hardy, *Scripture-Account of the Nature and Ends of the Holy Eucharist* (London 1784), pp. 348–51; for an interesting allusion to reservation for the sick at St Clement Dane's, see letter from Campbell to Brett, 3 February 1730, MS Eng. Th. c30 f. 495 (Bodleian). On confession, cf. Wheatly, *Rational Illustration*, ch. 11, sect. 4 §4; T. Coney, *Companion for a Sick-Bed*, 5th edn (London 1747); N. Spinckes, *The Sick Man Visited*, 6th edn (London 1775).
45. Wickham-Legg, *English Church Life*, pp. 21–76; C. W. Dugmore, *Eucharistic Doctrine in England from Hooker to Waterland* (London 1942); W. Jardine-Grisbrook, *Anglican Liturgies of the Seventeenth and Eighteenth Centuries* (London 1958).
46. Wheatly, *Rational Illustration*, ch. 6, 10 §4 (mixture); ch. 6, sect. 11 §2 (prayer for the dead) (cf. also Wickham-Legg, *English Church Life*, pp. 315–33); ch. 6, sect. 22 §3 (oblation).
47. T. Wilson, *Short and Plain Instruction*, 24th edn (London 1796), pp. 142, 179; id. *Week's Preparation*, 'Monday Morning: "bread and wine so offered and blessed" '.
48. R. Nelson, *Companion for the Festivals and Fasts*, 13th edn (London 1726), pp. 580–1; id. *Great Duty of Frequenting the Christian Sacrifice*, 13th edn (London 1756), p. 98.
49. Wheatly, *Rational Illustration*, ch. 6, sect. 10 §4.
50. Wheatly to Brett, 31 October 1739, cited in H. Broxap, *The Later Nonjurors* (Cambridge 1924), p. 212.
51. Waterland, *Review of the Doctrine of the Eucharist*, ch. 12.
52. Wheatly, *Rational Illustration*, ch. 14, 'Introduction' §1.
53. Richard Hooker, *Lawes of Ecclesiastical Polity* (London 1593–7), Book V, §68.
54. Wheatly, *Rational Illustration*, 'Appendix to Introduction', p. 24.
55. *The Mitre and Crown, or, Great Britain's True Interest* (1748), pp. 88ff.
56. *Gentleman's Magazine* (1776), pp. 59–61; E. Cobden, 'And Sacrilege for

Idols Must Atone', in *An Essay, sacred to the Memory of Queen Anne, for her Bounty to the Clergy: Discourses and Essays* (London 1757), p. 350.

57. Gloucester Ridley, *A Letter to the Author of the Confessional* (London 1768), pp. 76ff.; N. Sykes, *William Wake*, 2 vols (Oxford 1957), I, pp. 252–314.

58. For Le Courayer, cf. Nichols, *Literary Anecdotes*, II, pp. 39f.; for Cole, cf. ibid. I, pp. 657–701, and F. G. Stokes, ed., *The Bletchley Diary of the Rev. William Cole* (London 1931); id. *A Journal of my Journey to Paris in... 1765* (London 1931); Edward Rowe-Mores, another Anglican eccentric, cf. Nichols, *Literary Anecdotes*, V, pp. 389ff.

59. G. V. Portus, *Caritas Anglicana* (London 1912).

60. W. Roberts, *Memoirs of . . . Hannah More* (London 1836), p. 176.

61. D. W. Bahlman, *The Moral Revolution of 1688* (London 1957); Wickham-Legg, *English Church Life*, pp. 345–50.

62. Sermon III by Samuel Johnson, cited by M. J. Quinlan, *Samuel Johnson: a layman's religion* (Wisconsin 1964), p. 165; Joseph Trapp, *The Nature, Folly, Sin and Danger of being Righteous Over-Much* (London 1734), p. 7.

63. Wheatly, *Fifty Sermons*, I, p. 348.

64. W. Law, *A Serious Call to a Devout and Holy Life* (London 1920), p. 136.

65. T. Sharp, *Life of Archbishop Sharp*, II, pp. 281f.

66. Philip Burton, 'A Letter Supposed to be Wrote by a Gentleman to his Friend with a Scheme of a Protestant Nunnery', July 1766, MS Add 8134/N/1 (Cambridge Univ. Lib.).

67. W. Hanbury, *History of the Rise and Progress of the Charitable Foundations at Church-Langton* (London 1767); W. Woty, *Church-Langton* (Leicester 1767); J. Nichols, *History and Antiquities of the County of Leicester*, 4 vols (London 1795–1811), II, pp. 645f.; J. H. Hill, *History of the Parish of Langton* (Leicester 1867).

68. Fitzwilliam Museum, Cambridge, *The Ingenious Mr Essex: a bicentenary exhibition catalogue* (Cambridge 1984); Georgian Group, *A Gothic Symposium at the Victoria and Albert Museum* (London 1983); C. L. Eastlake, *A History of the Gothic Revival* (London 1872); K. Clark, *The Gothic Revival*, 4th edn (London 1974); M. Whiffen, *Stuart and Georgian Churches* (London 1948), ch. 5.

69. M. Pennington, *Memoirs of the Life of Mrs Elizabeth Carter* (London 1807), pp. 155–6.

70. C. W. Chute, *A History of the Vyne in Hampshire* (Winchester 1888).

71. *Town and Country Magazine* (1769), pp. 122–3; Thomas Percy, *The Hermit of Warkworth* (London 1771); B. Jones, *Follies and Grottoes*, 2nd edn (London 1976).

72. Thomas Warton, *Poems*, ed. Cooke (London 1800), pp.100–1.

73. J. Britton, *Graphical and Literary Illustrations of Fonthill Abbey, Wiltshire* (London 1823).

74. L. Stephen, *Hours in a Library*, 2nd series, *Horace Walpole*, 3 vols (London 1874–9); see also Wickham-Legg, *English Church Life*, p. 159, for Mrs Delany's description of a 'Fop's Chapel' in 1768.

75. Walpole to Cole, 12 July 1778, in W. S. Lewis, ed., *The Yale Edition of Horace Walpole's Correspondence*, vols I– (New Haven 1937–   ), III, p. 98.

76. On Jennens, see Nichols, *Literary Anecdotes*, III, p. 120n.; on Holdsworth, see ibid. III, pp. 68–9.

77. On Jacob, cf. *Dictionary of National Biography*.

78. H. J. Rose to Newman, 9 May 1836, cited in Burgon, *Lives*, p. 110; Sykes, *Edmund Gibson*, p. 1.

2

The Oxford Movement:
historical background 1780–1833*

Peter Nockles

The passage of time is normally conducive to the attainment of a balanced and objective historical perspective. However the commemoration of great historical events can be a powerful barrier against it, and in this respect the Oxford Movement has proved no exception. For the celebration of the centenary in 1933 was productive of some glaring historical misconceptions, partly, be it noted, out of the very focusing of the participants on what happened in 1833 and the years following. For while on the one hand outright enemies of the Catholic tradition in Anglicanism, such as Bishop Knox, berated the movement as innovatory and alien to the true Protestant spirit of the Church of England as bequeathed by the Reformers and Elizabethan settlement,[1] on the other the hagiography which Dean Church, Pusey's biographer, Liddon, and Canon Ollard had firmly established was carried to new lengths. What both had in common was their propagation of the view that 1833 was *the* magic year that marked a radical, if not revolutionary break from what had gone before in English church history. Shane Leslie epitomised this historical treatment of the movement when he described it as having been 'born out of fallow and dust'.[2] The older high church tradition in Anglicanism that remained alive throughout the so-called 'tunnel-period' of the mid-eighteenth century was too often either ignored or derided. When its existence was recognised it was found to be theologically ambiguous, Erastian, 'high and dry' – a favourite epithet – worldly, and in matters of ritual and spirituality cold and dull, when judged by the apparently higher standards later set by the Catholic revival after 1833. Although the Swedish historian Archbishop Brilioth, in his work, *The Anglican Revival*, published in 1925, sought to question some of these presuppositions and to exonerate the pre-Tractarian Church of England from some of the standard aspersions made against it, his more sympathetic understanding of the older high churchmanship was not echoed by many. Even he dwelt heavily on the supposed sterility of that older tradition, in contrast with what he termed the 'Neo-Anglicanism' of the Oxford Movement.[3] At best, the old high church tradition was treated as a

* © 1986 Peter Nockles

mere backcloth or background to what followed after 1833.[4] For instance, Canon C. P. S. Clarke, the first contributor in 1933 to the volume of centenary studies of the movement, called *Northern Catholicism*, set the tone by brushing aside Brilioth's portrait of the older high church tradition as too flattering, and rested content with the aphorism of a Scottish geologist, Hugh Miller, whom he quoted as having 'compared the pre-Tractarian High Churchmen to bulbs in a drawer, and the post-Tractarian High Churchmen to the same bulbs after they were planted out and were in flower'.[5] Such an assumption needs some questioning. Not only was there genuine high church continuity in the late eighteenth century but an actual high church revival – to use Miller's analogy, a real 'flowering of the bulbs' in the forty to fifty years immediately prior to 1833; a revival, one might add, which in origin dated from the accession of George III, but which was also a fruit of the general conservative reaction against the French Revolution. At the centre of this revival were the leaders and associates of the so-called 'Hackney Phalanx', Joshua Watson, Henry Handley Norris, Thomas Sikes, John Hume Spry, William van Mildert and Christopher Wordsworth, to which Nancy Murray has drawn attention,[6] and like-minded allies such as Charles Daubeny. They are commonly referred to and given due recognition in the histories of the movement, but rarely without at least the underlying hint that their teaching was in some ways defective, their temper over-rigid and narrow. It was these apparent negative qualities in them that led the Tractarians, with their enormous sensitivity to what they called ethos, to dub both them and their successors in the era of the movement, such as Edward Churton, William Palmer of Worcester and R. W. Jelf, as 'Zs'[7] or conservative churchmen.

It is time to look at some of these figures anew, and thereby to set the Oxford Movement more firmly within the context and perspective of the rich and varied high church tradition which they represented in their day. One of the most revealing entries in the manuscript diaries of Joshua Watson's niece Mary is that the leader of the 'Phalanx' was by the early 1840s expressing extreme disquiet at what he called 'the inclination to make a great era of the year 1833'. Indeed Mary Watson records her uncle as repeatedly saying in his latter years, 'I am only solicitous to get rid of all the history of the agitation'.[8] Watson's concern was shared by many old high churchmen of the younger generation who went far in support of the movement in its early stages. For instance, Benjamin Harrison, appointed chaplain to the Archbishop of Canterbury in 1838 but the actual author of No. 49 of the *Tracts for the Times*, by 1843 was complaining of the widespread 'notion, which it is most desirable to get rid of, of church principles being altogether a creation of the last ten years'. He felt that what was then wanted was 'to have the "Tracts", if possible, forgotten – merged, at least, in the view of Christian Faith, and the Christian church, and the long course of

eventful history and warfare which they have passed through'.
Harrison wished that thinking men would but 'look a little deeper
than the opinions and efforts of any individuals, or combination of
individuals, ten years ago, as the source and spring of the late movement'.[9] Other old high churchmen reiterated the point with telling
insistence. In 1840, in a work ostensibly written in defence of the
Tractarians, the rector of Leigh, Essex, James Beaven, argued that
their real influence had been 'very much overrated, both by friends
and foes'.[10] Perhaps still more striking though, was the testimony of
Edward Churton, rector of Crayke, who in 1846 tried to temper the
zeal of his Tractarian-minded friend William Gresley, by impressing
upon him the example of another Oxford-inspired high church movement, that of the so-called 'Hutchinsonians' of the previous century.
The Hutchinsonians comprised the high church followers of the
mystical theories of the Hebraist John Hutchinson,[11] led by George
Horne, President of Magdalen College and later Bishop of Norwich,
William Jones, vicar of Nayland, and the layman William Stevens.
They were the natural predecessors of the 'Hackney Phalanx'. It was
natural for Churton to invoke their name to the Tractarians, in
order to press the idea of continuity and to detract from Tractarian
assumptions of novelty and thereby alleviate the growing anxieties
of the original 'Phalanx'. As he told Gresley:

> The value of the labours of Bishop Horne, Jones of Nayland and
> their friends, will not be forgotten by any faithful historian of the
> church of the eighteenth century . . . I want you to refer to such
> good men's names . . . not only as a matter of justice but because
> I believe nothing will tend more to make what you are now doing
> more acceptable to my good old friends . . . Nothing is more
> important in my mind, than to show that Anglicanism, as it is now
> called, is not a new party, but has come down to us in regular
> descent from the Reformation, from Hooker to Andrewes,
> Andrewes to Laud, Bramhall, and Hammond, thence to Pearson
> and Jeremy Taylor, thence to Bishop Bull, thence to Hickes and
> Robert Nelson, Leslie and other names . . . After the succession of
> George III these principles were again enquired for, and Horne
> and Jones answered to the call. Horne and Jones have their
> disciples still living. Tell the world this.[12]

If we look at the three main themes or facets of Tractarianism –
the doctrine of the church, its apostolicity, unity, independence and
relation to the State; the rule of faith, role of tradition and the
Fathers; and finally, spirituality and its different elements, along with
sacramentalism and the symbolic significance of rite and ceremony
– we can find ample evidence of renewal and resurgence in each,
within the high church tradition in the forty or fifty years preceding
the dawn of the movement. Of all the doctrines inculcated by the
early Tractarians, none was given greater prominence than that of

the apostolical succession, constitution, order and spiritual independence of the Church Catholic. As is well known, in the face of the
Whig-Erastian reforms and constitutional changes of the early 1830s
they urged the clergy of the Church of England, in the words of No.
1 of the *Tracts for the Times*, to rely only on their 'apostolic descent',
and not merely worldly position. They assumed in doing this that
they were rousing discussion, in the words of the Advertisement to
the second volume of the Tracts, 'on points which had long remained
undisturbed'.[13] However the evidence from the previous half-century
shows just how mistaken they were in this assumption. Much too
much reliance has been placed upon Bishop Blomfield's supposed
and oft-quoted remark, apparently made to Joshua Watson on the
eve of the Oxford Movement, to the effect that the number of clergy
who still believed in the doctrine of the apostolical succession could
be counted on two hands.[14] Moreover one should be equally sceptical
about the validity of Gladstone's contention in the famous article in
the *Foreign and Colonial Review* in 1843, that few bishops and archdeacons in their pre-Tractarian era ever touched upon this subject
in their charges and sermons.[15] Significantly the old high churchmen
or so-called 'Zs' resented these assumptions about the period which
most of them had lived through, and in private correspondence with
their Tractarian friends went to enormous lengths to refute them.
For instance, in May 1836 one of the old high churchmen most
sympathetic to the new movement, Hugh James Rose, after perusing
No. 71 of the *Tracts for the Times*, wrote to Newman, its author: 'I wish
that you had somewhat more represented the Apostolic Succession
as a regular, undoubted doctrine, held undoubtingly by all true
churchmen, and only a little neglected – than as a thing to which
we were to recur as a sort of ancient novelty – a truth now first
recovered.'[16]

The charges of the bishops relating to the movement, which were
delivered in the years 1841 to 1843, were especially insistent upon
this point. The leaders and followers of the movement at the time,
and many later historians, were able to perceive little more than a
blind and negative Protestant spirit of condemnation in those
charges.[17] I do not propose to demonstrate the weakness of this view
here, but suffice to say that there were many contemporaries who
recognised in those charges positive statements of classical high
church teaching, and a generous anxiety to uphold what was good
and true in the movement, and in conformity with the old high
church tradition. A good source in this respect is an interesting work
entitled *Testimonies to Church Principles selected from Episcopal Charges and
Sermons*, published in 1843, which found the great bulk of them to be
much more in accord with the Tractarians than their Evangelical
opponents.[18] Even the extreme Tractarian Frederick Oakeley was
prepared to admit, early in 1843, that 'the general tenor of the charges
delivered during the past year has been in a most unprecedented

degree in favour of catholic views'.[19] Certainly many Evangelicals
were critical of the bishops for being too lenient. For instance, Archdeacon Browne could complain to C. P. Golightly in 1843: 'What an
afflicting consideration it is that no measures are taken by the bench
of bishops collectively for arresting the progress of either [Tractarian-
ism or Popery]. What indeed is to be expected, when the Primate
has a Puseyite for his chaplain, and the calumniator of Foxe for his
librarian.'[20]

Moreover the Evangelical divine William Goode made the point
still more strongly, when he complained that the 'culpable apathy or
worse, of the heads of the church in this matter is making our church
an object of wonder and I might almost say derision to the whole of
Protestant Europe and America'.[21]

All this is not surprising, considering that many of these bishops
in their earlier years had themselves been closely linked with the
'Hackney Phalanx', and what William Molesworth aptly described
as the 'Canterbury party' of Establishment high churchmen centred
around the court and government circles in the 1810s and 1820s.[22]
None the less this background made them keen to play down the
significance of what happened in 1833 and afterwards. The attitude
of Christopher Bethell, Bishop of Bangor, who as a member of the
'Phalanx' had been raised to the bishopric of Exeter in the 1800s,
was a case in point. As one who in his charges in that period had
emphasised the doctrines of the Church and succession, Bethell had
every right to complain of the Tractarians in his charge of 1843, that:

> Some of their encomiasts have spoken of them as truths which had
> been forgotten and lost to the church till they were rescued from
> oblivion by the authors of the Tracts. It may be allowed that they
> were kept much in the background but they never ceased to be
> held and avowed . . . in illustration of this, we need only refer to
> the writings of Archdeacon Daubeny, and Mr Jones of Nayland,
> whose works on the church were widely circulated, and received
> with great approbation.[23]

In fact we may cite among many others William Stevens's *Constitution
of the Catholic Church* (1784), Daubeny's *Guide to the Church* (1798) and
Sikes's *Parochial Communion* (1812), as examples. Another instance
illustrative of their real priorities was the especial concern of Horne,
Jones, Stevens and Daubeny, for the disestablished and recently
persecuted Episcopal Church in Scotland. Not only did they give
generous aid but they were active, along with another high
churchman, Bishop Horsley, in persuading parliament finally to
repeal the major disabilities on Scottish episcopacy in 1792.[24] Both
the Hutchinsonians and the leaders of the 'Phalanx' valued Establishment but still insisted that, in the end, it was only a most valuable
appendage. They were sensitive to charges of Erastianism levelled
against the Church of England of their day. For instance, in a letter to

Joshua Watson in 1815 Christopher Wordsworth actually complained that there was too much stress in SPCK publications on the Church as an Establishment.[25] Significantly in his memoir of Bishop Horne, first published in 1795, Jones of Nayland laid particular stress on his part in the restoration of the Scottish Episcopal Church to favour:

> In order to show not only that the bishops of Scotland are true Christian bishops, but that the bishops of England, from the part they kindly took in the affair, do little deserve the clamour which some have raised against them, as if they were so dazzled by their temporalities, as to lose sight of their spiritual character, and bury the christian bishop in the peer of parliament.[26]

The essential anti-Erastianism of these old high churchmen deserves emphasising, since from what the Tractarians themselves, and then later writers in the Catholic tradition, have assumed, they have been made to appear tainted in this respect.[27] The Tractarians felt that they were actually substituting what they called 'apostolicity' for what had passed as high churchmanship, but was really 'high establishmentism'[27] or Erastianism – Z-ism in Froude's vocabulary. The Zs, they assumed, were prepared to compromise the spiritual integrity and independence of the Church in order to preserve its mere temporal well-being, the trappings and privileges of Church Establishment. Seeking inspiration not only in the nonjurors but in St Ambrose and St Athanasius and even Hildebrand and Becket, the Tractarians found it, in William Copeland's words, 'a relief to contrast' those figures with 'the cold heartedness and semi-infidel conservatism of many of the maintainers of our so-called happy establishment'.[28] Indeed John Mason Neale even went so far as to claim that the old high church tradition, even its pure Laudian form, was infused by what he termed a 'fearful Erastianism'.[29] Yet the Tractarians and their successors have tended to pose a false dichotomy between zeal for the inherent spiritual rights of the Church and a loyal and hearty belief in Establishment and the positive role of the State, especially the crown, in matters ecclesiastical. The two co-existed quite happily, side by side, in old high church teaching. The royal supremacy was viewed in a positive light, as a reflection of the monarch's sacral and quasi-religious character as 'Defender of the Faith', whose duty was laid down in the coronation oath to watch over and protect the Church as a 'nursing father', not imperious tyrant.[30] The non-established Episcopal Church in America and especially one of its leading figures, John Henry Hobart, are usually seen as potent forces of inspiration for the Tractarians. However, unlike the Tractarians, old high churchmen were not always impressed by the example of that church[31] and they reacted angrily to Bishop Hobart's strictures on Church-State relations in England in 1826.[32] Watson, for instance, was apt to refer disparagingly to the 'pseudo-anti-erastianism of America'.[33] Disestablishment played into the hands of ultra-Protestants and republicans. Thus, they would disagree with those Tractarians who ascribed all the evils they faced in the 1830s to the tyranny of State laws. As Edward Churton reminded William Copeland in 1840:

> The religion of Ultra-Protestantism is essentially a religion against all ordinances, whether of Pope, Prelate, or Caesar, and the man who adopts it, calls history an old almanac, and writes the year of his own conversion or first formation of a system as the year one of Christianity. It is not the result of an Establishment, but pride of reason and spiritual wickedness and rebellion.[34]

Thus in a real sense prelate and Caesar, church and king, stood or fell together, and of course, the lessons of the French Revolution seemed to provide exclusive proof for the axiom. Yet for all their strictures on 'Z' attitudes the early Tractarians themselves were in fact remarkably in accord with this more political facet of old high churchmanship. Virtually to a man, they were high Tories,[35] and ardent royalists – W. G. Ward causing great offence by his irreverence to the memory of the 'Royal Martyr'[36] Charles I. For it was devotion to the principles enshrined in the coronation oath, almost as much as to the notion of 'apostolical descent' that was at stake for the Tractarians in 1833.[37] It was only later that the view developed that the origin of the movement had no connection with the political changes of the time.[38]

Above all we should recognise, as Edward Norman has reminded us, 'that it was the interdependence of church and state, and not the dependence of the church upon the state' that underlay the old high church position.[39] In fact so interchangeable did the two often appear that there is no doubt that the very term 'Establishment' was often used as much to denote the actual episcopal regimen and spiritual constitution as the merely temporal framework of the Church. Therefore we should not be surprised to find startling assertions of Church independence in even those pre-Tractarian high churchmen who had the worst reputation for being merely Establishment-minded, 'high and dry' and worldly. Godfrey Faussett, Lady Margaret Professor of Divinity in the University of Oxford, and the author of a bitter attack on the Tractarians in a notorious sermon called *The Revival of Popery*, preached from the university pulpit in 1838, appeared to 'apostolicals' as a prime case in point, the personification of the pampered aristo-crat in ecclesiastical dress. The Tractarians much disliked Faussett's ethos, and in an article in the *British Critic* in 1841 Thomas Mozley made a scurrilous parody of him[40] which caused widespread offence and embarrassed Keble and Newman. However there was much more to Faussett than the Tractarians, and especially Newman who wrote a famous reply to his *Revival of Popery* sermon, realised. At that time Faussett had over thirty years of writings in defence and propagation of high church principles behind him – writings which reveal him to have been no mere Erastian, political churchman. In his Bampton Lectures of 1820 Faussett maintained that the union of Church and State was a union of independent powers on the principles of federal, not incorporating, union. Certainly his ideal was that of Hooker and the Elizabethan settlement, not that of the later nonjurors, as it was for the Tractarians, but he was not complacent or prepared to temporise.[41] He frankly castigated the practical deviations from the Elizabethan ideal that had occurred, such as the silencing of Convocation since 1717, the persecution of the Scottish Church and establishment of presbyterianism in Scotland, and the prolonged failure to send bishops to America. He complained of 'the listless apathy, the blind security, and latitudinarian spirit of these alarming times', and lamented 'a complete confusion of ideas between the church as a society of divine institution, and the church as a political establishment, or rather, perhaps a disposition to consider the church, so far as its outward polity is concerned, as left altogether to human discretion'.[42] Clearly the utilitarian arguments for Establishment of Warburton, William Paley and their school were abhorrent to him.

On the question of apostolical succession Faussett was especially explicit. Even Newman's apparently radical suggestion in No. 41 of the *Tracts for the Times*, that the Thirty-Nine Articles be amended to include an explicit statement of the doctrine,[43] had been prefigured by Faussett in these lectures.[44] Moreover John Hume Spry, rector of Marylebone and also considered to be very 'high and dry', made the same call in his own Bampton Lectures for 1816, entitled *Christian Unity Doctrinally and Historically Considered*. Like works such as Daubeny's *Guide* and Sikes's *Parochial Communion*, it contained an explicit enunciation of the classic high Anglican 'branch theory',[45] by which catholicity was made dependent on a strict adherence of the churches to episcopal order and succession, and as a result of which Protestant dissenters were effectively 'unchurched' while Rome as well as the Orthodox were deemed true in foundation, if corrupt in practice. In fact all the evidence suggests that the late 1810s and 1820s witnessed a steady growth in popularity and acceptance of the doctrines of the Church, a point actually insisted upon by a writer in the high church periodical journal, the *Christian Remembrancer*, in 1821.[46] Two other works that had particular influence were Joshua Watson's brother, Archdeacon John James Watson's *Divine Commission and Perpetuity of the Christian Priesthood* (1816) – a work which owed much in spirit to that of the nonjuror George Hickes's *Christian Priesthood* of 1712 – and John Oxlee's *Three sermons . . . on the Power, Origin and Succession of the Christian Hierarchy* (1821). The kinship of Watson's work to Tractarian publications on the same theme in the 1830s was such that it was republished in 1839, precisely because, as Joshua Watson told Henry Handley Norris, 'the 30 years which have crossed over our heads since its delivery would save it from the

prejudice of being only the product of the current controversy'.[47]
However the writings of the obscure rector of Scrawton, Yorkshire,
John Oxlee, reveal him as a still more remarkable precursor of the
movement on the same theme. This was so, not simply because of
his almost monotonous emphasis on apostolic succession and endeav-
ours to prove in table form what he described as 'a continued and
uninterrupted list of Christian bishops from the blessed Apostles,
Peter, Paul, and John, down to the present prelates of Canterbury,
York and London'.[48] This in itself could be dry, uninspiring work.
What is striking about Oxlee and a whole number of other pre-
Tractarian high churchmen is another more imaginative, out-going,
truly Catholic dimension, not often fully recognised.

It was to be a familiar criticism of old high churchmen by the later
Tractarians that, holding the apostolical succession in only a negative
sense and failing to draw out its consequences, they were incorrigibly
insular. They were considered only to value the doctrine as a weapon
in the Anglican armoury against Rome, to glory too much in the
isolation of the English Church from the Continent, and to be infected
by what John Mason Neale described as a 'Donatist temper'.[49] It is
true that to a great extent the old high churchmen's very sense of
kinship with Rome on account of a common apostolical heritage
through the channel of episcopal order, led them to emphasise Rome's
supposed doctrinal and practical 'corruptions', and thereby shield
the Church of England from the charge of schism at the time of the
Reformation.[50] Some of them, such as Thomas Burgess, Bishop of
Salisbury, seemed to fit Neale's description and wrote lengthy treatises asserting the apparent original independence from Rome, of
primitive, apostolically ordered British churches.[51] Nevertheless it
was hard for even the most anti-Romanist of pre-Tractarian high
churchmen entirely to overlook or deny the fact that the English
Church had depended on Rome for many centuries,[52] both for the
reconversion of England by Roman missionaries in Anglo-Saxon
times, and above all for the lineal transmission of her apostolic
succession. There were many strikingly candid admissions of indebt-
edness to Rome. Thus John Oxlee looked forward to a reunion of
Christendom on the basis of a mutual intercommunion of episcopally
constituted 'branch' churches, once Rome had been shorn of her
supposed later 'corruptions' and had returned to her original 'pure'
state. Oxlee's readiness to commend what he called 'the glorious
episcopate of Gregory the Great' and 'the venerable see of Rome',[53]
made him rejoice that the Church of England had derived her orders
through such a source, and poured scorn on Protestant cavils at the
fact. Stephen Hyde Cassan made the point more forcefully in an
aside in his *Lives of the Bishop of Winchester*, published in 1827:

She [Rome] is our Mother-Church, in as much as it is through
her, and through her alone, as a connecting link that we can, with

any degree of certainty, derive the right of administering the word of God and the sacraments. Those who would thus disclaim our Romish parentage seem to forget that the further they remove us, in the superabundance of their zeal, from the Roman Catholic Church, the lower they sink us, and the nearer they cause us to approach to the degraded and precarious position of Dissenters.[54]

However perhaps the most remarkable figure of all was Samuel Wix, rector of St Bartholomew-the-Less, London. In his significantly entitled *Christian Union without the Abuses of Popery*, published in 1820, Wix maintained that 'no solid objection prevails against the Church of England attempting an union with the Church of Rome, since the Church of Rome is acknowledged by the Church of England to be a true apostolical church'.[55] Wix even went so far as to predate the very argument employed by Newman in 1841, in Tract 90, when Newman had sought to distinguish between the so-called practical corruptions of the popular Roman religious system, which both labelled 'popery', and the more 'catholic' or 'primitive' official teaching of the Roman Church as enshrined in the Council of Trent. Newman sought to justify this position by appealing to the authority of Charles Lloyd, Bishop of Oxford, from whom he and other future Tractarians first imbibed Catholic Anglican principles in the 1820s.[56] In fact Newman's views were more closely anticipated by Wix rather than Lloyd. For both argued that Rome in her official teaching actually disowned this supposed popular system. What mattered was that many of these later corruptions such as the invocation of saints and communion under one kind, were not always '*de fide*' matters anyway. As long as they could simply be dismissed as 'things indifferent' on the Anglican principle of adiaphora, then here was a basis for reconciliation.[57] Clearly from all this the concept of the 'via media' as formulated by Newman in his *Prophetical Office of the Church*, by which the Church of England was firmly detached from the level of the Protestant churches of the Continent, and defined as at least as far removed from Geneva as from Rome, was very much a living reality for high churchmen in the half-century prior to the movement. Henry Handley Norris made this point quite as uncompromisingly as any of the Tractarians, as early as 1812, when he wrote:

> If names had any weight, I much more highly prize the title of a Catholic than that of a Protestant, which later appellation I am by no means fond of, as it confounds one with those from whom Christianity, I verily believe, has suffered more outrages than from the papists themselves. The distinguishing title of a member of the Church of England is a Reformed Catholic – and this places him in a central situation from which the Papist and the larger portion of that mixed multitude known by the name of protestant diverge, in opposite directions indeed but to equal distances.[58]

Another important aspect of the way in which the high church tradition prefigured Tractarianism in the half-century preceding 1833 was in its deference to antiquity, and especially the writings of the early Fathers, as either testimonies to fundamental doctrines or as standards of faith and practice. No. 78 of the *Tracts for the Times* was devoted to a *'catenae patrum'* of Anglican divines who had upheld the so-called Vincentian rule – *'quod semper, quod ubique, et quod ab omnibus'* – the principle formulated by Vincent of Lérins in the fifth century. High churchmen had long appealed to this rule for a Catholic consent of Fathers and councils as the basis of Catholic truth. Unlike ultra-Protestants, they did not rest content with the testimony of Scripture alone. In Tract 78, in Keble's famous Visitation sermon of 1836, *Primitive Tradition recognised in Holy Scripture*, and in Newman's controversy with the Abbé Jager between 1834 and 1836, due acknowledgement was made to the Caroline divines and nonjurors for their witness to this rule. However the witness of high churchmen of the previous half-century was almost entirely overlooked. Works which did uphold it in that period included Kett's Bampton Lectures (1793), Daubeny's *Guide* (1798), Van Mildert's Boyle Lectures (1804), Martin Routh's *Reliquae Sacrae* (1814), Oxlee's *Christian Priesthood* (1816), Spry's Bampton Lectures (1816), Archdeacon Pott's *Grounds and Principles of the Church of England* (1824) and Bishop Kaye's *Ecclesiastical History of the Second and Third Centuries* (1826).

However there were two vitally important works to which the Tractarians did acknowledge their debt – Bishop Jebb's sermon, published in 1815, entitled *The Peculiar Character of the Church of England as distinguished from other branches of the Reformation, and from the modern Church of Rome*;[59] and the later Provost of Oriel Edward Hawkins's sermon of 1819, *The Use and Importance of Unauthoritative Tradition*. Many of Hawkins's latitudinarian friends such as Whately and Arnold were dismayed and embarrassed by the use which the Tractarians were to make of this sermon in the 1830s. For instance, in 1835 Thomas Arnold complained that Hawkins's sermon had 'served the cause of schism and error',[60] while in 1836 he told Whately that Hawkins had 'contributed to their mischief by his unhappy sermon on Tradition'.[61] Hawkins was sensitive to these criticisms, and complained to Whately in 1836, 'Keble has published a very puerile sermon on Primitive Tradition, which makes me more desirous of following your advice and rewriting "unauthoritative Tradition" '.[62] Yet though Hawkins might try to retract or shift his ground his influence on Newman, as Louis Bouyer has shown, remained profound. Significantly Newman defended his view of the *'disciplina arcani'*, the idea of a secret tradition within the bosom of the Church, which he first formulated in his *Arians of the Fourth Century* in 1832[63] by direct reference both to the writings of Bishop Kaye,[64] and to Hawkins's sermon on Tradition.[65] Moreover he was able to go to the same source in order to defend the *'argumentum ad hominem'* which he employed in No. 85 of the *Tracts for the Times*,[66] to justify such doctrines as the Trinity on the basis of tradition alone, on the grounds that they were not clear from the text of Scripture only.[67]

Yet perhaps surprisingly it was in its character as a primarily religious, spiritual movement that Tractarianism owed its greatest debt to the high churchmanship of the preceding half-century. Following the verdict of the Tractarians themselves many later writers have taken for granted a massive degeneration from the ideal of primitive holiness after the revolution and Hanoverian succession, even within the ranks of the high church party.[68] Brilioth drew heavily on the testimony of Bishop Jebb and his lifelong friend and correspondent Alexander Knox, who both had strong formative influences on the movement, and were both very un-'Z'-like in the almost Evangelical warmth and feeling of their piety. In comparison the men of the 'Phalanx' and their associates seemed very 'high and dry'. It was Brilioth's contention, after showing the comparison, that:

> the weakness of that kind of High Churchmanship which was preached by Daubeny and his likes, and its inability to win the ear of the age, rested perhaps not least on the fact that they so entirely cut themselves off from the spiritual well which streamed forth from the Evangelical revival of the eighteenth century.[69]

There was a certain truth in this; a deep seated prejudice against any so-called 'enthusiasm' in matters spiritual was responsible for some lowering of the religious temperature among many old high churchmen. Yet the charge of worldliness and coldness has been over-played, and Brilioth's estimate is in need of distinct modification. The Hutchinsonians, George Horne especially, retained an almost Evangelical warmth of religious expression in devotion, but perhaps more surprisingly even Daubeny, whom Brilioth described as clinging to 'a narrow ecclesiasticism',[70] was no exception in this respect. One of his first actions on becoming a prebend of Salisbury in 1784 was to transcribe Bishop Andrewes's Morning Prayer for daily use.[71] Moreover his aids to devotion read like a catalogue of the richest treasures of Caroline and nonjuring spirituality – Jeremy Taylor's *Holy Living and Holy Dying*, Bishop Wilson's *Sacra Privata*, Bishop Ken's *Manual for Winchester Scholars*.[72] In fact it was Brilioth's main source for his verdict – Knox and Jebb – that needs scrutiny. On his visits to England the famous Bishop of Limerick recorded his favourable impression of Henry Handley Norris, but also his criticisms of him and the 'Phalanx' as a whole, Sikes and Spry especially, for rigidity and dryness,[73] but it was Daubeny who attracted his severest strictures. However the attitude of Alexander Jolly, the Scottish episcopalian Bishop of Moray, towards Knox and Jebb's criticism of Daubeny and the 'Phalanx' is most revealing. After sorting through Jolly's papers after his death in 1838 James Walker, Bishop of Edinburgh, wrote to Henry Handley Norris, to reassure him just how much Jolly had disapproved of Knox and Jebb's criticisms of Daubeny as contained in their recently published *Thirty Years Correspondence*.[74] Another high churchman of an apparently similar dry mould, Daubeny's diocesan Thomas Burgess, Bishop of Salisbury, has been similarly misunderstood. He was much more than a narrow 'high and dry' anti-Roman polemicist. According to Burgess's biographer James Harford, when the future Bishop of Salisbury had been rector of Winston, Co. Durham, his spiritual reflections 'were chiefly written in the blank leaves and in the margins of some of his favourite devotional writers, among whom may be enumerated Bishop Wilson's "Sacra Privata" . . . Payne's Thomas à Kempis, Nelson's "Practice of True Devotion", Law's "Serious Call" '.[75]

It is the influence of William Law, the nonjuror's *Serious Call* (1728) on old high churchmen, that provides an important piece of evidence to their continued adherence to the ascetic element in spirituality which was especially to characterise the Oxford Movement. It was not the Tractarians who first rediscovered Law, as is often supposed. For instance, George Horne moulded his spirituality on Law's ascetic example,[76] while it was Thomas Rennell, Dean of Winchester 1805–40 and a leading member of the 'Hackney Phalanx', who first introduced the young W. F. Hook to Law's *Serious Call*, while Hook was a curate on the Isle of Wight in the early 1820s.[77] Examples of the value set upon fasting and celibacy can repeatedly be found. Both Horne and William Stevens frequently referred to the latter in their writings, as a worthy spiritual ideal.[78] We can even find surprisingly favourable views of at least the original monastic ideal. Certainly there were some robustly Protestant, 'high and dry' denunciations of it in any form, notably from Robert Southey in his *Book of the Church* of 1824. Thus Southey attacked monasticism even in what he termed 'its first stage, when it had nothing useful or ornamental to compensate for its preposterous austerities'. He poured scorn on those pilgrims of the early Church who went 'to behold and reverence, like a living idol, a maniac in Syria, who, under that burning climate, passed his life upon the top of a lofty column, and tied with the goguecs of India in the folly and perseverance with which he inflicted voluntary tortures upon himself'.[79] Yet even Southey advocated religious sisterhoods in the Church of England, and 'the first Anglican convent was established as his posthumous memorial'.[80] Clearly there was a tension between medievalism and anti-catholicism in Southey. However, more typical of the better type of old churchman was Edward Churton's love of Anglo-Saxon saints such as Bede and Alcuin.[81] Churton condemned what he called Southey's 'absurd vulgar trash about St Dunstan' and for following 'no system of distinguishing between the age of credulity and the age of imposture'.[82] Churton was quite prepared to defend the ideal of early monasticism. He wrote:

It is impossible for a serious mind to suppose that a rule of life so early introduced into the Christian church, so approved by the most eminent Fathers and confessors of those early times, and so long kept up in almost every christian country, can have been allowed without some providential purpose.[83]

Moreover both Watson and Norris were favourably disposed towards the Tractarian plan for the revival of sisterhoods. Watson was even sympathetic to a revival of monasticism itself. As Charles Marriott told Newman, after staying at the home of Watson's sister-in-law at Daventry: 'I was desirous to know what he thought of the monastic life . . . I found the good old man . . . spoke decidedly in favour of some institution of the kind. I told him what you were doing at Littlemore, and he seemed to like the notion of it much.'[84]

Another characteristic theme of Tractarian spirituality was of course that spirit of awe and reserve in sacred matters, borne out of a reaction to the apparently profane over-familiarity of popular protestantism. Newman seized upon the concept of the '*disciplina arcani*' in the Fathers, according to which there had to be reserve or restraint in the communication of religious knowledge, so as to avoid a situation whereby 'pearls' might be 'cast before swine'.[85] As is well known, the notion was given full expression in No. 80 of the *Tracts for the Times*: Isaac Williams, *On Reserve in Communicating Religious Knowledge*. The Tractarians, especially Keble, recognised a debt to Bishop Butler on this,[86] but it is wrong to assume that they were the first to rediscover it. The Hutchinsonians had all witnessed to it, in practice as well as theory. There were some at the time who realised that this was so. For instance, in 1846 at the time when the Tractarian position on this question was widely assumed to be novel William Teale, in a memoir of Jones of Nayland, with somewhat heavy irony cited Jones as an example of the fact 'that English churchmen had condemned the irreverent admixture of things sacred and profane long before some late assailants of the same offences against decorum and religious feeling were born to denounce them to the world as the results of the English Reformation'.[87] Particularly striking was the precise way in which the central argument of Tract 80 was prefigured by Daubeny in a charge which he delivered to the clergy of Salisbury archdeaconry in 1824, when he attacked what he called 'the unreserved and indiscriminate application of strong evangelic language to Christians who might be in the infancy of their growth' and therefore could not 'be supposed to have attained in any degree to that stage of spiritual proficiency, to which that language originally belonged'.[88] Moreover this ethos of reserve was central to the spiritual make-up of the 'Hackney Phalanx'. It lay at the root of their opposition to propagate the Scriptures without any comment or guidance among the unlearned, and thus determined their resistance to the activities of the British and Foreign Bible Society in the thirty years

prior to the movement. It was thus indicative of Newman's new
adherence to the high church camp when in 1829 he formally cut his
links with that organisation. Certainly Newman, Keble or Williams
in the mature stage of Tractarianism could not have bettered the
reasons given by Henry Handley Norris for his opposition to the
Bible Society, in a letter to his friend Ralph Churton, the father of
Edward, in 1813. Scripture, he wrote:

> is not in the purpose of God, the instrument of conversion – but the
> repository of divine knowledge for the perfecting of those already
> converted. I mean that it is the children's bread and not to be cast
> to dogs . . . the Scriptures are not a self-sufficient means of grace
> and salvation but co-ordinate only with the appointed ministry
> who must superintend the cultivation of the Divine word in order
> to procure for it the blessing of increase from the Almighty.[89]

Another important element in Tractarian religion, wholeheartedly
embraced by old high churchmen of the preceding years, was its anti-
rationalist emphasis. It needs to be recognised that a depreciation of
the eighteenth-century cult of unaided human reason and perfecti-
bility, a rejection of mere moralism and utilitarianism as the basis of
faith and conduct, as exemplified in the writings of William Paley,
was as much a feature of the Hutchinsonians and Hackney Phalanx
as of the Oxford Movement. Froude's Essay on Rationalism,
published in his *Remains*, and a famous university sermon of
Newman's of 1830 on the subject, set the characteristic Tractarian
tone of emphasis on childlike humility and reverence for truth. As
such they are usually regarded as complementary to, and the true
successors of, those eighteenth-century Evangelicals who assailed the
standard moralism and evidential theology of the day, a theology to
which not only outright latitudinarians but the so-called 'high and
dry' apparently subscribed. It is often forgotten that the Hutchinsonians and the 'Phalanx' also joined forces with Evangelicals, in
asserting the absolute supremacy of faith over verifiable external
evidence. In short, they were quite as antagonistic to Paleyism as
Evangelicals and Tractarians alike. As George Horne put it:

> Reason can no more find out, without the help of Revelation,
> the original state and constitution of man, the changes that have
> happened in his nature, and the counsels of God, that have taken
> place in consequence of these changes . . . than she can prove
> metaphysically, that William the Conqueror vanquished Harold,
> at Hastings, in Sussex.[90]

Significantly the two most lasting products of the high church revival
of the 1790s – the foundation by Horne and Jones of the periodical
British Critic in 1792, and the Society for the Reformation of Principles
in 1795, with its series of publications entitled *The Scholar Armed against
the errors of the times* – both had as their original leading aim the

reversal of the rational spirit of the age. It is interesting to note that the Tractarian William Copeland, in his *Narrative of the Oxford Movement*, specifically acknowledged the close affinity of the *Scholar Armed* in its aims and spirit with the *Tracts for the Times*.[91]

The final aspect of Tractarian spirituality which the older high churchmen foreshadowed was an emphasis on the importance of mysticism, allegory and typology, and what might be called the sacramental principle of the symbolism of rites and ceremonies. This aspect of Tractarian teaching, as is well known, found expression in Pusey's unpublished lectures of 1836, on types and prophecies, and in Keble's No. 89 of the *Tracts for the Times*, *On the Mysticism of the Fathers*. At its root lay a consciousness that not only was man's reason and his ability to glimpse into the spiritual and even visible creation necessarily limited, but that for the man of faith there was another method of perceiving spiritual truth. This method lay through the typological principle which Keble defined in a well-known phrase, 'as the doctrine that material phenomenon are both the types and the instruments of things unseen'.[92] The Tractarians found this principle to have been employed by Hooker[93] and later Bishop Butler,[94] but overlooked the contribution of the Hutchinsonians and members of the 'Phalanx' such as Van Mildert. It was given perhaps its fullest expression in a course of lectures given by Jones of Nayland preached in Nayland parish church in 1786, entitled *On the Figurative Language of Holy Scripture*. Like Pusey in his lectures in 1836, Jones of Nayland argued that the language of Scripture consisted not merely in words themselves but 'signs or figures taken from visible things'.[95] To explain his meaning, he demonstrated that religious rites and ceremonies were far more than 'things indifferent' as some held, but divinely-ordained visible signs of 'things unseen':

> Priests and singers in our church wear a white linen garment as a sign of purity, and to give them a nearer alliance to the company of heaven. Chanting by responses . . . was intended to imitate the choir of angels, which cry out to one another with alternate adoration. The primitive christians turned towards the east, in their worship, to signify their respect to the true Light of the World. They set up candles as a sign of their illumination by the Gospel; and evergreens are still placed there at Christmas, to remind us that a new and perpetual spring of immortality is restored to us, even in the middle of winter, by the coming of Jesus Christ.[96]

This theoretical sacramentalism was reflected in the attention to ritual and ceremonial practice by old high churchmen. In his university sermon of 1830 on the subject Newman argued that Christians 'must receive the Gospel literally on their knees, and in a temper altogether different from that critical and argumentative spirit which sitting and listening engender'.[97] Accordingly he always made a point of kneeling or bowing to the altar in St Mary's for long periods,[98] a

practice which George Home and then Dr Routh observed in
Magdalen Chapel.[99] Thomas Sanders had made precisely the same
point as Newman in a sermon before the University of Oxford in St
Mary's in 1801. Sanders condemned the modern practice of congre-
gations sitting when they should kneel, arguing, like Newman was
to, that it was 'essentially necessary that our outward deportment
should indicate humility, and correspond with the inward disposition
of the soul'.[100] It was this same conviction that led many old high
churchmen to state their preference for the spirit of Roman Catholic
rather than Presbyterian worshippers. For instance, Daubeny, after
a tour of the Continent in 1788, lamented that the Swiss Reformed
were not what he called 'kneeling Christians', but rather, 'peripatetic
Christians'.[101] Thus it is not surprising that high churchmen should
have become actively engaged in a movement towards ritual and
ceremonial renewal and restoration, long before the ecclesiological
arm or ally of the Oxford Movement, the Cambridge Camden
Society, took up this cause in the 1840s. Both Watson and Norris
had for long been involved in just such a cause, the former being
responsible for restoring the print of the communion office in the
Book of Common Prayer to large bold type.[102] Watson's own career
and experiences made him most impatient of the assumption of
Tractarians and ecclesiologists that all was cold and dead in ritual
before their own emergence. As he put it, in the early 1840s at the
time of the so-called ritual controversy, 'much of the evil we now
deprecate arises from those who are now agitators not having seen
the church in her beauty in their own early days'.[103] He was especially
critical of the Camden Society for their attitude in this respect – 'the
impertinence of these Camdenians', he wrote, 'is perfectly unendur-
able . . . they would almost seem to take to themselves the language
of the prophetess, and say that the highways were unoccupied, and
the people wandered in byways, until the Camdenians arose, masters
in Israel'.[104]

In conclusion, the degree of high church continuity throughout the
half-century prior to the movement has been seriously underesti-
mated, and the extent to which the Tractarians owed a direct debt
to the high Anglican tradition upheld by their precursors, for too
long overlooked. It was a debt which Pusey warmly acknowledged
when he wrote to Joshua Watson in the summer of 1839 after a visit
to the venerable old high churchmen at Brighton. Pusey told Watson,
'how cheering' it was:

to be recognised by you as carrying on the same torch which we
had received from yourself, and those of your generation, who
had remained faithful to the old teaching. We seemed no longer
separated by the chasm from the old times and old paths to which
we wished to lead people back; the links which united us to those
of old seemed restored.[105]

None the less there were important differences in both temper and teaching, between the new and old high churchmen. The differences were evident as early as 1833, and Keble implicity recognised them when in that very year he informed Newman that, in the manner of Burke's pamphlet with regard to differences among the Whigs in the 1790s, he was planning 'an Appeal from the New to the Old Churchmen, or some such thing'.[106] These differences widened and deepened as the years passed. Only Watson's generosity of spirit prevented him from spelling them out more clearly to his Tractarian friends. Above all the older men of Hackney lamented a spirit of youthful impatience with, and even growing insubordination towards, episcopal authority.[107] They sighed over their apparent want of discretion, practical sense and sound judgment. As Edward Churton told William Copeland in 1841, 'I love them, but how is it possible to keep them, when their conduct tomorrow may contradict the defence you have made for them today?'[108] In particular the old high churchmen regretted that the Tractarians, for all their sincere professions that they were but following in 'the old paths', had not been better grounded in the older tradition. As a writer in the *Christian Remembrancer*, a periodical which reflected the older standpoint, put it in 1841:

> The leading minds among these writers had not the advantage of being trained themselves in the Anglo-Catholic school; they had to grope for their principles, as men suddenly beset by nightly robbers catch at such weapons as the moment allows ... Their sentiments therefore had not been worked out by a previous development of the English system, but were taken up by persons who came rather as allies than as subjects to the defence of the church.[109]

Joshua Watson made the same point himself, complaining in private that the Tractarians 'begin to fight before they scarcely know the weapons wherewith they should arm themselves'.[110] In consequence he felt that they did less than justice to the vigour and achievements of the high church tradition in the previous century,[111] while Hugh James Rose was especially critical of Newman's contention in the introduction to his *Lectures on the prophetical office of the Church*, that Anglicanism had never had a wide influence historically while both Romanism and dissent had.[112] The old high churchmen as a whole insisted that the Tractarians exaggerated not only the extent of decay in the past but the evils of the present condition of the Church. Significantly Churton later told William Gresley how fond Watson was of quoting, against the Tractarians, Hooker's dictum: 'He who goes about to persuade the young that they are ill-governed, shall never want hearers.'[113] Essentially, because they came to similar views but by very different routes, the Tractarians were never likely to rest content with the careful bounds and limits observed by the

old high churchmen. Moreover the fact that so many of them had
been reared in an alien religious tradition in itself caused them to
misunderstand the high church tradition, and led them to pervert it
to some extent. In the end, what Churton called a 'practical "beau
ideal" of catholicity'[114] that was to be strived after, was substituted
for what old high churchmen were content to respect as the concrete
and living catholicism of the Church of England as she already was.
However the question of the full extent to which the Oxford Movement in its mature and later phases came to diverge from the old
high church tradition is beyond our scope here. Yet that which we
have touched upon, and especially the alarm and response of the
bishops, many of whom, such as Christopher Bethell, had been
associated with the 'Hackney Phalanx', leaves us justified in at least
posing the question as to whether in the final analysis this later
divergence was not to prove as significant as the broad continuity
we have outlined.

For if the evidence of Joshua Watson from the manuscript diary
of his niece Mary, and the testimony of others in the 'Phalanx' is
anything to go by, then George Tavard was absolutely right when
he maintained that the most powerful theological opposition to the
movement actually came from those who had always professed what
had hitherto passed as high churchmanship, and not 'from the Evangelicals, who were far too far from it to be able to understand it, or
from the latitudinarians, who were not equipped to treat it as
anything but as crypto-Romanism'.[115] Thus whereas in its basic
themes and temper this chapter shows the movement to have been
clearly the heir of a rich and varied pedigree of high Anglicanism,
this always needs to be qualified by the reflection that its later growth
and development was by no means always on the lines that older
adherents of that tradition would have considered sound or legitimate. In the end we must agree with George Ayliffe Poole, friend of
W. F. Hook and an old high churchman who keenly supported the
movement in its early stages. For Poole, with the advent of the Oxford
Movement, 'a modification of High Churchmen arose, which we are
obliged to recognise as another party'.[116] For all the debt that movement owed the high Anglican tradition, Tractarianism and the Anglicanism of that tradition were not identical.

1. E. A. Knox, *The Tractarian Movement, 1833–1845: a study of the Oxford
   Movement, as a phase of the religious revival in western Europe in the second
   quarter of the nineteenth century* (London 1933), ch. 18.
2. S. Leslie, *The Oxford Movement* (London 1933). See also S. Ollard, *The
   Anglo-Catholic Revival* (London 1925); F. L. Cross, *The Oxford Movement
   and the Seventeenth Century* (London 1933); C. B. Moss, *The Orthodox
   Revival, 1833–1933* (London n.d.); H. L. Stewart, *A Century of Anglo-
   Catholicism* (London 1929); D. Morse-Boycott, *The Secret Story of the*

Oxford Movement (London 1933); T. H. Whitton, *The Necessity of Catholic Reunion* (London 1933).

3. See Yngve Brilioth, *The Anglican Revival: Studies in the Oxford Movement* (London 1925), ch. 2 and 4.

4. See for example, F. W. Cornish, *The English Church in the Nineteenth Century*, 2 vols (London 1910), I, pp. 62–76; G. Worley, *The Catholic Revival of the Nineteenth Century* (London 1894), ch. 2; G. Wakeling, *The Oxford Church Movement: sketches and recollections* (London 1895); J. H. Moorman, 'Forerunners of the Oxford Movement', *Theology*, 25 (1933), pp. 6–11; B. Reardon, *From Coleridge to Gore: a century of religious thought* (London 1971), pp. 31–41.

5. Quoted by C. P. S. Clarke, 'The Genesis of the Movement', in N. P. Williams and C. Harris, *Northern Catholicism: centenary studies in the Oxford and parallel movements* (London 1933), p. 8.

6. N. Murray, 'The Influence of the French Revolution on the Church of England and its Rivals, 1789–1802' (unpublished D. Phil. thesis, Univ. Oxford 1975). The term 'Hackney Phalanx' was used to denote the large and rather amorphous group of pre-Tractarian high churchmen, based in, or linked to, the metropolis of London, which was particularly active in the years, c. 1805 until c. 1835. The 'Hackney Phalanx' took its name from the vicar (afterwards rector) of Hackney, Archdeacon John James Watson, elder brother of Joshua Watson, its unofficial leader, and from the rector of South Hackney, Watson's close friend, Henry Handley Norris.

7. Hurrell Froude first used the slang epithet 'Z' to describe conservative or old high churchmen, while Evangelicals were labelled 'Xs' and the Tractarians or 'apostolicals' were termed 'Ys'. cf. *Remains of the Late Reverend Richard Hurrell Froude*, MA [Part I], 2 vols (London 1838), I, p. 429.

8. Quoted in A. Webster, *Joshua Watson: the story of a layman* (London 1954), p. 29.

9. B. Harrison to W. E. Gladstone, 16 November 1843, MS Add. 44204 ff. 114–15. Gladstone MSS (British Library). Typical of the Tractarian attitude which Harrison deplored was Manning's remark to Newman in 1843, 'that the church has passed under a fearful influence for 150 years is sadly true; but surely the last ten years have dispelled much, and brought the living church back again?' H. E. Manning to J. H. Newman, 23 October 1843, Manning MSS V, 26 (Bodleian).

10. J. Beaven, *A Calm Exposure of the Unfairness of the 'General Reply to all Objections' of 'Ancient Christianity'* (London 1840), p. 37.

11. For an account of Hutchinsonianism, see E. Churton, *Memoir of Joshua Watson*, 2 vols, (Oxford 1861), I, pp. 39ff. cf. R. Spearman, *Life of John Hutchinson prefixed to A Supplement to the Works of John Hutchinson Esq.* (London 1765), pp. i–xiv.

12. E. Churton to W. Gresley, 25 May 1846, Pusey MSS (Pusey House).

13. *Tracts for the Times*, II, p. ii.

14. W. Copeland to T. Bowdler, 6 December 1841. Copeland MSS (Pusey House). cf. W. Copeland, MS, 'Narrative of the Oxford Movement' (n.pl. n.d.), Copeland MSS (Pusey House). Newman helped to give credence to the alleged remark. See John Henry Newman, *Apologia Pro Vita Sua* (London 1864), p. 94.

15. Draft of Gladstone's article, 'Present Aspect of the Church', in *Foreign and Colonial Review* (1843), MS Add. 44360 f. 250, Gladstone MSS (British Library).

16. H. J. Rose to J. H. Newman, 9 May 1836, in J. W. Burgon, *Lives of Twelve Good Men* (London 1889), p. 108.

17. See Newman's comment about 'the growing consensus of the episcopal bench against catholic truth', J. H. Newman to E. B. Pusey, 24 August 1842, Pusey MSS (Pusey House). cf. J. H. Newman to H. A. Woodgate, 8 November 1841, MS Eng. Lett. d. 102 f. 103 (Bodleian). See Keble's comment on the bishops: 'I see few signs of good information among them', J. Keble to J. T. Coleridge, 24 November 1841, MS Eng. Lett. d. 134 f. 37 (Bodleian).

18. *Testimonies to Church Principles, selected from Episcopal Charges and Sermons* (London 1843), p. 5.

19. *British Critic*, 33 (January 1843), p. 274.

20. J. H. Browne to C. P. Golightly, 9 June 1842, MS 1804 f. 106, Golightly MSS (Lambeth Palace).

21. W. Goode to C. P. Golightly, 29 May 1843, MS 1804 f.108, Golightly MSS (Lambeth Palace).

22. W. N. Molesworth, *History of the Church of England from 1660* (London 1882), p. 317.

23. C. Bethell, *A Charge to the Clergy of the Diocese of Bangor* (London 1843), pp. 15–16.

24. W. Stevens to J. Boucher, 11 September 1793, B/3/38 Boucher MSS, Locker-Lampson Coll. (East Sussex County Record Office, Lewes).

25. C. Wordsworth, *Annals of my Early Life 1806–1846* (London 1891), p. 330. cf. E. Churton, *Memoir of Joshua Watson* (1861), I, pp. 130–1.

26. W. Jones, *Memoirs of the Life, Studies, and Writings of the Rt. Rev. George Horne*, DD (London 1795), p. 22.

27. In 'Home Thoughts from Abroad', first published in *British Magazine*, Newman argued that the 'element of high-churchmanship (as that word has common been understood) seems about to retreat again into the depths of the Christian temper, and apostolicity is to be elicited instead, in greater measure ... high churchmanship looking at the matter historically – will be regarded as a temporary stage of a course ... I give up high-churchmanship'. *British Magazine*, 9 (March 1836), p. 358. Newman later came to identify the Anglican system per se, as Erastian: John Henry Newman, *Certain Difficulties Felt by Anglicans in Catholic Teaching Considered* (London 1850), p. 112.

28. W. J. Copeland to M. A. Copeland, 3 May 1836, Copeland MSS (Pusey House).

29. J. M. Neale, 'The Laudian Reformation Compared with that of the Nineteenth Century', in *Lectures Principally on the Church Difficulties of the Present Time* (London 1852), p. 172.

30. For a classic statement of this high church interpretation of the supremacy, see J. Reeves, *Considerations on the Coronation Oath to maintain the Protestant Reformed Religion and the Settlement of the Church of England* (London 1801), p. 22.

31. G. D. Faussett, *The Alliance of Church and State Explained and Vindicated* (Oxford 1834), p. 11. cf. S. Wilberforce, *A History of the Protestant Episcopal Church in America* (London 1844).

32. H. J. Rose to H. H. Norris, 4 November 1826, Norris MSS (Bodleian). W. F. Hook, staunch old high church friend of the Tractarians and admirer of the American church, also dissociated himself from Bishop Hobart's criticisms. See J. McVicar, ed., *The Early and Professional Years of Bishop Hobart . . . with a Preface Containing a History of the Church in America, by W. F. Hook* (Oxford 1838), p. iii. For Hobart's strictures, see J. H. Hobart, *The United States of America Compared with Some European Countries, Particularly England; in a Discourse Delivered in Trinity Church, in the City of New York, October 1825, with an Introduction and Notes* (London 1826), pp. 19–35.

33. M. Watson, MS, 'Reminiscences', J. Watson to C. Wordsworth (jun.), 7 September 1852, f.348 Watson MSS (Torquay). For Watson's attempt to convert Hobart to the old high Anglican ideal of Establishment, see E. Churton, *Memoir of Joshua Watson*, II, p. 155.

34. E. Churton to W. J. Copeland, 30 May 1840, Churton MSS (Sutton Coldfield).

35. For evidence of the high, divine-right, 'Jacobite' Toryism of the early Tractarians, see especially Edward Bouverie Pusey, *Patience and Confidence the Strength of the Church: a Sermon preached on the fifth of November, before the University of Oxford at St Mary's* (Oxford 1837). Even prior to Pusey's sermon, the moderate Evangelical *Christian Observer* was accusing the Tractarians of wishing 'to restore the doctrines and practices of Laud and Sacheverell'. Among these doctrines the old Tory notions of non-resistance and passive obedience were listed as figuring prominently: *Christian Observer*, 37 (September 1837), p. 586. In similar vein, Thomas Arnold referred to the Tractarians as 'Church Tories' in the mould of the 'high flyers' of the reign of Queen Anne: T. Arnold, 'The Oxford Malignants', *Edinburgh Review*, 63 (April 1836), p. 235. On this politically Tory aspect of early Tractarianism, see Peter Nockles, 'Pusey and the Question of Church and State', in Perry Butler, ed., *Pusey Rediscovered* (London 1983), pp. 275–82.

36. W. Ward, *William George Ward and the Oxford Movement* (London 1889), p. 214. Newman went to great lengths to keep what for high churchmen was a special day of observance, King Charles the Martyr's day, on 30 January. The entry in his diary for 30 January 1836 reads: 'The martyrdom. Tried to find church open in vain'! T. Gornall (ed.), *The Letters and Diaries of John Henry Newman* (London 1981), V, p. 216. The cult of the 'Royal Martyr' in high church Anglicanism was manifested as late as 1879, with Charles Phillimore's edition of the Royal 'Martyrology', *Eikon Bazilikeh: the Portraiture of his Sacred Majestie in his Solitudes and Sufferings*, first published in 1648, and claimed by high churchmen to have been the spiritual manual of Charles I himself, while imprisoned by the Parliamentarians in the Isle of Wight.

37. See Newman's declaration in a letter to the *British Magazine* in 1834: 'If it be said that the act of settlement secures to the people certain liberties, I reply that the coronation oath has secured to the church its liberties also to the utter annulment of all former precedents of tyranny – and that we stand by that oath as our law as well as our sovereign's sanction and acknowledgement of it, and that any power in the state that innovates on the spirit of that oath tyrannises over us.' T. Gornall, ed., *Letters and Diaries of J. H. Newman*, V, p. 164.

38. See Copeland's comment to Pusey in 1864: 'The political element, the reform bill, had not any effect in producing the "Tracts for the Times".' W. Copeland to E. B. Pusey, 30 October 1864, Pusey MSS (Pusey House). For discussion of this point, see Peter Nockles, 'Pusey and the Question of Church and State', pp. 257–61.

39. E. R. Norman, *Church and Society in England, 1770–1970: an historical study* (London 1976), p. 22.

40. 'The Oxford Margaret Professor', *British Critic*, 30 (July 1841), pp. 214–43. cf. E. A. Knox, *The Tractarian Movement*, pp. 302–3.

41. G. D. Faussett, *The Claims of the Established Church to Exclusive Attachment and Support, and the Dangers which Menace her from Schism and Indifference*, Bampton Lectures (Oxford 1820), p. 313.

42. ibid. p. 316.

43. John Henry Newman, Tract 41, *Via Media II*, pp. 3–4.

44. Faussett, *The Claims of the Established Church*, pp. 9–12.

45. J. H. Spry, *Christian Unity Doctrinally and Historically Considered*, Bampton Lectures for 1816 (Oxford 1817), p. 189.

46. *Christian Remembrancer*, 3 (March 1821), p. 157.

47. J. Watson to H. H. Norris, n.d., Norris MSS (Bodleian Library). cf. J. J. Watson, *The Divine Commission and Perpetuity of the Christian Priesthood as Considered in a Charge to the Clergy of the Archdeaconry of St Albans at his Primary Visitation . . . in . . . 1816*, reprinted (London 1839).

48. J. Oxlee, *A Sermon, in which all Due and Lawful Claim of the Protestant Dissenters to any Part of the Christian Ministry is Further Disproved and Rejected* (York 1821), p. 71.

49. J. M. Neale, 'The Laudian Reformation Compared with that of the Nineteenth Century', in *Lectures on Church Difficulties*, pp. 181–3.

50. As Ralph Churton explained, 'this charge, unfounded, as it is, can only be refuted by showing . . . that the points which compelled us to separate from the Church of Rome, were matters not merely wrong, but highly sinful'. R. Churton, *An Answer to a Letter from Francis Eyre of Warkworth* (London 1796), p. 12.

51. See especially T. Burgess, *Tracts on the Origin and Independence of the Ancient British Church, on the Supremacy of the Pope, and the Inconsistency of all Foreign Jurisdiction with the British Constitution, and on the Differences between the Churches of England and Rome* (London 1815).

52. Bishop Burgess does appear to have been a notable exception, as Bishop Kaye's comment to W. F. Hook in 1842 makes clear: 'it is well for you that Bishop Burgess is not alive. You would otherwise be called to strict account for setting forth Augustine, as the founder under God, of the Church of England'. J. Kaye to W. F. Hook, 22 January 1842, No. 15 Hook MSS (Bucklebury-Coatalen).

53. J. Oxlee, *Three Letters addressed to Mr C. Wellbeloved, Tutor of the Unitarian College, York; Being Occasioned by his Epistolatory Attack on a Late Visitation Charge of the Ven. and Rev. Francis Wrangham*, MA, *Archdeacon of Cleveland* (York 1824), pp. 42–3.

54. S. H. Cassan, *Lives of the Bishops of Winchester*, 2 vols (London 1827), II, p. 16.

55. S. Wix, *Christian Union without the Abuses of Popery: a Letter to the Rt. Rev. The Lord Bishop of St David's, in reply to his Lordship's Letter entitled 'Popery Incapable of Union with a Protestant Church'* (London 1820), pp. 16–17. cf.

B. and M. Pawley, *Rome and Canterbury through Four Centuries* (London 1974), pp. 110–11.

56. J. H. Newman, *A Letter Addressed to the Rev. R. W. Jelf in Explanation of No. 90 in a Series called the 'Tracts for the Times' by the Author* (Oxford 1841), pp. 8–12. On Bishop Lloyd as a formative influence in the origins of the Oxford Movement, especially by instilling knowledge of the Roman breviary, see F. Oakeley, *Historical Notes on the Tractarian Movement* (London 1865), pp. 12–14. cf. id. 'Catholicism Fifty Years Ago', *Contemporary Review* (June 1879), p. 469. See also W. J. Baker, *Beyond Port and Prejudice: Charles Lloyd of Oxford, 1784–1829* (Orono, Maine 1981), pp. 214–15.

57. S. Wix, *Reflections Concerning the Expediency of a Council of the Church of England and the Church of Rome Being Holden, with a View to Accommodate Religious Differences, and to Promote the Unity of Religion in the Bond of Peace* (London 1818), p. 13.

58. H. H. Norris to R. Churton, 30 September 1812, Churton MSS (Sutton Coldfield).

59. Francis Huyshe republished the sermon as *A Tract for All Times, but Most Eminently for the Present* (London 1839).

60. T. Arnold to E. Hawkins, 4 November 1835, in A. P. Stanley, *Life and Correspondence of Thomas Arnold*, DD, 2 vols (London 1845), p. 17.

61. T. Arnold to R. Whately, 4 May 1836, in ibid. II, p. 34.

62. R. Whately to E. Hawkins, 11 September 1836, Hawkins MSS (Oriel College).

63. J. H. Newman, *The Arians of the Fourth Century* (London 1833), pp. 147–9.

64. See Newman's defence of the principle to Hugh James Rose: 'I have no reason to change my mind about it – and that the Bishop of Lincoln [Kaye] grants that Clement holds it.' J. H. Newman to H. J. Rose, 15 December 1836, in Gornall, ed., *Letters and Diaries of J. H. Newman*, V, p. 178.

65. J. H. Newman to J. E. Tyler, 5 March 1836, Newman MSS, No. 84 (Birmingham Oratory).

66. John Henry Newman, Tract 85, *Lectures on the Scripture Proofs of the Doctrines of the Church*, p. 5.

67. E. Hawkins, *Dissertation Upon the Use and Importance of Unauthoritative Tradition* (Oxford 1819), p. 64.

68. cf. C. J. Abbey and J. H. Overton, *English Church in the Eighteenth Century* (London 1878), I, p. 136.

69. Brilioth, *The Anglican Revival*, p. 45.

70. ibid.

71. C. Daubeny, *A Guide to the Church in Several Discourses . . . to Which is Prefixed Some Account of the Author's Life and Writings* (London 1830), p. xi.

72. ibid. p. lxvi.

73. J. Jebb to C. A. Ogilvie, 16 June 1820, MS Eng. Lett. d.123 f.141 (Bodleian). cf. C. Forster, ed., *Thirty Years' Correspondence between John Jebb and Alexander Knox*, 2nd edn, 2 vols (London 1836), II, p. 4.

74. Bishop J. Walker to H. H. Norris, 25 September 1839, Norris MSS (Bodleian).

75. J. S. Harford, *Life of Thomas Burgess* (London 1840), p. 182.

76. W. Jones, *Memoirs of George Horne* DD, p. 22.

77. Quoted in W. R. Stephens, *Life and Letters of Walter Farquhar Hook*, 2

vols (London 1878), I, p. 97. cf. *Catalogue of the Extensive and Valuable Library of the Late Thomas Rennell* DD, *Dean of Winchester* (London 1840), p. viii.

78. W. Jones, *Memoirs of George Horne* DD, p. 44.

79. R. Southey, *Book of the Church*, 2 vols (London 1824), I, p. 16. For similar anti-ascetic attitudes among pre-Tractarian high churchmen, see G. Nott's Bampton Lectures for 1802, *Religious Enthusiasm* (Oxford 1803), pp. 339–40. cf. R. Polwheele, ed., *The Enthusiasm of Methodists and Papists Compared*, new edn of Bishop Lavington's 1749 work (London 1833). See Hook's explanation of his high church mother's view of the movement, to Pusey: 'She has the old notions of the last century, considers all you are doing as enthusiasm', W. F. Hook to E. B. Pusey, 10 October 1840, Pusey MSS (Pusey House).

80. S. Gilley, 'Nationality and Liberty, Protestant and Catholic: Robert Southey's "Book of the Church" ', in S. Mews, ed., *Religion and National Identity*, Studies in Church History, XVIII (Oxford 1982), p. 420. For Southey's advocacy of Church of England nunneries and celibacy of the clergy, see R. Southey, *Sir Thomas More; or Colloquies on the Progress and Prospects of Society*, 2 vols (London 1829), I, pp. 93, 154–5, 339–40; II, pp. 37, 228.

81. E. Churton to W. Gresley, 10 May 1842, Pusey MSS (Pusey House).

82. E. Churton to W. Gresley, 7 April 1840, Pusey MSS (Pusey House).

83. E. Churton, *Biography of the Early Church* (London 1840), p. vi.

84. C. Marriott to J. H. Newman, 10 January 1842, Ollard MSS (Pusey House).

85. Newman, *Arians of the Fourth Century*, pp. 149–52. As Copeland explained, 'People have got to learn that true piety lies too deep to be always in the tongue, and is too sublime to be talked about.' W. Copeland to M. A. Copeland, 4 November 1836, Copeland MSS (Pusey House).

86. W. Copeland, MS, 'Narrative of the Oxford Movement', Copeland MSS (Pusey House).

87. W. Teale, 'William Jones', in *Lives of English Divines* (London 1846), p. 363.

88. C. Daubeny, *A Charge Delivered to the Clergy of the Archdeaconry of Sarum* (London 1824), p. 8.

89. H. H. Norris to R. Churton, 4 March 1813, Churton MSS (Sutton Coldfield).

90. G. Horne, *An apology for Certain Gentlemen in the University of Oxford, Aspersed, in a Late Anonymous Pamphlet* (Oxford 1756), p. 14. cf. G. Watson, *A Seasonable Admonition to the Church of England: a sermon preached before the University of Oxford at St Mary's* (Oxford 1751), p. 14. Edward Churton's view of the impact of Horne's sermons and writings at Oxford is significant: 'Bishop Horne, long before he was bishop, had as much influence on the minds of the young men at Oxford, as ever Newman or Pusey have lately had', and was 'attacked much in the same way by the high and dry or latitudinarian party', E. Churton to W. Gresley, 25 May 1846, Pusey MSS (Pusey House).

91. W. Copeland, MS, 'Narrative of the Oxford Movement', Copeland MSS (Pusey House).

92. Quoted in J. Coulson, *Newman and the Common Tradition: a study in the language of Church and society* (London 1970), p. 58.

93. J. Keble, ed., *Works of . . . Richard Hooker*, 3rd edn, 3 vols (Oxford 1845), I, pp. xci–xcii.

94. See Newman's remark to Sir James Stephen, how Butler's 'wonderfully gifted intellect caught the idea which had actually been the rule of the primitive church, of teaching the more sacred truths by rites and ceremonies'. J. H. Newman to J. Stephen, 16 March 1835, MS Add. 7349 f.138. (Cambridge Univ. Lib.).

95. W. Jones, *A Course of Lectures on the Figurative Language of Holy Scripture and the Interpretation of it from Scripture Itself, Delivered in the Parish Church of Nayland in Suffolk, in the Year 1786* (London 1786), p. 9.

96. ibid. pp. 318–19. cf. T. Wilson, *Ornaments of Churches Considered: A Sermon Preached Before the University of Oxford, at St Mary's* (Oxford 1761), p. 97. Another late-eighteenth century 'Hutchinsonian' high churchman, the American loyalist Jonathan Boucher, likewise stressed the 'peculiar sacredness of places of worship', and was highly critical of latitudinarianism, indifferentism or mere utilitarianism, on the subject, *Anti-Jacobin Review*, 2 (March 1799), p. 411.

97. J. H. Newman, *Parochial and Plain Sermons* (London 1879), p. 28.

98. For evidence of this, see E. B. Pusey to Bishop R. Bagot, 26 September 1837, Pusey MSS (Pusey House). cf. P. Maurice, *The Popery of Oxford Confronted, Disavowed and Repudiated* (London 1837).

99. R. D. Middleton, *Magdalen Studies* (London 1936), p. 15.

100. T. Sanders, *A Practical Sermon on the Nature of Public Worship* (Oxford 1801), pp. 11–12.

101. C. Daubeny, *A Guide to the Church*, p. xviii.

102. W. Copeland, MS, 'Narrative of the Oxford Movement', Copeland MSS (Pusey House).

103. E. Churton, *Memoir of Joshua Watson*, I, pp. 139–40; II, p. 131. For instance, an American churchman, Philander Chase, noted on a visit to Manchester in 1823, 'Prayers are read and the psalms chanted every day in the Old Cathedral Church', *Bishop Chase's Reminiscences*, 2 vols (Boston 1848), I, p. 218. Magdalen College Chapel under George Horne also set a high ceremonial standard. See R. D. Middleton, *Newman and Bloxam* (London 1947), p. 26; and H. Best, *Four Years in France* (London 1826).

104. Quoted in E. Churton, *Memoir of Joshua Watson*, II, pp. 201–2.

105. E. B. Pusey to J. Watson, 30 October 1839, Pusey MSS (Pusey House). cf. E. B. Pusey to J. H. Newman, 11 September 1839, Pusey MSS (Pusey House); and E. B. Pusey, *A Letter to Richard, Lord Bishop of Oxford, on the Tendency to Romanism of Doctrines held now as of old in the English Church* (Oxford 1839).

106. J. Keble to J. H. Newman, 8 August 1833, in I. Ker and T. Gornall, eds., *Letters and Diaries of J. H. Newman*, IV, p. 23.

107. See Churton's comment, 'The Church at large will think, as I feel more than half inclined to think myself, that the principles of the juniors at Oxford has destroyed all natural respect for the aged and honourable.' E. Churton to E. B. Pusey, 9 December 1841, Pusey MSS (Pusey House).

108. E. Churton to W. J. Copeland, 10 August 1841, Churton MSS (Sutton Coldfield).
109. *Christian Remembrancer*, 3 (April 1841), p. 426. See Thomas Mozley's comment in 1841, that those who joined the movement were 'not what was called high church some thirty years since', *British Critic*, 30 (July 1841), p. 226.
110. M. Watson, MS, 'Reminiscences', f.166, '16 May 1845', Watson MSS (Torquay).
111. E. Churton, *Memoir of Joshua Watson*, II, p. 169.
112. H. J. Rose to H. E. Manning, 20 March 1837, V, No. 40, Manning MSS (Bodleian).
113. E. Churton to W. Gresley, 5 June 1846, Pusey MSS (Pusey House).
114. E. Churton to J. C. Crosthwaite, 13 April 1842, MS Eng. Misc. e.117 f.135, Crosthwaite MSS (Bodleian).
115. G. H. Tavard, *The Quest for Catholicity: a study in Anglicanism* (London 1963), p. 173.
116. G. A. Poole, *The Present State of Parties in the Church of England*, 2nd edn (London 1842), p. 11.

3

The Classical High Church Reaction to the Tractarians*

Reginald H. Fuller

I

During the twenties of this century there hung in the parish room of St Mary the Virgin, Horsham, a picture of Hugh James Rose, vicar of Horsham 1821–30. That picture used to excite my fascination as a choirboy, and some time later – at the time of the centenary of the Oxford Movement in 1933 – I learnt about him as one of the leaders of the Church revival of 1833. Soon after that I read Ollard's chapter on 'The Beginning of the Movement' and found that same familiar picture appearing opposite page 23.[1] Later still, around 1947, Alec Vidler, when editor of *Theology*, recommended J. W. Burgon's *Lives of Twelve Good Men* for Lenten reading and once again Rose's picture peered out at me as I read of him as the 'Restorer of the Old Paths'.[2] My New Testament studies under Sir Edwyn Hoskyns at Cambridge had in the meantime prepared me to enter sympathetically into the mentality of the older high churchmanship which Rose represented, for by that time Hoskyns, with his Tractarian upbringing, had rediscovered the Reformation. I read – and have frequently since re-read – Burgon's short life of Rose and discovered there one who puts his finger on exactly what is right and what went wrong with the Tractarian movement, from the standpoint of the older high-churchmanship.

II

Burgon's life of Rose contains a vivid account of the Oxford Movement written from the point of view of one who was related by marriage with Rose and whose attitude to the Oxford Movement was profoundly influenced by his Rose relatives. To Burgon 'Church feeling was EVOKED, not CREATED by the movement of 1833'.[3] And for the first two years of the Tracts Burgon saw them as proceeding along sound lines. But about the beginning of 1836 a change set in, and the movement began to develop in non-Anglican directions.

* © 1986 Reginald H. Fuller

Burgon's own opinions are well summed up by his biographer Dean Goulburn, and are worth quoting as typical of the view Burgon had imbibed from Rose:

> What was said of him [Burgon] when he unfolded his ecclesiastical views at some party of Oxford men, 'Why I declare, Burgon, you are quite a primitive Tractarian', represented very accurately his whereabouts in Religious opinion. He had strong sympathy with the Tractarian movement at its outset, in its revival of discipline, in its recognition of the value and blessing of the Apostolic Succession, and above all its re-instatement of the Daily Office, and its teaching on the subject of the sacraments; but further than that he could never be induced to go.[4]

The reason why Burgon remained a 'primitive Tractarian' and did not advance further along the Tractarian path is to be found in some important letters which Hugh James Rose wrote to John Henry Newman and which are reproduced by Burgon in his life of Rose. In 1836 Rose was already alarmed by some of the effects that the Tractarian appeal to antiquity was having upon some of the younger men. It was dangerous to let them loose 'among the spacious pastures of Antiquity', for 'All that is in Antiquity is not good; and much that was good for Antiquity would not be good for us. Antiquity must therefore be studied with guidance, otherwise the young men will *affect* Antiquity.'[5] The younger men were thinking that 'ancient Novelties' such as apostolic succession, were being introduced for the first time, whereas in point of fact these things were truths held by all churchmen and only a little neglected. Another effect was that the younger men were discovering things in antiquity that had never been part of the Anglican system and were seeking to introduce them, thus going behind the Reformation. The purpose of the Tracts until 1835 had been to 'pour the light of Antiquity through your own windows'.[6] What the early Tractarians had shown was that what the Church of England taught since the Reformation was what had always been taught by the Catholic Church. Now some were beginning to suggest that there were Catholic teachings that the Church of England had lacked since the Reformation and which she needed to recover from antiquity in order to make her fully Catholic.

Later in the same year, on 13 October 1836, Rose wrote again to Newman protesting at the altered tone manifested in Newman's Tract 71 and in his 'Home Thoughts from Abroad'. Newman had spoken of the Church of England as 'safe' and nothing more. Rose deplored Newman's hankering after things we do not have: monasteries, a better liturgy, a different confession of faith and so on. Rose points out that we do have the sacraments and the ministry: these are not additions to our present faith. We have to bring out what we now have, feasts and fasts, more frequent communion, more understanding of the sacraments.[7] And again: 'We are not like our

Reformers, *looking* for the truth and not knowing where the truth is.'[8]
Here Rose has put his finger on the basic difference between older,
classical high churchmanship, and the later type of Tractarianism
which began to come in during 1835. The difference is that the older
high churchmen took as their standard of catholicity the Anglican
formularies, and supported them from Scripture and antiquity,
whereas the later Tractarians used the appeal to antiquity to correct
and supplement the Anglican formularies.

Another good barometer to test the classical high church reaction
to the Tractarian movement is Walter Farquhar Hook. Hook, too,
initially welcomed the Tracts. He wrote about his reactions to Samuel
Wilberforce:

> We agree in insisting upon important doctrines, the authority of
> the Church, the Apostolic Succession, and the Sacraments. And
> now let me ask, what right have you to identify me with the Oxford
> Movement then? I love Pusey, Newman and Keble with all my
> heart but I call no man my Master. Christian is my name, Catholic
> my surname: when my Oxford friends are acting as Catholic Chris-
> tians then I agree with them; when they act otherwise, their great
> names have no influence upon me.[9]

Hook was a more truly Evangelical high churchman than Rose, and
not so scholastic in his theology. He had a strong grasp of the
Reformation's recovery of the Pauline message of justification *sola
gratia*, So he can write about Newman and his younger followers
thus:

> On the subject of justification the Church of England and the
> Church of Rome stand in direct contrast. There are two theories
> on the subject:
>
> 1. The Protestant theory, which is that of the Church of England,
> that when we are sincerely endeavouring through grace to serve
> God, God is pleased to account us righteous, so that we may
> approach him through prayer and the sacraments etc., as if we
> were, what we can never become, righteous persons. The righteous-
> ness of sanctification, though a righteousness, as far as it goes, is
> always imperfect, and therefore we always appear before God in
> the righteousness of Christ imputed to us.
>
> 2. The Romish theory, i.e. the theory that by the Holy Spirit, we
> may become entirely righteous, and that by this righteousness,
> given by the Holy Spirit, we can stand as righteous before God.
>
> Our Romanizing young men repudiate the doctrine of justification
> by Faith because they think it is not reconcilable with sacramental
> religion. But who was a greater supporter of sacramental religion
> than Hooker, and where can we find a stronger advocate for the
> Protestant view of justification by Faith?[10]

Hook agreed with Rose on the question of theological method, that it is the Anglican formularies that provide us with the Anglican statement of the Catholic faith. Hook too saw a difference in the *later* Tracts. By 1841 he could write:

> A new party seemed to be arising, as different from the teaching of the original Tractarians as they had been from the Evangelicals; a party pointing to the mediaeval rather than the primitive Church as a pattern of all that was excellent; viewing the English Reformers and their work with suspicion if not aversion, the Romanists with leniency or favour.[11]

Perhaps we can here detect, what was not clear when Rose reacted in 1836, that Richard Hurrell Froude was the source of the great change. But Hook went significantly further than Rose, the restorer of the old paths did, in recognising that the Church of England might eventually come to accept officially something of what the later Tractarians had rediscovered in antiquity and if and when such matters were officially adopted Hook would be willing to go along:

> The Church was reformed on the right principles, therefore I bow to her decisions. The Reformers who applied that principle (viz., the appeal to Antiquity) were more learned than I, and to their judgment I defer. If the proper authorities see fit to make changes to meet the exigencies of the time, all that I require of them is that they adhere to the principle of our Reformation, and then I will obey them.[12]

The Book of Common Prayer of 1928 of the Protestant Episcopal Church in the USA introduced prayer for the dead. The 1979 Book of Common Prayer of the same Church permitted the reservation of the sacrament for delayed communion. Hook could presumably have accepted these changes as adhering to the principle of our reformation.

Let us close our examination of Hook's reaction to the Tractarian movement with his own self-testimony:

> When I was called a High Churchman, we meant by the word one who, having ascertained that the Church of England was reformed on the right principle, cordially accepted the Reformers. We meant by a High Churchman one who, thinking the Church wiser than himself, observed her regulations and obeyed her laws, whether we understood them or not.[13]

Therein, I think, lies the quintessential difference of spirit between the classical high churchmen and the later Tractarians. In so far as the early Tractarians reasserted this position, to that extent the older high churchmen welcomed their work wholeheartedly. But when they began to rediscover and revive from antiquity things that the Reformed Church of England had rejected as inconsistent with Scripture as interpreted by antiquity, there came a parting of the ways. This parting was to become all the more evident as Tractarianism passed into the next phase, namely that of ritualism. High church bishops of the older school like S. Wilberforce, Christopher Words-worth and Harold Browne in England, and W. R. Whittingham and Cleveland Coxe in the USA, fulminated against ritualism in their charges later in the century. Behind this was the later Tractarian introduction of doctrines rediscovered in antiquity or in the medieval Church which the Reformers had rejected. A mine of information on this subject will be found in the collections published in 1908 by J. C. Sharpe under the title of *A Vindication of Anglo-Catholic Principles*.[14]

III

The classical high church tradition in America goes back to 1722, when seven Congregationalist theologians of Yale University read themselves by a study of the Church Fathers into the conviction that their orders were invalid and made the hazardous voyage to England to receive episcopal ordination. It was out of this tradition of Connect-icut high churchmanship that Samuel Seabury (1729–96) came, the first American bishop, who was consecrated by the nonjuring bishops of Scotland in 1784 and who took back to the States the Scottish liturgy.[15] After the American revolution the infant Protestant Epis-copal Church fell on hard times and was a prey to latitudinarianism until about 1810. Around then an Evangelical revival sprang up in Virginia, and a high church revival in New York, inspired by Connecticut churchmanship under the leadership of John Henry Hobart, Bishop of New York 1811–30.[16] This was before the Trac-tarian movement, of course, though Hobart had visited England and met Hugh James Rose in 1825. The mantle of Hobart fell upon the high churchmen who were contemporary with the rise of Tractari-anism, such as Bishop W. R. Whittingham of Maryland (1805–79), mentioned above, who edited the American edition of William Palmer's *Treatise of the Church*, and who promoted the publication of the *Tracts for the Times* in the USA.[17] It is worth noting the preface to the American edition of the first volume of the *Tracts for the Times* (1839):

> In the bosom of the Episcopal Church in this country, and from our Church having no connection with the state, it has resulted that some of the leading doctrines of the Oxford divines relating to the constitution of the Church and to the Ministry, have been better preserved than in the English Establishment.[18]

The American high churchmen had already had to produce an apolo-getic for the authority of the Church independent of any connection with the State, and this offered a fertile ground for the Tractarian

insistence on the Church's spiritual independence and authority.
Before that, Bishop Hobart, on his visit to England, had been viewed
as something of an anomaly, as one who, though a high churchman,
was nevertheless a Republican!

We now turn to John Henry Hopkins (1792–1868), Bishop of
Vermont from 1832. I choose him because in an episcopal charge
and in a series of open letters he responded at some length and with
considerable scholarship to the Tracts and other writings of the
Oxford school. He was also a clear example of a pre-Tractarian
high churchman in the Connecticut-Hobart tradition. His son and
biographer correctly emphasised his sympathy with the Tractarians,
but mentioned only in summary terms the points on which he took
issue.[19] Fortunately the pamphlets in question are all preserved in
the library of the Virginia Theological Seminary, and what follows
is a summary of what I found there.

In the charge of 1842 Hopkins praised the Tracts in general terms:
'I hold the Tracts in high esteem.'[20] But then he goes on to reassert
against them Hooker's and the classical Anglican doctrine of episcopacy. Episcopacy, he says, notwithstanding its divine institution, is
not essential to the existence of a church, although it is to her
integrity.[21] The baptisms of non-episcopal churches are not invalid
(this was directed against certain enthusiasts among the students at
General Theological Seminary who had had themselves rebaptised
because of their non-episcopal baptisms). Heresy and schism, though
grievous sins, may, Hopkins asserts, co-exist with the essential unity
of the Church Catholic. Tradition is not binding religious truth unless
it is founded in holy Scripture. The doctrine of the objective real
presence is open to serious objection. Here Hopkins reasserts
Hooker's classical doctrine that by consecration the elements are not
changed essentially, but become instruments which convey the body
and blood of Christ to the faithful receiver after a heavenly and
spiritual manner. The real presence is to be sought not in the sacrament but in the faithful receiver. In general terms but without spelling
out his own position, Hopkins castigated as objectionable the Tractarian teaching on priestly power of absolution, prayers for the dead,
auricular confession, additional saint's days, Tractarian views on
papal supremacy and their negative judgments on some Reformers.
On Tract No. 90 he agrees that 'the ground work is admitted' but
goes on to declare his own adherence to 'the doctrines of our Church
as interpreted by the great body of our standard divines' and
concludes with a special commendation of Richard Hooker.[22]

In 1844 Hopkins elaborated his attack on the Oxford divines in
four open letters published by Herman Hooker of Philadelphia under
the title, *The Novelties that Disturb Our Peace*. Of these, Nos 2 and 3
are of particular relevance to our concern. No. 3 elaborates in opposition to William Palmer's *Treatise of the Church*, and with extensive
quotations from the standard Anglican divines from Hooker onwards,

the doctrine that episcopacy, while of divine right, belongs to the integrity rather than to the being of the Church and protests against the theory that would deny the name 'church' to those without bishops in historical succession.

Here is a typical passage: 'While our Mother Church provided for the strictest adherence to apostolical order in her own case, she yet granted the name and character of Church to the various Christian sects which sprang up in the difficulties and struggles of the Reformation.'[23] And again: 'those portions of Christendom, which retain the fundamental verities of the Christian faith, are entitled, for the faith's sake, to be called Churches, although they have lost the apostolic order of the ministry'.[24]

In view of the later but differently applied use of the same terminology at Vatican II it is interesting to find Hopkins stating that 'without episcopacy, the Church may *subsist* notwithstanding' (italics mine).[25] Later he wrote: 'This (sc. the lack of apostolic order of episcopacy) was a defect, but yet it did not destroy them as Churches. The title Church was applied to them not only by Hooker, but by all the English episcopalians of that and long subsequent times.' Hopkins then proceeds to quote Chillingworth, Mede, Usher and Bramhall, noting that these same divines were also quoted in the Tracts. But, Hopkins asks, is the ecclesial recognition of non-episcopal bodies simply the private opinion of individual divines? He adduces two pieces of evidence that this is the official doctrine of the Church of England. The first is the loyal address of Convocation at the accession of William III, thanking the king for his services to the Church of England and asserting that by this 'the interest of the Protestant religion in all other Protestant Churches would be better secured'. The second is from Canon 55 of 1604, which includes Protestant Churches within Christ's holy Catholic Church. There is also American evidence. The Preface of the Book of Common Prayer of 1789 accords to non-episcopal bodies the title of churches. For it states that when the American States became independent with respect to civil government: 'the different religious denominations of Christians in these States were left at full liberty to model and organize *their respective Churches*' (italics mine).[26]

Hopkins understandably goes on to criticise Palmer's *Treatise* and its 'branch theory in particular'. In volume I, chapter 8, Palmer asserts that a ministry in apostolic succession is essential to the Church. In chapter 12 he states that the Lutherans, Zwinglians and Calvinists could not be considered as churches, and in chapter 13 he states that dissenters 'are not part of the Church of Christ'. Such views Hopkins considers novelties.

Later Hopkins accuses the Oxford men of frequently disparaging the work and character of the Reformers, and remarks that 'It was not the usurpation of the Pope . . . It was the corruption of the faith of the gospel, that justified the separation of the blessed

Reformation.'[27] The older high churchmen were not ashamed to call themselves Protestants, Protestant Catholics, of course.

Before we leave this third letter it is worth noting that the same ecumenical thinking that activated Hopkins lies behind the ecclesial recognition that was accorded by the General Convention at New Orleans in 1982 to the Lutheran churches in America, a recognition which has made possible what is called interim eucharistic fellowship.

As was to be expected there has been some malaise about this recognition of churches without bishops in apostolic succession. But we can claim that this is in accord with the classical Anglican tradition and with past official Anglican pronouncements. We have not abandoned our conviction that episcopacy is of divine right and of the integrity of a church, or that its absence is a very real defect which we hope and pray will eventually be remedied. We found there was so much of the substance of apostolicity in the Lutheran churches – Scripture, the creeds and the confessions, and even a sacramental view of holy order, to justify this ecclesial recognition. This is something that Bishop Hopkins and pre-Tractarian high churchmen like him would have endorsed.

IV

The third letter of Hopkins in the series, *The Novelties that Disturb our Peace*, deals with the Tractarian teaching on the holy Eucharist. It was a response to the doctrine of the Eucharist set out in W. Palmer's *Treatise of the Church*, for the learning of which Hopkins had a very high regard; and in Tracts Nos 10 and 90. Against the doctrine of the 'objective Real Presence', which he regards as a novelty, Hopkins sets forth the classical Anglican doctrine in these terms:

> The elements of bread and wine, by virtue of the act of conse-cration, become the Holy Symbols of the Body and Blood of our crucified Lord. Thus far we hold the same view as the Zwinglians. But in the more important question of the inward and spiritual graces received in the Sacrament, we go incomparably further; believing that by the due reception of the representative Body and Blood, the faithful communicant is made, by the Holy Spirit, a partaker, verily and indeed, of the Body and Blood of Christ, after a heavenly and spiritual manner, so as to become mystically one with his divine Lord, and to strengthen the bonds of that glorious incorporation more and more with each repetition of the Holy Communion; provided he approach it with genuine repentance, lively faith, and fervent charity.[28]

Hopkins contrasts this view with that of Palmer and the Tracts. For them, by consecration the elements became really the blood and body of Christ. The real presence is found in the consecrated elements, on the communion table or altar; they are then offered up as an unbloody sacrifice. This is opposed to the doctrine of the eucharistic sacrifice contained in the American (following the Scottish) rite, in which, after the words of institution, in the oblation paragraph, before the invocation, the words occur: 'We thy humble servants do celebrate and make here before thy divine majesty, with these thy holy gifts, which we now offer unto thee, the memorial which thy Son hath commanded us to make.' Hopkins does not provide an alternative statement of the eucharistic sacrifice to that of the Tractarians, but the difference was later brought out in the ritualistic controversy. Among the collection of materials published by J. C. Sharpe in 1908[29] there is an excerpt from the Revd J. Le Mesurier, vicar of Bembridge in the Isle of Wight. He distinguishes three aspects of the eucharistic offering: (1) our alms, contrite hearts etc.; (2) the commemorative or representative sacrifice (expressed in the oblation paragraph of the Scottish and American eucharistic prayers, but barely implicit in 1662, which Le Mesurier and the other old-fashioned English high churchmen were using), in which with the consecrated symbols we make a commemoration of Christ's sacrifice before God; (3) there is what God does as we receive the communion, the application of the efficacy of Christ's sacrifice on the cross.[30]

Le Mesurier makes some very interesting comments on the primitive liturgies, which would apply equally well to the Scottish and American eucharistic prayers:

> the commemoration of Christ's death was always made in early liturgies as the offering of the elements before the completion of the consecration (i.e. although after the recital of the Lord's words of institution, yet before the invocation or prayer that they might become the Body and Blood of Christ to the good of the receiver) such offering cannot be called by any strict propriety of speech the oblation of the Body and Blood of Christ.[31]

To return to Hopkins's pamphlet of 1844, he noted that however strongly the Tractarians might protest that their doctrines of the objective real presence was not the same as the Romish doctrine of transubstantiation (the difference being that the Tractarians espoused no philosophical definition of the mode of the presence), its *practical* effects would be indistinguishable from those of the Roman doctrine of transubstantiation itself. He foresaw the following consequences of the Tractarian doctrine: every particle of the consecrated elements would be regarded as the body and blood of Christ and would be fussily protected from profanation. There would be an exaggerated reverence for the altar and for the communion vessels. Genuflexion would be introduced; the reservation of the sacrament (Hopkins did not differentiate between delayed communion, a practice wholly consonant with the classical Anglican doctrine of the sacrament, and the use of the reserved sacrament for cultic purposes);

and finally what he calls 'processions of Corpus Christi'.[32] Hopkins
goes on to refute the claim that the Tractarian doctrine is in accord
with the doctrine of the Church of England as expressed in her
formularies: 'The Church confines the idea of the Real Presence of
the Body and Blood of Christ to the faithful receiver of the sacrament,
while our Tractarian brethren place the Real Presence in the Sacrament itself, that is, in the consecrated elements on the Communion
Table or Altar.'[33] Next Hopkins proceeds to defend the Church of
England doctrine in the light of the Church Fathers, complaining
that Pusey takes the Fathers' language 'always in the highest possible
sense'. He quotes their highest figures 'without the slightest qualifi-
cation, and applied in the most literal sense' – despite the fact that
Pusey claims that he adheres to the Articles. Pusey holds that

> by virtue of the act of consecration, the divine and human natures
> of our LORD JESUS CHRIST become united to the sacramental
> elements, on the altar and in the hands of the officiating priest: a
> doctrine which I believe to be thoroughly inconsistent with Scrip-
> ture, with the Reformers, with the Fathers, and with the standards
> of our Church.[34]

Hence Hopkins states that he cannot join with those who protest at
the censure of Pusey's sermon of 1843, and believes that it would
have been better if the Church had formally censured the doctrinal
innovations of Tract No. 90.

Later on, during the ritualist controversy and towards the end of
his life, Bishop Hopkins received from his son, John Henry Hopkins
junior, Dr Pusey's two works, *The Doctrine of the Real Presence as
contained in the Fathers*, and *The Real Presence of the Body and Blood of
Our Lord Jesus Christ: The Doctrine of the English Church*, together with
John Keble's *Eucharistical Adoration*.[35] Hopkins junior invited his father
to note in the margins wherever he thought these two authors had
'gone too far'. The bishop returned them without comment and with
only verbal remarks. He said he was especially delighted with the
scrupulous fairness with which Pusey quoted passages which seemed
to take a contrary position. J. H. Hopkins junior was disappointed
that he 'had not a measure of his difference of opinion as sharply' as
he wished.[36] In subsequent conversation the elder Hopkins acknowledged that the doctrine of Pusey and Keble was 'clearly within the
comprehensiveness of the Church of England' and also that the ritual
which expressed it was by logical implication allowable.[37] But in the
younger Hopkins's words there was 'some shade of difference'
between Bishop Hopkins and the two Tractarian theologians. The
bishop strongly maintained the 'Real Presence' and called it such.
He acknowledged that it was objective, that is, not merely in the
heart of the faithful receiver. But it was 'not so rigidly or locally
identified with the consecrated Elements'.[38] He preferred, in his son's
words, to 'think of Christ as Himself so present that, at the instant

when the Priest gave the consecrated Element, Christ gave himself to the faithful receiver'.[39] We must remember that Hopkins's remarks have been filtered through his post-Tractarian son's mind. The younger Hopkins seems to be trying to minimise the difference between the doctrine of Hopkins senior and that of the Tractarians. But something of the classical position shines through.

Hopkins was of course not alone in his eucharistic doctrine among the old-fashioned high churchmen of his day. We find essentially the same doctrine in Martin Routh, H. Philpotts, J. W. Burgon, W. F. Hook, and in America in Bishops W. R. Whittingham of Maryland and Cleveland Coxe of Western New York. But I have selected Hopkins because he was deliberately reacting to Tractarianism. That the Tractarian form of the doctrine of the real presence was a novelty in Anglicanism is clearly evidenced by the history of J. Keble's poem for 5 November, the Gunpowder Plot. He had originally written that the Church of England, as distinct from the Church of Rome, held that in the Communion we receive Christ:

not in the hands, but in the heart.

Only at the end of his life and reluctantly did he consent to alter the wording to:

in the hands as in the heart

thus bringing the poem in conformity with his later doctrine as stated in *Eucharistical Adoration*.[40] One wonders how far Keble was conscious of the change of doctrine. Had the whole issue become blurred in his mind? Many failed to see the difference between the two doctrines, either reading the later Tractarian doctrine back into the older classical doctrine or explaining the older formulations as due to looseness of expression.

It is interesting to note that the new American Prayer Book, which has clearly benefited so much from the positive results of the Anglican revival of the nineteenth century, still remains in its explicit state-ments within the parameters of the classical Anglican doctrine of the real presence. To take Rite II, eucharistic prayer A, the most frequently used prayer in the new rite, the invocation, which in the American tradition comes after the words of institution and the oblation, says:

Sanctify them [these gifts] by your Holy Spirit to be *for your people* [i.e. for the purposes of reception] the Body and Blood of your Son, the holy food of new and unending life in him.[41]

And the first of the post-communion prayers states that 'you have fed us with the Sacrament of his Body and Blood', while the alterna-tive reads, 'we thank you for feeding us with the spiritual food of the most precious Body and Blood of your Son our Saviour Jesus Christ'. The reservation of the sacrament for delayed communion is permitted in a number of circumstances, for the sick, for the so-called deacon's masses, a necessity in remote parts, and for Good Friday communion. But outside of the context of communion the elements are invariably referred to as 'consecrated Bread and Wine'. Of course it is possible and within the limits of Anglican comprehensiveness to read into the language of the Prayer Book the Tractarian doctrine. But this is not what it explicitly asserts.

V

Conclusion

The classical high churchmen welcomed the Oxford revival of church life; the Prayer Book services performed with careful observance of the rubrics, the daily office and weekly communion; they welcomed the new emphasis on the centrality of the Eucharist and many of the new standards of devotional life. But there were certain points at which the Tractarians innovated, going beyond the Anglican reformation to recover for themselves doctrines and practices which the Reformers had rejected. Here the classical high church reception was negative. At the most, as we have seen with W. F. Hook, they would be prepared to accept such matters (e.g. prayer for the departed) when they were sanctioned by proper authority and were shown to be consistent with our previous formularies. Prayer for the departed has, fortunately, been accepted in the American Prayer Book since 1928, and since 1979 the ministry of reconciliation has been fully restored with one of the alternative absolutions in the form, *ego absolvo te*, a form which has recently been rejected in the Church of England. Thus far we have welcomed into our life new things that came out of the Oxford Movement. But other innovations, especially those to which Bishop Hopkins called attention, have not found official acceptance. I have concentrated upon episcopacy and the real presence because these are the areas in which the changes introduced by the Tractarians are often overlooked in post-Tractarian historiography. Let us remember however that there was much in the Tractarians that the classical high churchmen welcomed and accepted as their own. Hopkins for one spoke of the 'startling energy of Froude, the lovely poetry of Keble, the learned mysticism of Pusey, the profound yet simple eloquence of Newman'.[42] For all of this we can indeed thank God on this 150th anniversary of John Keble's Assize Sermon.

1. S. L. Ollard, *A Short History of the Oxford Movement* (London 1915).
2. J. W. Burgon, *Lives of Twelve Good Men* (London 1888), pp. 62–146.
3. ibid. p. 82; cf. p. 94.

4. E. M. Goulburn, *John William Burgon*, 2 vols (London 1892), I, p. 179.
5. Burgon, *Lives*, p. 110.
6. ibid. p. 111.
7. ibid. p. 112.
8. ibid. p. 114.
9. W. R. W. Stephens, *The Life and Letters of Walter Farquhar Hook*, 2 vols (London 1880), II, p. 28.
10. ibid. II, p. 251.
11. ibid. II, p. 103.
12. Ibid. II, p. 489.
13. ibid. II, p. 80.
14. J. C. Sharpe, *A Vindication of Anglo-Catholic Principles*, 3rd edn (Oxford 1898).
15. See E. E. Beardsley, *Life and Correspondence of Samuel Seabury* (Boston 1882).
16. See J. M. Norton, *Life of the Rt. Rev. John Henry Hobart, Bishop of New York* (New York 1857).
17. See W. F. Brand, *Life of William Rollinson Whittingham, Fourth Bishop of Maryland*, 2nd edn (New York 1886).
18. 'Advertisement to the American Edition', *Tracts for the Times*, 2nd edn, 5 vols (New York 1839ff.), I.
19. See J. H. Hopkins, jun., *The Life of the Late Reverend John Henry Hopkins, First Bishop of Vermont* (New York 1875).
20. J. H. Hopkins, *The Novelties that Disturb Our Peace* (Philadelphia 1844), Letter I, pp. 4ff.
21. ibid. Letter II, p. 26.
22. ibid. Letter II, pp. 1, 77.
23. ibid. Letter II, p. 22.
24. ibid.
25. ibid. Letter II, p. 8.
26. ibid. Letter II, p. 23.
27. ibid. Letter II, p. 70.
28. ibid. Letter III, p. 7.
29. See note 14 above.
30. Le Mesurier, in Sharpe, *Vindication*, p. 98.
31. ibid.
32. Hopkins, *Novelties*, Letter IV, p. 5.
33. ibid. Letter IV, p. 6.
34. ibid. Letter II, p. 78.
35. Hopkins, jun., *Life of Hopkins*, p. 376.
36. ibid.
37. ibid. pp. 384–5.
38. ibid. p. 385.
39. ibid.
40. cf. W. H. McKean, *The Eucharistic Doctrine of the Oxford Movement: a critical survey* (London 1933), p. 127.
41. *The Book of Common Prayer and Administration of the Sacraments . . . According to the Use of the Episcopal Church* (New York 1979), p. 363.
42. Hopkins, *Novelties*, Letter IV, p. 3.

4

Ye shall be Holy:
reflections on the spirituality of
the Oxford Movement*

Frederick H. Borsch

We know two things of the Angels – that they cry Holy, Holy, Holy, and that they do God's bidding.[1]

Seeking better to understand and appreciate the spirituality of the Oxford Movement and its first leaders we become quickly implicated in the complexities of their personalities as well as of the sociological and intellectual currents which helped to shape the movement. Especially is this true if we define spirituality sufficiently broadly, so as to be inclusive of not only conscious acts of prayer, meditation and devotion, but of the whole human effort to live lives that seek to realise and be faithful to God's purposes in creation. 'Spirituality', John Macquarrie maintains, 'is the process of becoming a person in the fullest sense.'[2] That breadth of vision for the life of the Spirit – the sense that all life must be consecrated to God and offered for his glory, we soon come to recognise as the guiding force in the lives of Newman, Keble, Pusey and many of their companions and followers.

This inclusive view makes more difficult, however, the task of trying to sort out predominant influences and strains of thought and practice. We are forced, first of all, to realise how distinctive were the personalities of the Oxford Movement leaders and how much their individual circumstances and motivations varied. Whatever else brought these men together into a good measure of common cause, it was not some obvious similarity of temperament or character. Moreover each personality was intricate in its own right. Newman continues to defy biographers and other commentators who wish to establish his personality type. But it is also becoming increasingly clear that the caricatures of Keble as the self-effacing equanimous parson and Pusey as the doctrinaire devotionalist distort more than inform the complexities of their lives. Nor do their better known followers, men like Richard Hurrell Froude and Isaac Williams, readily match up in terms of personality or background with Keble, Pusey or Newman.

In turning from the personalities to the sociological and intellectual context, we again find a number of strands. In order to explain the character of the Oxford Movement different analysts have stressed the background of Newman in evangelicalism and the response of the leaders of Tractarianism to the Evangelicals' piety and view of the Church, the continuing power of the older high church tradition's view of Catholic England (with an important strand coming from the nonjurors), that tradition's devotional practice leading from Lancelot Andrewes through William Law, the Romantic movement (with all its complexities and contradictions), the influence of the Oriel Noetics and a reaction to some of that group's liberalisms, a desire to prove that faith and reason are not incompatible coupled with a sometimes fierce rejection of the dominance of rationalism in faith issues, and the writings of a number of early Christian teachers. These and other factors have been seen as having critical influence on the formation and direction of the Oxford Movement and its spirituality.

Certainly it is also important to recognise that, in their different ways (Newman's urban middle-class background was hardly the same as Keble's intimate connections with the country squirearchy), the leaders of the movement were all sufficiently affiliated with the established upper socio-economic groups of the time so that the attitudes and emotionalism associated with the piety of at least many of the Evangelicals were regarded with grave suspicion. While the Oxford Movement leaders could certainly be emotionally demonstrative in their personal lives and make use of strong sentiment and feeling in their poetry, prayers and homiletic appeals, they were cautious about the role of excitement or overt passion in religious practice and especially as a basis for a way of demonstrating religious conviction. Since they were also distrustful of the rationalism, which they regarded as a corrosive force in contemporary religion, they found themselves on a narrow course – guarding against both an excess of emotion and of intellectualism in religion. Yet they were men with well-trained minds and passionate feelings. Much of the force of their preaching and writing may indeed issue from this tension of powerful emotion constrained by the strength of the intelligence of men who were at the same time not convinced that intellectual effort led to God, and who thus could not satisfy their longing in the exercise of reason alone.

Part of the interest that the Tractarians continue to hold for us may lie just here. In their suspicion of either too much emotionalism or reason in the practice and understanding of religion, they anticipate aspects of the dilemma of contemporary men and women of faith. Newman in particular, with his fear of the road opened by Hume, his belief that all the rational discussion of the 'evidences' of religion had not made one new disciple, and his strong if uninformed distrust of the new German theology and historical criticism, still held reason to be a way of expositing and partially confirming faith. But it was not its instigator. Undirected by faith's commitment, reason easily led away from God. Undisciplined emotion and feeling were still more unreliable. Newman, whose sermons could enthral with their intensity of passionate feeling suppressed in a web of delicate argumentation, yet found in neither emotion nor intellect a path to the confirmation of faith and relationship with God that were his life's preoccupations. Still God and the transcendent world of divine realities seemed so tantalisingly near. With the different emphases of their temperaments this dilemma was also experienced by Keble and Pusey.

How then could God be known and made known in the world?

Owen Chadwick looks to find a dominant strain in the diversity of the lives of the Tractarians and comes at least close to identifying a primary means they all chose to bring them nearer God. 'It would be too sharp a dissection,' he writes, 'but not therefore without its truth to say that Newman represented the moral and intellectual force of the Movement, Keble the moral and pastoral, Pusey the moral and devotional.'[3] The common element in their religious quest is their concern for the authenticity of discipleship manifested in the moral life. Moreover it is the will to be disciples, to seek sanctification and holiness through the following of conscience which leads individuals to God. 'Conscience, not logical reason – the ethical judgment rather than the argumentative judgment – is for all these Tractarians the chief road to religious knowledge.'[4]

This emphasis on conscience was inherited from Bishop Joseph Butler whose *The Analogy of Religion, Natural and Revealed, to the Constitution and Course of Nature*, the appended *Of the Nature of Virtue*, and *Fifteen Sermons*, were textbooks for Newman, Keble and others. Their understanding of the relationship between the natural and supernatural worlds and the sacramentalism of nature was strongly influenced by the bishop, but his teaching about the compelling authority of conscience may have had an even greater effect upon their epistemology and spirituality.

Butler was concerned to refute Thomas Hobbes's argument that self-interest could be a proper moral guide. Butler wanted to believe that true self-love and the dictates of conscience would one day be seen to be in harmony, but in the present human condition conscience must be regarded as the supreme authority calling forth an obedience which did not consider the consequences for self. True benevolence and love of one's neighbour were strictly disinterested. The Tractarian leaders also believed that conscience was from God and that obedience to conscience led to the sense of God's nearness and presence. Faith was kept on the right course by dutifulness. It was those who were pure of heart who could see God.[5] 'It is holiness,' maintained Newman, 'or dutifulness, or the new creation, or the spiritual mind, however we word it, which is the quickening and illuminating principle of true Faith, giving it eyes, hands, and feet.'[6]

. . . [R]eal Faith [Newman held was] a reaching forward, yet not of excitement or of passion – a moving forward in the twilight, yet not without clue or direction . . . kept in the narrow path of truth by the Law of dutifulness which inhabits it, the Light of heaven which animates and guides it . . . it takes its character from the moral state of the agent. It is perfected, not by mental cultivation, but by obedience.[7]

The obedient conscience is not the only guide to religious truth but it certainly is critical.

Similarly Pusey preached that 'Scripture gives us but one rule, one test, one way of attaining the truth, i.e. whether we are keeping God's commandments or no, whether we are conformed to this world, or whether we are by the renewing of our mind, being transformed into his image.'[8] As he did at other times, Isaac Williams put the thought more directly, while stressing the theme of self-denial which was so central to Tractarian morality and spirituality: 'Actions of self-denial dispose the heart to prayer, prayer to the love of God, and the love of God to the knowledge of Him.'[9] These words come from Williams's Tract 80, the first part of his controversial essay, 'On Reserve in Communicating Religious Knowledge', which held that certain religious teachings could not and should not be imparted until persons were in the right moral state.

The reverse corollary was, of course, also true. 'One thing only deafens us to the voice of God, untunes all, sets us out of harmony with all . . .' taught Pusey, 'sin.'[10] The remedy was a disciplined, obedient life. So Keble instructed Thomas Arnold that he could best cure himself from doubt not by 'reading and controversy, but by diet and regimen, i.e. holy living'.[11] Similarly Newman in his sermon 'Obedience the Remedy for Religious Perplexity' advised, 'To all those who are perplexed in any way soever, who wish for light but cannot find it, one precept must be given – OBEY. It is obedience which brings a man into the right path, it is obedience keeps him there and strengthens him in it.'[12] Repeatedly in their sermons Newman, Keble and Pusey stressed the necessity of obedience to conscience and moral living in even the smallest details of life. 'Whoso is faithful in little, is faithful also in much' (Luke 16:10) was a favourite text. 'Is not holiness', Newman asked rhetorically in his sermon 'Holiness Necessary for Future Blessedness', 'the result of many patient repeated efforts after obedience, gradually working on us, and first modifying and then changing our hearts?'[13] Only by means of such conscientious living could God's presence and the reality of the transcendent realm be realised.

As an epistemology such an approach to religious truth may seem somewhat naive and to leave much to be desired. By seeking to prove in life the reality it has already assumed – to interpret life on the basis of prejudgments of faith – the approach fully partakes of what today we call the hermeneutical circle. The believer-interpreter stands within the world of faith as a participant and has no platform outside that world view from which it might be objectively criticised.

Again however the Tractarians may be seen to be our precursors, for a century and a half of philosophy, science and theology later it has become more clear that there is no escaping the circle. All knowing results from expectations and prejudgments about what is to be known.[14]

This awareness need not lead to sheer relativism and the setting aside of all discrimination and critical judgment, for we can still ask about consistency and whether what is being believed can be authentically lived. Verification becomes at least partially dependent on how one lives. If, for instance, I believe that God is trustworthy, am I able to live in such a fashion as to show that I depend on that trust? If I believe that there is a God who desires to share his will with humanity through prayer, do I pray? Does such prayer give to my life a deeper awareness of the divine reality and strengthen me to live a life of sanctification? Does my belief make me different in these ways from those who do not believe? Am I willing to make the sacrifices and undergo the disciplines that are evidences of faith?

Now we begin to feel the dynamics of the moral seriousness and *earnestness* (a word often used to describe the Oxford leaders) which impelled the Tractarians and powered their spirituality. What was most dangerous to faith – most likely to disprove its claims – was inauthentic Christian living. But if they could begin to live lives of sanctification – if their lives could evidence the differences in purity and charity that Christianity was supposed to make – then at least the authenticity if not the truth of Christian believing could be seen. The value that Newman placed upon celibacy (knowing it was not for everyone, he still severely tested his relationships with Keble and Henry Wilberforce in his displeasure at their marriages), and Pusey, for instance, on fasting, lay especially here. Austerity and rigour of discipline were signs of complete commitment. 'Try yourself daily in little deeds to prove that your faith is more than a deceit,' preached Newman in his 1833 sermon 'Self-Denial: the Test of Religious Earnestness'. And again, 'A rigorous self-denial is a chief duty, nay, that it may be considered the test whether we are Christ's disciples, whether we are living in a mere dream, which we mistake for Christian faith and obedience, or are really and truly awake, alive, living in the day, on our road heavenward.'[15] The importance of almsgiving, though properly unostentatious, still had to be thoughtfully stressed. Keble and Newman ran the dangers of scrupulosity in the care with which they exercised their pastoral and parochial responsibilities. It is hard to overemphasise the effects of these life styles (what they called then 'ethos' upon others, especially its attractiveness for the young men of Oxford. Here was holy living. Here was 'singleness of purpose' (another favourite Tractarian phrase). Here was no *cheap grace*, no mere formalism – not just respectability or moralism posing as true religion, but instead fully committed authentic Christianity. With respect to Christian zeal no Tractarian need stand in the shade of any Evangelical!

Of course, the Tractarians did not offer their way of life as a definitive argument for the authenticity of their faith. In addition to all else it would have seemed immodest to suggest that one could so establish Christianity's truth claims through our own life, and the Oxford leaders had a keen sensitivity to the dangers of public piety. They were caught in the dilemma of those who wish to let their lights shine but for God's glory, not their own – to evidence the virtues of faith, among which is humility. They would also have recognised better than most how open such an argument was to the attacks of logic. 'The Oxford men', Chadwick writes, 'did not affirm, that which helps men to be saints must be true. But they had much sympathy with the proposition, and would probably have agreed that it contained more than a seed of truth.'[16] It is the thesis of this essay that in their daily living – as a motivation for their spirituality – this seed had taken deep root in the lives of the Tractarians.

Such a motivation could lead to a high level of hypocrisy if our primary audience were other men and women. The Tractarians however had a far more difficult audience to convince with their moral argument for the validity of Christian faith: they were acting the parts of Christian disciples for themselves. In the first and last analysis it was their own doubts that had to be overcome by the power of Christian believing for holy living. Because their backgrounds and personalities were different, this heavy responsibility bent their lives in particular ways, but we can still discern the similar shape of the burden of their earnestness and their developed capacities for introspection. Pusey grew steadily more determined to find no pleasure in this world which might distract his vision from the transcendent – a determination which at times had been taken to extremes by the enthusiasms of Hurrell Froude. Keble was generally more willing to see God present in nature and some of life's simple pleasures while yet experiencing not infrequent depressions because of what he regarded as his failures. This sense of heavy responsibility is most evident in the emphases we find among them all on conscience as the best guide to God's purposes, on the duties of Christian discipleship and the role of obedience. Through such obedience others would see again the vital nature of Christian faith. Isaac Williams summed up the task of evangelism with these words:

> If people were now asked what was the most powerful means of advancing the course of religion in the world, we should be told that it was eloquence of speech or preaching . . . Whereas, if we were to judge from Holy Scripture of what were the best means of promoting Christianity in the world, we should say obedience; and

if we were asked the second, we should say obedience; and if we were to be asked the third, we should say obedience.[17]

As has happened before and since with those seeking so seriously to lead lives of Christian discipleship, what they sadly came to know as their chief obstacle to holy living was sin. It could not be ignored or minimised. Indeed perhaps nothing proved the validity of the Christian way more than the strength of the obstacle it must over-come. Superficial and unexamined human life does not even begin to understand this. Rigorous honesty, obedient perseverance, self-denial and severity of discipline are the weapons in a fierce battle. The arena is the human will.

Of course human beings do not struggle unaided. In one sense the whole point of the contest is to show forth the power of the grace of God. All the Oxford men, Keble especially in his poetry and Newman in his sermons, knew how to express their joy in the experience of that gracefulness. Yet here also is that paradox known by so many Christians beginning with St Paul: 'Work out your own salvation with fear and trembling: for God is at work in you, both to will and to work for his own good pleasure' (Phil. 2:12–13). Keble, having imbibed from infancy his understanding of God's grace working through the Church and sacraments, may have had a somewhat easier time dealing with the problem of the role of the human will in interaction with God's grace than did Newman, although Newman certainly came to stress the graceful presence of Christ in the Eucharist and the importance for believers of experiencing that relationship. Pusey's sacramental mysticism sometimes drew near to ecstasy as he used biblical imagery to tell of dying and rising with Christ in baptism and continuing in relationship with that body of Christ through the Eucharist. His words point beyond themselves to his faith in that mystery by which God penetrates into this physical world and then draws his faithful ones into his divine life.

Yet there has to be this faithfulness. Christians can cut themselves off from the grace of the sacraments and therefore must be exhorted to their reception. The true efficaciousness of the sacraments was only realised as disciples entered upon the imitation of the way of the cross, for which suffering the sacraments were also types – the chalice and baptism of tribulation and passion. Such dying to the world in order to be reborn to the risen life of Christ required, as we have seen, self-denial and disciplined obedience.

Newman, with his defensive attitude towards Lutheran teachings and the strong influence of Calvinism on his early life, can be seen wrestling with this paradox of grace both in theory and practice. A number of his most carefully constructed sermons are balanced on the horns of the dilemma. The issues have rarely been argued more delicately than in his *Lectures on Justification*. Eugene Fairweather calls these discourses 'the most important attempt to find the theological expression of [the Oxford Movement's] piety',[18] for they focus on these critical questions regarding God's grace and the human will. Unaided sinful humanity cannot even begin to do God's bidding. Only God's grace can offer justification and the life of righteousness, and that grace is given through the Church in the sacraments of baptism and especially Holy Communion. Yet individuals must accept the sacraments and are called to obedience in order to show forth the light of grace by holy living. '[S]uch co-operation is the condition, not of our acceptance, or pardon, but of the continuance of that sacred Presence which is our true righteousness.'[19]

We must not expect, however, some sudden outward moral change, but there begins an inner transformation as when a light enlightens a room.[20] It is then 'our blessedness to have our glory swallowed up in Christ's glory, and to consider our works and our holiness, to avail merely as securities for the continuance of that glory . . . as tokens that His grace is not in vain.'[21] Newman explicitly rejects both what he understands to be the Lutheran teaching of justification by faith alone and the Roman justification by obedience, especially when either is held exclusively.[22] In his thought the doctrine of justification becomes one of sanctification through sacramental grace and, viewed in the right way, 'to believe and to obey be but different characteristics of one and the same state of mind'.[23]

Still, why is it that some accept this way of life and others do not? At some fundamental level Newman's Calvinistic background may have continued to whisper to him that it must be a matter of divine choosing. God enables some to accept grace. Yet Newman seems also to have experienced the classical Calvinistic *angst*: one can only know election by God's grace if one manifests that grace and not just to others but to oneself. Therefore one must show forth and experience within oneself the obedience and character of God's chosen. As with many Christians before and since, the doctrine of grace appreciated theologically becomes difficult fully to accept in daily life. The grace may be a gift, but the individual must take a great measure of responsibility for being receptive to that gift. Again God becomes real to those who will commit themselves to live out their faith in God's reality.

This concern with grace was also orchestrated by the Oxford men into that more complex symphony which in some ways soothed but in other ways heightened their personal difficulty, for God's grace did not act just through individuals. It moved through history and especially in the life of the Christian community. (Here more than anywhere else the Tractarians differed from the Evangelicals who stressed individual salvation and the personal holiness of an invisible gathering of disciples.)[24] 'Speak to all the congregation of the children of Israel, and say unto them, ye shall be holy: for I the Lord your God am holy', reads the text (Lev. 19:2). The appeal and the challenge were to the visible church as the body of Christ and the new

Israel to show forth by its obedience the power of God's grace and holiness.

The music is now more intricate but the fundamental counterpoint can still be heard. Is it God's grace or human effort which makes the Church holy? Perhaps it must be some dance of both, at least theologically speaking, but surely it is God's grace which has to lead while the Church must regularly be urged and chastised to respond to God's call. Since it is a matter of God's grace and the Church's holiness, the will to show forth this spiritual character cannot come from without the Church – from society-at-large or the State. Reform, however much needed, can only come from within the Church. In this context Keble's Assize Sermon is preached.

The Church is not primarily a human institution. However lethargic and even corrupt the Church may appear it is divine in origin and is the theatre for the drama of God's special acts of grace. The apostolic succession is a vital doctrine ensuring this continuity of divine purpose, and so the Church of England was not to be viewed as some part-Protestant and part-Catholic quasi-political entity produced in reformation conflict. It is more than a *via media*. It is a living extension of the ancient Church. It is God's Church.

Keble and Newman could differ on the political steps that should be taken to help maintain the divine character of the Church. Newman still hoped for a 'Churched-England' while Keble recognised that separation was likely the only answer. But they were one in believing that State interference, however well intended, and the mixing in Church affairs by Roman Catholics and dissenters were, at the least, a threat to their view of a Church whose true leadership reached back through the centuries to the authority and purpose of the Son of God. They were also largely at one in their vision of what the Church ought to be. The clarification of that vision and exhortation in the hope that it might become practice were the purposes of the Tracts.

In his 'Advertisement' or preface to the publication of the first collection of the Tracts, Newman set forth their intent while also sketching the circumstances they were trying to improve: 'The neglect of the daily service, the desecration of festivals, the Eucharist scantily administered, insubordination permitted in all ranks of the Church'.[25] Two of the Tracts (25 and 26) were reprints of the seventeenth-century Bishop William Beveridge's sermons on the importance and value of the daily service and frequent communion. Fasting, together with other forms of austerity and ascetical practice, and auricular confession were important not only for their benefits but as signs that this was a church in continuity with both the early church and its developing life through the centuries. Excommunication had its purpose in maintaining the necessary authority and discipline of the body of Christ. And all this was to be carried out through a devoted, dignified and meticulous pastoral care. St Mary's and then even more evidently Littlemore were testing and training grounds. In quite different circumstances Keble's Hursley was meant to be the ideal apostolic parish. Among a group of friends concerned about the course of Church events, Keble is reported to have exclaimed, 'If the Church of England were to fail altogether yet it would be found in my parish.'[26] Generations of clergy were to be enlightened by this vision, and, in time, the concern with incarnating God's love through pastoral care would become a wellspring for social action ministries and spirituality expressed through them.

Much of the Tractarian's faith in how God would accomplish this renewed Church centred around the sacraments. In a mystical, sometimes almost quasi-physical manner, the Eucharist, which was the sacramental channel between the divine and creaturely worlds, was seen as the focus of God's grace. This was above all how Christians came into contact with the living God. For Keble much of the importance of the apostolic succession lay in its guarantee of the validity of the Eucharist.[27] Froude, who often took his friends' concerns two steps further, was ready to urge the benefits of daily communion.

In all this however little effort was made to call attention to these practices in terms of their outward performance. The Tractarian clergy celebrated the sacraments, said the offices, preached and went about their pastoral duties with restraint and a minimum of ceremonial. It was as if to call attention to their outward form might detract from the inner grace which was all important. Theirs was not a this-worldly religion. The divine services and sacraments pointed not to themselves but beyond to the more important and lasting world. As we have noted, for Pusey especially it was important to seek to die to things of this world in order to realise the reality of the divine. 'The less we live for things outward, the stronger burns our inward life. The more we live to things unseen, the less hold will this world of sense have over us.'[28] It would be left to another generation to give a more incarnate character to their reverent sacramentalism through church decoration, ritual and devotional acts.

Yet while in their priestly offices and personal lives the Oxford leaders remained distrustful of display, the almost magnetic energy produced by so much passionate intensity held under control by a restraining simplicity of life was a source of powerful attraction. To many who gathered about them it made them appear to glow with an inner light. They seemed to make the unseen world real. They stood close to the holy God.

Yet what if, after all their exhortation and effort to bring people to God's grace, the Church, which is meant to be at least a penetration of the invisible world into what is seen, appears no holier? Might it then not be God's chosen way of grace? In response to such doubts one can appeal to the Church's holiness in the past and the connection of the present Church with that past – stressing the signs and means of continuity while conversely disparaging the importance of the abrupt changes of the reformation. One can realistically recognise that the Church must remain imperfect in an imperfect world while still calling for a new holiness of life for the present-day Church modelled on and developing from the earlier Christianity.

But what if the Church seems largely deaf to those challenges, and the signs of apostolicity and continuity appear dim at best? Newman can ameliorate the doubt and pain of his individual dilemma about salvation by projecting it on to the screen of the Church as a historical and present-day institution. There secure grace might be known and the response of holiness be thought of more corporately. Yet if there remain doubts as to whether that grace is genuinely manifested in a particular church and might instead be found in another, then the pain is experienced again in a different form. As Newman drew closer to Roman catholicism, the question of the signs of the Church's holiness and saintliness became more and more important to him. He pondered as he edited and worked during this period on the *Lives of the English Saints*. While W. G. Ward's views are hardly a reliable guide for Newman's, the contention in Ward's *Ideal of a Christian Church* (1844) that the Church of Rome better carried forward and exemplified saintliness than did the Anglican Church was clearly a potent factor in Newman's agonised thinking.

We began this chapter with the understanding that the spirituality of the Oxford Movement can only be viewed as a complex development. No one theme can fully characterise it. No one cause can fully explain it. We have, however, seen how the hope that God's grace could be realised through individual and corporate holiness in such a manner as to evidence the authenticity of Christian faith served as an important dynamic at the heart of the movement. We have also recognised the ways in which the search of the Oxford leaders for authentic Christian living, as a response to the rising tides of relativism, the scientific method and historical criticism, anticipated many of the concerns about the bases for faith which were also to be problems for later Christians. The Tractarians too lived among circumstances which created for them the clangour of *cognitive dissonance*,[29] that is a sharp want of harmony between many of the truth claims of Christianity and the apparent realities of the world and the Church.

To the extent that their best response to religious uncertainty was to try so to live as to affirm 'that which helps men to be saints must be true', we, with them, can be aware of some of the unsatisfactory aspects of that answer. Yet we can also recognise that this response is far from insignificant. In a number of areas of human experience we can only know what may be true by attempting rigorously to live as if it is true. That is no simple tautology but rather part of the awareness of the hermeneutical circle of the interpretation of life which everyone must enter in order to know at all. 'I have more understanding than the aged, *because* [his emphasis] I keep thy commandments' (Ps. 119:100) is the text for Newman's sermon, 'Inward Witness to the Truth of the Gospel'. 'By obeying the commands of Scripture, we learn that these commands really come from God; by trying we make proof; by doing we come to know.'[30]

The Bible taught the Oxford Movement's leaders that holiness of life is the pathway to the Lord's presence. 'Follow peace with all men and holiness, without which no man shall see the Lord' (Heb. 12:14) served as the text for one of Pusey's first formative sermons.[31] Holiness and its disciplines brought the gift of the vision of God's otherwise invisible kingdom. The Tractarians also realised, better than some who lived before and after them, that Christian experience is meant to take on its true depth and colour in forms of community. Anselm's 'I believe that I may understand' had for them become 'we will seek holiness that we my believe'.

What is rightly to be remembered in the life of the Church is how earnestly and sacrificially the Oxford leaders invested themselves in that way of exploration and, with all their frailties and insecurities, sought to show forth what they believed to be the action of God's grace in their lives through authentic Christian spirituality. In retrospect their appeal to the Church's authority and many of their ecclesiastical and doctrinal teachings had little lasting effect on the Church. A different world view was coming into being even as they wrote and preached, and a new order of response was needed to meet the challenges of science and relativism and to the inspiration of the Bible. Events soon superseded their kind of conservatism with respect to biblical interpretation and their metaphysical perspective. Even their appeals to the teaching and practice of the ancient Church have had to be fully re-evaluated. Many Christians of the later nineteenth and twentieth centuries have been searching for spiritualities which seek to experience God through the world rather than by transcending the material creation. They have been looking for a sense of authority which arises through the activity of the Spirit, from within the ongoing body of the Church rather than being seen only in a hierarchical manner. Yet the responses of the Oxford leaders to the challenges of their times in terms of single-hearted discipline, sacrifice and devotion, their sense of God's sacramental presence and their basic theological awareness that the authenticity of Christian faith had to be tested through serious commitment in the examples of their lives together with their call of a church to holiness – these deeply rooted themselves in many hearts and imaginations, sending up shoots to bear fruit in subsequent generations.

1. John Henry Newman, *Parochial and Plain Sermons*, new edn, 8 vols (London 1878), VIII, pp. 264–5.
2. John Macquarrie, *Paths in Spirituality* (New York 1972), p. 47.
3. Owen Chadwick, ed., *The Mind of the Oxford Movement* (London 1960), p. 48.
4. Chadwick, *Mind*, p. 36. See also Yngve Brilioth, *The Anglican Revival: studies in the Oxford Movement* (London 1925), esp. pp. 210–79.
5. John Keble, Tract 89, *On the Mysticism Attributed to the Early Fathers of the Church*, p. 135. Here Keble speaks of the moral means of repentance, devotion and self-denial necessary for a right reading of Scripture.
6. John Henry Newman, *Sermons Chiefly on the Theory of Religious Belief, Preached before the University of Oxford* (London 1843), p. 228.
7. ibid. pp. 243–4.
8. Edward Bouverie Pusey, *Parochial Sermons*, rev. edn, 3 vols (London 1878), III, p. 202. See also Newman's sermon 'Faith and Obedience', on the text, 'If thou wilt enter into life, keep the commandments' (Matt. 19:17), *Parochial and Plain Sermons*, III, pp. 84–97.
9. Isaac Williams, Tract 80, *On Reserve in Communicating Religious Knowledge*, pp. 40–1.
10. Edward Bouverie Pusey, *Sermons during the season from Advent to Whitsuntide* (London 1848), p. 280.
11. Quoted by Georgina Battiscombe, *John Keble: a study in limitations* (London 1963), p. 63.
12. Newman, *Parochial and Plain Sermons*, I, p. 267.
13. ibid. pp. 12–13.
14. See, for example, the discussions by A. C. Thiselton, *The Two Horizons: New Testament Hermeneutics and Philosophical Description with Special Reference to Heidegger, Bultmann, Gadamer and Wittgenstein* (Grand Rapids, Michigan, and Exeter 1980), pp. 16–19, 103–14 *passim*.
15. Newman, *Parochial and Plain Sermons*, I, pp. 65–82.
16. Chadwick, *Mind*, p. 12.
17. Isaac Williams, Tract 87, *On Reserve in Communicating Religious Knowledge* (conclusion), p. 82. See also Newman, *Parochial Sermons*, I, p. 12.
18. E. R. Fairweather, ed., *The Oxford Movement* (New York and Oxford 1964), p. 215.
19. John Henry Newman, 'Righteousness Viewed as a Gift and a Quality', Lecture VIII, in *Lectures on the Doctrine of Justification* (London 1838), p. 214.
20. ibid., 'The Characteristics of the Gift of Righteousness', Lecture VII, p. 196.
21. ibid., Lecture VIII, p. 231.
22. cf. ibid., Lecture I, pp. 1–31.
23. id., *Parochial and Plain Sermons*, III, p. 95.
24. See J. E. Linnan, 'The Search for Absolute Holiness: a study of Newman's evangelical period', *Ampleforth Journal*, 73 (1968), pp. 161–74, who illustrates from Newman's first sermons strong parallels with the Evangelicals' call to personal holiness.
25. John Henry Newman, 'Advertisement', in *Tracts for the Times*, I, p. iv.
26. See Battiscombe, *John Keble*, p. 303.
27. See M. R. O'Connell, *The Oxford Conspirators: a history of the Oxford Movement 1833–45* (London 1959), p. 213.

28. Pusey, *Sermons from Advent to Whitsuntide*, pp. 299–300.
29. On cognitive dissonance, cf. L. Festinger, in L. Festinger, H. W. Riechen and S. Schachter, *When Prophecy Fails: a social and psychological study of a modern group that predicted the destruction of the world* (New York 1956); and L. Festinger, *A Theory of Cognitive Dissonance* (California 1957).
30. Newman, *Parochial and Plain Sermons*, VIII, pp. 112–13.
31. See O'Connell, *Oxford Conspirators*, p. 99.

5

The Sacraments in the
Tractarian Spiritual Universe*

Alf Härdelin

Introduction

John Keble, who had penetrated deeply into the hermeneutics of the
Fathers as well as into the nature of literary language in general, has
the following remarkable words to say in his tract, *On the Mysticism
Attributed to the Early Fathers of the Church*, which appeared in 1839.
He writes:

> Consider how very differently the same words sound in our ears,
> according to our different moods of mind; how much more meaning
> we find, not only in a text of Scripture, but in a chance passage
> of a book or a stray remark of a friend, when we recall it by and
> by, more seriously than at first we listened to it; nay, and how
> much beyond what we suspected we discover occasionally in our
> own words, uttered perhaps at first by instinct, we hardly knew
> how; so that not only are we always uncertain whether any two
> persons receive exactly the same impression – the same moral
> impression, that is – from any given words, but even whether to
> the same person the same ideas are conveyed by them twice. And
> yet there is truth and definite meaning in the words so spoken,
> although they go so much deeper with one man than they do with
> another.[1]

These are observations entirely of one accord with those of modern
hermeneutic philosophers.[2] What they perhaps would want to add is
that the same words sound differently in our ears, not only 'according
to our different moods of mind' but also to the changes in our
historical situation, both corporate and individual. However, Keble
as well as modern philosophers remind us of the inexhaustible richness of meaning in words and texts. Any re-reading of ancient texts
will therefore open up to us dimensions hitherto unnoticed; new
personal or historical or social experiences will direct the eyes of the
investigators to levels of meaning that previously had not been
observed or clearly grasped.
    With a view to looking afresh at the achievements of the Trac-

tarians we have thus to perform that task, not only as historians armed with the usual technical skills of that profession but also as people conscious of discoveries and reorientations in recent thought and scholarship. Let me then state briefly some of these discoveries and reorientations in the field of theology. In so doing I am convinced we shall be assisted in our attempt to map out that spiritual universe in which the Tractarian doctrine of worship and of the sacraments is rooted.

In the first place we have to remind ourselves of a significant change which the very concept of theology has undergone during the last decades.[3] That change is not unconnected with the intensification of the study of the Fathers and with the rediscovery of that monastic theology, which during the early Middle Ages was the continuation of patristic theology. My meaning is this: sources, which we were inclined earlier to consider as mere 'edification', or perhaps as unscientific 'spiritual theology' – a strange expression – we have now learned to read as authentic records, not only of the Christian kerygma, but of deep theological reflection. Generally this was not the attitude of most academic theologians as late as a few decades ago. And Newman, as we know, repeatedly asserted in his time, that he was not a 'theologian'.[4] For our part we need not excuse ourselves any longer if we take his sermons and those of his fellow-Tractarians as documents of primary theological importance. And it is no longer a surprise to us to find therein well reflected theological insights.

Closely related to this deepened knowledge of patristic theology as it is discovered in sermons and biblical commentaries – indeed an essential aspect of it – is a new understanding of the kind of exegesis which pervades all these works. After recent thorough studies, above all by Cardinal de Lubac in his *Exégèse Médiévale*, it is, I dare say, no longer possible to reject indiscriminately the so-called allegoris-ation as a work of mere pious fancy.[5] At any rate I think it is legitimate to say that, with regard to the re-evaluation of classical Christian exegesis, de Lubac was anticipated in no small degree during the nineteenth century; by Newman in his book on the *Arians*, but even more by Pusey in his unfortunately still unpublished 'Lectures on Types and Prophecies of the Old Testament',[6] and above all by Keble in Tract 89. Of these, Keble's tract is the most extensive and thorough and, from my point of view, the most rewarding; I know of no other nineteenth-century work which has in such a remarkable way perceived, not the technicalities perhaps, but the *inner theological point* in patristic and early medieval hermeneutics and exegesis. However all the three writers mentioned (and to that list we could also add the name of Isaac Williams) agreed that the ancient 'spiritual' exegesis was no mere device of text-interpretation, but that it rested on firm christological and ecclesiological foun-dations. They saw too, like Andrew Louth and other theologians of today, that its rejection and its fall into disrepute during former centuries was not unconnected with the rise of what they regarded as a rationalistic spirit.[7]

The two points I have mentioned are important for what I am going to say. For though they have to do with theology in general they also form the immediate background for two or three other more specific concerns of contemporary theological reflection. The first I would like to mention is basic to our understanding of the nature of the sacraments and of worship in general. It can be expressed briefly in the form of a question: What is the relation between the saving mysteries of Christ and the liturgical mysteries? Are the sacraments above all to be understood as instrumental causes mediating grace from the cross of Christ, or are they, together with liturgical celebrations in general, to be viewed as mysterious re-presentations, not merely of the passion of Christ, but of the whole economy of salvation? I would like to suggest that the Tractarians have left us some interesting if tentative indications of a line of thought which *we* tend to connect with a modern 'mystery theology'. And this is no strange coincidence, for just as the modern mystery theology is basically a result of renewed study of patristic thought, so also it was the Fathers above all who opened new and similar vistas to the Tractarians.

Another modern problem concerns the relation between these mysteries of Christ, conceived of as in some sense present in the liturgical celebrations on the one hand, and the moral, ascetic, or spiritual life of the Christian on the other. In other words the problem concerns the relationship between christology, liturgical theology, and spirituality.[8] And there is no doubt that the Tractarians even here, and not least through their study of the Fathers, recovered a more organic relationship between mystery and life. For, like the Fathers, the Tractarians connected the Christian life and Christian ethics with the mysteries of Christ, present in the Church. Not only was Christ to be regarded as an ideal pattern for imitation but, in all his mysteries, as a principle of life, to be realised through an authentic transformation of the personal existence, in Christ.

One last point has to be added here, namely the recovery of the eschatological dimension of the mysteries of salvation. Once again it is a question of something that is common to Tractarianism and certain endeavours in contemporary theology.[9] For, being celebrations of the mysteries of salvation, wrought in history and represented in the liturgy, worship cannot but be directed *also* towards that vision, in which the Church no longer has to walk by faith but will see these mysteries in their fulfilment, not only in Christ, the head, but also in those who are his members.

Sources and Hypothesis

As I implied in my introductory remarks, I would prefer to speak about the Tractarian doctrine of the sacraments, and of the liturgy in general, in a broader context than the usual one. The reasons for this have been suggested already. However a more formal one has to do with the character of the sources themselves: there are indeed, before the works by R. I. Wilberforce, published around 1850, no strictly systematic, speculative treatises on any of the sacraments from the pen of any Tractarian. Thus I do not regard Pusey's Tract *On Baptism*, first published in 1836, as such for it has an exegetical, historical, and controversial, rather than a systematic character. We find limited aspects of a sacramental theology in different tracts and treatises of a more or less controversial kind; I mean works such as Newman's *Letter to Dr Faussett*, from 1838, and Froude's *Remains*, published after his death. These I will *not* take into account again.[10]

However the Tracts by Pusey and Keble that I have already mentioned are of the greatest importance for my purpose, because we find in them some of the deepest and best treatments of that spiritual universe of which the sacraments form an integral part. Above all we find in them clear statements of those basic exegetical and theological principles which the authors considered they had recovered primarily through their fresh examination of the Catholic Fathers of the Church. These principles we find practically applied in their homiletic works, which will be my second principal group of sources. For if we read the Tractarian sermons we shall discover that though they might sometimes appear to be 'simple', compared with the works formerly mentioned and others of a similar kind, yet they are not just 'unscientific' popular discourses but texts offering an organic unity of thought. We shall find that in them certain things are deliberately kept together, and not because the authors have failed as proper theologians. And this is the hypothesis I would like to test, namely, that according to such leading Tractarians as Newman, Keble and Pusey, the sacraments belong to a complex living organism, and therefore cannot be treated without distortion as a detached and self-contained section in a treatise of systematic theology.

The Theological Basis of the 'Spiritual' Exegesis

There is neither space nor, I believe, need to enlarge upon the subject of the Tractarian doctrine of the Bible.[11] For it is well known that influences from contemporary Romanticism in combination with the study of the Fathers, not least those of the Alexandrian school, led the Tractarians not only to 'a symbolic or sacramental view of nature', according to which the visible world can be regarded as 'an index or token of the invisible',[12] but also to a sacramental view of the Scriptures. 'Every word of Revelation has a deep meaning,' says Newman in his *Lectures on the Prophetical Office of the Church*. 'It is the outward form of a heavenly truth, and in this sense a mystery or Sacrament.'[13] The words and doing of Christ, says Keble:

> being as they are the words and doing of God, it cannot be but they must mean far more than meets the ear, or the eye: they cannot but be full-charged with heavenly and mysterious meaning, whether we are as yet competent to discern some part of that meaning or no; and to look at them in that light may be called Mysticism, but is it any more than the natural and necessary result of *considerate* faith in His divine nature?[14]

However it is not merely the words 'sacrament' and 'sacramental', used here, that make this view of the Bible of importance to our theme. The relation between the attitude of the Tractarians towards the Bible and their reading of it, on the one hand, and their view of the sacraments on the other, lies far deeper. For they had learned from the Fathers that the spiritual or allegorical interpretation of the Bible was no device to escape from the prosaic content of the letter, and neither was it a putting aside of the historical character of God's revelation of himself to mankind.[15] Rather it was that history itself that demanded such a spiritual interpretation. What prompted a spiritual reading was not only the insight that God's word, like every word, is by its nature necessarily inexhaustible in its meaning, but the insight too that God's revelation in Christ was itself an ever present spiritual reality in his Church, and not a passing momentary event in history. In other words, to allegorise the Scriptures was not only to relate everything in it to Christ but to maintain that his mystery, or rather his mysteries, were also and at the same time the mysteries of the Church, constituting her inner life.

That is what Keble means when he says that the allegorical mode of interpretation did not only arise from a deep sense of our Lord's divinity,[16] but also from another fundamental truth, which he calls that of 'the Communion of Saints'; for, he says:

> by the Communion of Saints, is here meant the real, but mysterious and supernatural union of Jesus Christ with his Body the Church, and with every member of that Body: by virtue of which, the actions and sufferings of the Head may be predicted of the Body, and conversely those of the Body, of the Head.

Due to the close relation between the head and the body, things referred in the Bible to Christ may apply also to the body, and vice versa. This is the way in which Christ is 'invisibly present' with us, Keble continues: 'so the unity between Him and His Church would lead us to inquire, from time to time, whether things which we find [in the Scriptures] happening to Him may not be prophetic tokens

of the future fortunes of the Church'.[17] In saying this he is of course
only maintaining that conformity of Christ with the Church which
is so central a theme in the writings of St Augustine, a thought which
was expressed, from a formal point of view, in the famous 'rules of
Tyconius'.[18] As everything in the Scriptures becomes transparent
when read in the light of Christ, so everything also belongs to the
Church, in communion with him.

The same thought can also be expressed by Keble in terms of
typology, but it is then a question of *double* typology. For not only is
Christ the fulfilment of everything in the old covenant, foreshadowing
him, but, being the head of his body the Church, *he* is also the type
of the Church. He is, says Keble, 'the end of the ancient types and
the beginning of a new series. In Him all that happened before was,
as it were, brought to a point; and all again that should come after,
was but so many developments of what He said, did, and suffered
among us'.[19] In this way Keble wants to express what was later to
be called 'the extension of the incarnation' in the Church. For Christ
is the 'type' of the Church in the sense that his mystery is effectually
present, and actually realising itself, in the Church.

As many patristic and medieval writers had spoken of Christ and
the Church as forming *una mystica persona*,[20] so in Keble's language
Christ, 'in union and communion with all His members', may be
said to constitute 'in a certain sense, one great and manifold Person,
into which, by degrees, all souls of men, who do not cast themselves
away, are to be absorbed'.[21]

Thus, to allegorise is to do no more than express the effectual
presence of the mysteries of Christ in the Church, or viewed from
the other angle to do no more than maintain the contemporaneity of
the Church, in every aspect of her existence, with Christ in the
mysteries of salvation.[22] Clearly this was not the perception of Keble
only. Quoting St Augustine, the great teacher of the *totus Christus*,
Pusey says in his Tract *On Baptism*: 'The ancient Church believed
that all [in Holy Scripture] was significant; that it was full of
mysteries, "some things referring to Christ, some to the Church and
thus the whole to Christ".'[23] This is the doctrine, Pusey asserts,
fundamental to Scripture, 'that we are "in Him"; of course in some
unearthly way, but still really and mystically. No mere external
relation (as the being members of the visible body, called by His
Name) exhaust the inwardness of the words "in Christ".' It is the
question of 'the hidden mystery of union with Christ, and of the
reality of our dwelling in Him, and He in us, which is not merely a
"unity of will", or a "mere conformity of mind" '.[24] All events
recorded in Scripture bear upon Christ, who, as Pusey says, is 'the
Sun and centre of the system'. But for him, as for Keble, Christ is
also communicating himself to the Church. For, says Pusey:

the events of His history gleam with His own effulgence upon His body, the Church. In that He had deigned to become her Head, it could not but be, that He had instituted a mysterious relation between Himself and His body, so that she should, in a manner, and as a whole, reflect Him, and His acts concern her.

And Pusey adds that in believing so, the ancient Church had her eye particularly fixed upon the sacraments, 'the means whereby He originally united her to Himself [that is, through baptism], or still nourished her, and cherished her, and maintained her in that union'.[25]

No doubt all this is nothing other than what was implied in authentic patristic 'allegory', as it was defined later, for example, by the Venerable Bede.[26] If sometimes it is called 'typology' by the Tractarians or by later scholars, this ought not to confuse us. But neither ought it to lead us astray, for the point is very important. What the Tractarians are anxious to teach is not only the fulfilment of the Old Testament in Christ, and not only that his mystery spreads its light over the whole of the New Testament. They are also anxious to stress the Church's being in Christ, sharing therefore the mysteries of his life, death and exaltation; in other words her essential and actual, and not merely moral, unity with Christ, the head.

This doctrine they thought they had learned from the Fathers, and therewith they turned against what they called 'the modern school'. Thus Pusey ends his Tract *On Baptism* by drawing a contrast between the harmonic beauty of the ancient system of scriptural theology on the one hand, and that of the moderns on the other. 'Certainly,' he says, 'a gradual abandonment of the types, and a less reverential and thoughtful appreciation of the reality, have gone together. In both we have declined, step by step, from the Ancient Church.'[27]

The Mysteries of Christ and the Liturgy

It has already been suggested what *kind* of sacramental theology would be expected to have flowed most naturally from this christology and ecclesiology, which the Tractarians had received from the Fathers. However theologies are not only the fruits of reading but also of the historic situation of the readers. All the leading Tractarians devoted themselves during the thirties to an intensive reading of the Fathers. But even had they so desired, no recovery of patristic thought could have obliterated from their minds what they had inherited as being the children of another age. As members of the nineteenth-century Church of England they were the heirs of a long tradition of theologising that no doubt contained many patristic elements but had received also some of its most characteristic traits from medieval scholasticism, traits which the Reformers had not questioned but had carried on to later times in a more or less modified form.

Now what is characteristic of a scholastic *and* reformed, or post-scholastic, sacramental thought, is, among other things, the need to *define* strictly what is a sacrament and to *separate* these sacraments – whether seven or two – from other rites and ordinances. But even more characteristic perhaps is the way in which sacraments are conceived, namely as means, or channels, or instruments for the communication of 'grace'. By way of *causality* the sacraments relate us with the past events of salvation, because, or in so far as, they mediate the virtues wrought by Christ, especially, if not exclusively, through the cross.[28]

It goes without saying that the Tractarians very often spoke about the sacraments in precisely this 'scholastic' way: as means or instruments of grace.[29] An important aspect of their struggle consisted indeed in their maintaining the sacraments as *effective* means of grace, versus the inclination of 'the moderns' to empty them of this reality.[30] This is too well known to need any further demonstration here.

At the same time however we have to notice occasional utterances showing that the Tractarians felt this way of conceiving the sacraments to be inadequate, or at least a little uncongenial to their thought. Thus we find Pusey saying in a sermon: 'This is the special gift of the Sacraments of our Lord, that they are not only means of grace, but that they invisibly join us on to Him.'[31] In another sermon he speaks about baptism as 'imparting to us the efficacy of [Christ's] Death, yea [as imparting] that Death itself'.[32] It is not at all difficult to understand the purport of these distinctions, for what Pusey wanted to express is that the sacraments are not just communicating grace but are mysteries by which we are made partakers of Christ in his deeds of salvation, and in particular of his death and resurrection.[33]

Here we are approaching a way of conceiving of the sacraments, as well as of worship and ordinances generally, which I suggest is more of one piece with that christology and ecclesiology which the Tractarians had learned from the Fathers. The key-word here can be said to be 'presence'. But it is not only a question, then, of the sacramentally mediated presence of a divine but nevertheless unspecific 'grace', but of a being present of Christ himself as a living person, in and through his mysteries of salvation. For conformity with him means sharing in all the mysteries of his life and exaltation. Historically he is gone, but through his Spirit he is sacramentally present in all the acts of his Church, and not only in the sacraments.[34] There are, particularly in Newman's sermons, many beautiful expressions of this belief. Thus, for example, in a sermon on 'Regenerating Baptism', he calls the sacraments, it is true, 'instruments of the application of [Christ's] merits to individual believers'. Yet this is not all he has to say, for he goes on to contend that though Christ is in heaven, he is also with his Church on earth. 'And as He is still with us,' Newman continues, 'for all that He is in heaven, so, again,

is the hour of His cross and passion ever mystically present', for 'time
and space have no portion in the spiritual Kingdom which He has
founded; and the rites of His Church are as mysterious spells by
which He annuls them both'.[35]

What was said here about the Church and its rites generally, Pusey
applied to the festivals of the Church calendar. In his usual way he
makes a contrast between the teaching of the ancient Church, this
time expressed in the old texts of the liturgy, and that of the modern:

> as the year flowed on [he says] the Festivals of our Lord did not
> simply commemorate (in modern phrase) events which took place
> 1,800 years ago, but showed Him to their purified hearts, as *even
> then* coming into the world, born, suffering, dying, rising, ascending:
> they longed for His coming; they suffered in His Passion; they rose
> with Him from the tomb; they followed His Ascension; they
> awaited His return to judge the quick and the dead, and to receive
> them to His kingdom.[36]

Though these utterances, and others of a similar kind that could
be adduced, might seem to be rather vague from the point of view of
systematic theology, I think they have a quite clear and unmistakable
bearing. It is obvious that for the Tractarians there is no question
here of a mere mental or imaginative presence of Christ. 'The
kingdom and Church of Christ', says Keble, 'is full of Christ: not of
the name only and profession, of the shadow and fancy, of the dreamy
and deceitful feeling, which some mistake for Christ; but of Jesus
Christ Himself, silently and mysteriously coming in and dwelling
there.' And if that is true of the Church at large it is also true, he
says, 'of every soul which is inwardly and spiritually conformed to
God's holy Church'.[37]

This presence could be called 'spiritual', not as if the Holy Ghost
had come, as Newman puts it, 'to supply Christ's absence. . . Let us
not for a moment suppose that God the Holy Ghost comes in such
sense that God the Son remains away. No; He has not so come that
Christ does not come, but rather He comes that Christ may come in
His coming.'[38] This of course applies most truly to the sacraments of
baptism and the Eucharist. It is worth repeating that the Tractarians
considered them as true and effectual means of grace. But such they
are precisely *because* they are mysterious representations of Christ's
entire economy of salvation.

As is well known the battle for baptismal regeneration formed an
important part of the Tractarian struggle, as is evidenced not least
by Pusey's Tract *On Baptism*. For:

> no change of heart, then [the writer says against the moderns] or
> of the affections, no repentance, however radical, no faith, no life,
> no love, come up to the idea of this 'birth from above' [through
> baptism] . . . it is not only the creation of a new heart, new affec-

tions, new desires, and *as it were* a new birth, but it is an *actual* birth from above . . . given to faith, through baptism.[39]

Thus Christ's birth is, as Newman says, 'a figure, promise, or pledge of our new birth, and it effects what it promises'.[40]

However this effectiveness of baptism is dependent upon its conveying 'a most intimate communion' with the saving events of Christ.

> It were much [says Pusey] to be buried, to be crucified, with Him, like Him; but it is more to become partakers of His Burial and Crucifixion; to be (so to speak) co-interred, co-crucified; to be included in, wrapt round, as it were, in His Burial and Crucifixion, and gathered in His very tomb [by baptism].[41]

This, it may be retorted, is nothing but the Bible's own 'mystery theology'. So it might be. However according to Pusey it was a doctrine forgotten by his contemporaries, who tended to see in such language 'a *mere* moral exhortation to conformity to Christ', but no allusion to that sacrament, which is 'the hidden spring of such action'.[42]

What then does this conformity of the Church with Christ mean with regard to the Eucharist? For it is obvious that the Tractarians did not merely contend for the real presence of Christ's body and blood. There is also with them a recovery of the sacrificial nature of the Eucharist, a recovery that can be best explained as the natural outcome of that grasp of the perpetual presence of Christ in the Church, which, as I have maintained, is the basis of their spiritual universe. This, I think, is particularly evident in Newman's works.

In words which reflect utterances of the Fathers and medieval theologians, Newman in one of his sermons represents the very incarnation and passion of Christ itself, as if it were a mass, indeed, the original mass of the Church. For this is what Newman says about God becoming man in Christ: 'He took it', namely our nature, 'consecrated it, broke it', that is to say, in his passion, 'and said, "Take, and divide it among yourselves" '.[43] In so doing Christ acted as the 'One proper priest' of the gospel. But as unity between head and body is, as Newman maintains in his *Lectures on Justification*, the 'characteristic sacrament' of the gospel, it is right to conclude:

> Christian Ministers also offer sacrifices, but it is their privilege to know that those sacrifices are not independent of Christ . . . but continuations, as it were, of His Sacrifice . . . and that though distinct as visible and literal acts, yet, as being instinct with that which they commemorate, they are absorbed and vivified in it.[44]

As the old priesthood, fulfilled in Christ, has a continuation in the Church and its ministerial services, so it is equally clear to Newman that the old paschal feast 'has not come to an end [in Christ] without leaving behind it a rite in its place, without reviving, as it were, in a new form' in the feast of Holy Communion.[45] Even though the Eucharist is related in particular to Christ's death and resurrection,[46] it reflects the entire economy of salvation, of which it is 'the effectual type'. Thus Newman asks his listeners to pray for 'a real and living insight into the blessed doctrine of the Incarnation of the Son of God, of His birth of a Virgin, His atoning Death, and resurrection', for no one realises 'that gracious Economy' without feeling disposed towards the mystery of the Eucharist.[47]

It is clear then that when Newman was speaking about the spiritual presence of Christ in the Eucharist he meant Christ in the fullness of his economy. To keep away from communion is thus to cut oneself off, not only from some unspecific 'grace', but from all the saving acts of Christ. This is what he says to those who abstain from coming to communion:

> I do not venture to say what you lose, but you lose something you know not what. You lose a mysterious entrance to the Court of the living God, you lose the overshadowing presence of Christ, your Saviour, you lose the privilege of that breath that once breathed upon His Apostles, of that heavenly manna which He promised the multitude when He miraculously fed them with bread, or the water of life which He promised . . . should become a well of water springing up into everlasting life. You lose all this, the close approach to the Holy Trinity, to the Saints and Angels, to the dead in Christ. Oh how great a loss, and how great a gain to those who enjoy it.[48]

Mystery and Spirituality

The preceding remarks and quotations are sufficient, I hope, to indicate that the sacraments were to the Tractarians more than just objective means for the communication of grace. Rather they constitute a liturgical world of signs, through which the Church is brought into effective contact with Christ in all the phases of his saving economy, and particularly in his death and resurrection. Yet worship and sacraments, necessary though they be, are not themselves the Church; rather they are there for the formation of that Church of living members which is to be conformed to Christ. They are the links connecting head and body. The mysteries of Christ are re-presented in the Church and through sacramental worship *in order to be* realised and interiorised in every member of the body. In *that* sense the sacraments are indeed means: means to an end, means to bring about the union and conformity between head and members.

If the Tractarians are comparatively vague in their sacramental theology, they are definite and clear with regard to the meaning of the Christian life. For what is it 'to be one of Christ's little ones'? It is, Newman answers:

> to become in a wonderful way His members, the instruments, or visible form, or sacramental sign, of the One Invisible Ever-Present Son of God, *mystically reiterating* in each of us all the acts of His earthly life, His birth, consecration, fasting, temptation, conflicts, victories, sufferings, agony, passion, death, resurrection, and ascension.[49]

Or, as Newman says in another sermon:

> What was actually done by Christ in the flesh . . . is in type and resemblance really wrought in us one by one even to the end of time . . . Christ himself vouchsafes to repeat in each of us in figure and mystery all that He did and suffered in the flesh.[50]

Thus the Holy Spirit is finishing in us 'what Christ had finished in Himself, but left unfinished as regards us'.[51]

Nothing, to be sure, is here explicitly said about the sacraments. And yet the sacramental vocabulary used already by Newman indicates the role of the sacraments as *links* between the mysteries of Christ and their realisation in the faithful. For of course there is no question here of a mere moral imitation of Christ but, as Newman said, of *him* 'mystically reiterating in us' his life and death, so that we ourselves become spiritual signs of his presence. And this is the work of the Spirit, through the sacraments. But that is not all; for though salvation, or justification, is, as Newman stressed, 'not *of* us', it is '*in us*'. Here then we can see the importance of the mystery theology for the Tractarians with regard to spirituality. For with the formula just quoted Newman expressly wanted to oppose two 'errors', those of the Pelagian and of the Evangelical, who both, in his opinion, deprived the 'Christian life of its mysteriousness'. Thus, while the former practically denies that salvation is of God, the latter 'considers that Christ's passion once undergone on the Cross absolutely secured his own personal salvation'. Such a person, says Newman, 'may see mystery indeed in that Cross . . . but he will see no mystery, and feel little solemnity, in prayer, in ordinances, or in his attempts at obedience'.[52]

But mystery there is for the Tractarians, not only in sacramental worship but also in the Christian's sanctification, for Newman says, 'we have to take the redemption offered us, and that taking involves a work. We have to apply [God's] grace to our own souls, and that application implies pain, trial, and toil, in the midst of its blessedness.'[53] And why? Because that taking and that application is nothing but the personal realisation of those mysteries, and in particular that of the cross, which are brought near by the liturgical mysteries, and which cannot be applied therefore without pain, self-denial, mortification.[54]

We are now I think in a better position to understand what Keble meant by the words quoted earlier. When he spoke about 'the Communion of Saints', as meaning the 'mysterious and supernatural union of Jesus Christ with His Body the Church', and of Christ as 'the type of the Church', he had in view the multidimensional character of Christ's work of redemption. The doctrine of the cross and of 'Christ crucified' is a doctrine which concerns not only Christ himself or the sacraments, but also Christian spirituality; it is, as Keble says, 'a doctrine of suffering in adherence to a crucified Redeemer'.[55] Again, as Pusey says: 'The whole of the Gospel is the doctrine of the Cross, but that two-fold' – he could have said threefold – 'the Cross borne *for* us, and the virtue and power of the Cross by the Sacraments communicated *to* us, and henceforth to be borne *by* us.'[56] However as the Tractarians themselves saw it this doctrine was not the fashion of their day. 'You hear men speak of glorying in the Cross of Christ', says Newman, 'who are utter strangers to the notion of the Cross as actually applied to them in water and blood, in holiness and mortification'.[57]

No Tractarian has more extensively laid down what all this means with regard to baptism than Pusey. In his Tract on that subject he saw it as his primary task to set right the proper *order* between the power and gift of baptism and the duties following upon them. He therefore opposed those 'moderns' who, in his judgment, 'see only duties of men' in those 'passages in which Holy Scripture speaks of gifts of God', conveyed through baptism.[58] Thus in interpreting Romans 6, Pusey sought support in the Fathers, who saw in the words of that text 'not only the death unto sin, which we *were* to die, but that also which in Christ we *have* died . . . not the life only which we *are* to live, but the actual life which, by Baptism, was infused in us'.[59] Thus there is according to Pusey not only a close connection between the historic work of Christ and the baptism by which that work is effectively re-presented. There is indeed also a death, which *we* have to die, and thus also a close connection between these mysteries and the Christian life. But the order of that connection is important, for 'our part begins with our new life in Christ, which we have received in Baptism; when in Him we have died', Pusey continues, '*then* begins that other death, which through Him we must continually die'.[60] Imitation of Christ follows, and *has* to follow, upon the conformity with him wrought through baptism.[61] And it is clear wherein that imitation consists, namely in that mortification and new life, which is nothing other than the realisation of the mysteries of Christ.

Thus Pusey has at least laid the foundations for what we could call a paschal spirituality. But although the details of such a spirituality were never worked out by any of the Tractarians, we find traces

of it everywhere, and particularly in their sermons. There we find
descriptions, or indications, of that temper of mind which they
consider to be the most appropriate for the disciples of Christ
crucified and risen. So, for example, Newman opposes those men 'in
these latter times' who make 'much of the free grace of the Gospel',
while they deny that 'it enjoined a work, as well as conferred a
blessing'.[62] So also he warns those who are 'feasting without fear'
and who 'would have all the glories of the Gospel without its austerities'. For what those people ought to remember is that 'even the
paschal lamb . . . was eaten with bitter herbs'.[63] A final example we
take from one of his most remarkable sermons, that on 'Bodily
suffering'. Here the author points out how all the gifts of God 'flow
from a fount of blood'. He continues: 'A work of blood is our
salvation . . . We must take Him, who thus suffered, as our guide;
we must embrace His sacred feet, and follow Him. No wonder, then,
should we receive on ourselves some drops of the sacred agony which
bedewed His garments.' Newman asks whether Christ himself did
not state 'this connection between nearness to Him and affliction',
when he asked the disciples if they were able to drink of his cup and
be baptised with his baptism. He paraphrases:

> Ye cannot have the sacraments of grace without the painful figures
> of them. The Cross, when imprinted on your foreheads, will draw
> blood. You shall receive, indeed, the baptism of the Spirit, and the
> cup of My communion, but it shall be with the attendant pledges
> of My cup and agony, and My baptism of blood.[64]

Newman, to be sure, did not only have literal martyrdom in view
here, but *any* pain involved in being brought into connection with
the mysteries of Christ in the sacraments and in following him. There
is no question here of Tractarian 'gloominess' and 'rigidity', but of
a spirituality and of a frame of mind nurtured by mystery theology.

Mysteries' End

For the Tractarians worship and sacraments are not only mysteries
related to the *past* history of salvation or mysteries to be realised in
every member of Christ's body. They are also, as preparations and
anticipations, related to the eschatological fulfilment in the beatific
vision. That aspect also forms an organic part of Tractarian mystery
theology.

That this is so is implied already by the very concept of sacrament
or mystery. For what is a mystery? It is, Newman says, 'a Truth
Sacramental: that is, a high invisible grace lodged in an outward
form'.[65] That was said with regard to doctrines, but certainly it has
a wider application. What is but 'imperfectly revealed' is
mysterious.[66] That applies to nature and the creation as well as to

the Bible, the Church and the sacraments. For only faith can penetrate that veil behind which God in this age is hiding himself, while at the same time revealing himself. Revelation gives us 'as in a figure, in the form of mysteries, what the Beatific Vision will then impart'.[67]

This then is the mysteries' end, to which worship and sacraments are conducting the Church on earth. For, as Newman says, 'in the worship and service of Almighty God . . . we are vouchsafed means, both moral and mystical, of approaching God, and gradually learning to bear the sight of him'. Thus the sacraments 'are not to be here for ever', but rather we ought to consider them as 'anticipations and first-fruits of that sight of Him which one day must be'.[68] This is a theme constantly alluded to by Newman, and not least when dealing with the Eucharist, as for example in his sermon entitled 'The Gospel Feast'. In that sermon Newman exposes the Old Testament types of the Eucharist, expounding not only their fulfilment in Christ and in the Eucharist but also their eschatological bearings. 'We Christians', he says, 'are both with the Church in the wilderness as regards faith, and in the Church in Canaan as regards enjoyment.'[69] And he ends by asking us to come in this way to the 'Blessed Sacrament', that it may 'be the first fruits of that banquet which is to last for ever and ever; ever new, ever transporting, inexhaustible, in the city of our God'.[70] Certainly to stress in this way the eschatological and anagogical aspect of worship and sacraments was no peculiarity of Newman's. It is clear that Pusey could not deal with baptism as the sacramental re-presentation of Christ's death and resurrection without including also its fulfilment in the resurrection, of which it is the earnest.[71] And to Keble the Eucharist is not only a 'perpetual witness of our Lord's return' and 'the ordained preparation for seeing His face with joy';[72] it is also 'a pledge of resurrection, a seed of immortal life to our vile bodies'.[73]

Thus I hope I have been able to show that the doctrine of the conformity between head and body was important to the Tractarians, not only with regard to ecclesiology, but also with regard to sacramental doctrine and to spirituality. The spiritual universe of the Tractarians is multi-dimensional in the same sense as that of the Church Fathers. For, just as God's *historia* is re-presented in the Church and its ordinances in order to be interiorised in the faithful, so also is it not fulfilled until all the members of the body are brought into complete union with him whom they now approach in worship, but whom they will then see face to face, when the veils of the sacramental mysteries are to be lifted.[74]

1.   John Keble, Tract 89, *On the Mysticism Attributed to the Early Fathers of the Church*, p. 177.

2.   See, for example, H.–G. Gadamer, *Wahrheit und Methode*, 4th edn

(Tübingen 1975); English tr. from 2nd German edn, *Truth and Method* (2nd English edn, with corrections, London 1981).

3. One of the first instances of the change I have in view was the 'kerygmatic theology' advocated – not without provoking disagreement – in the thirties by such as J. A. Jungmann, in his *Die Frohbotschaft und unsere Glaubensverkündigung* (Regensburg 1936).

4. See N. Lash, 'Was Newman a Theologian?' *Heythrop Journal*, 17 (1976), pp. 322–5.

5. H. de Lubac, *Exégèse Médiévale. Les quatre sens de L'Ecriture*, 2 parts in 4 vols (Paris 1959–64). Important also are the studies of F. Ohly, collected in his *Schriften zur mittelalterlichen Bedeutungsforschung* (Darmstadt 1977).

6. See D. Jasper, 'Pusey's Lectures on Types and Prophecies of the Old Testament', in Perry Butler, ed., *Pusey Rediscovered* (London 1983), pp. 51–70.

7. A. Louth, *Discerning the Mystery: an essay on the nature of theology* (Oxford 1983), esp. pp. 96–131.

8. See, for example, John Macquarrie, *Paths in Spirituality* (London 1972).

9. See, for example, G. Wainright, *Eucharist and Eschatology* (London 1971).

10. For a full treatment of the eucharistic doctrine of the Tractarians, see A. Härdelin, *The Tractarian Understanding of the Eucharist* (Uppsala 1965).

11. See, for example, J. Seynaeve, *Cardinal Newman's Doctrine on Holy Scripture* (Louvain 1953); and H. F. Davis, 'Newman and the Theology of the Living Word', *Newman Studies*, 6 (1964), pp. 167–77.

12. Keble, Tract 89, pp. 148, 152.

13. John Henry Newman, *The Via Media of the Anglican Church*, 2 vols (London 1901), I, p. 257.

14. Keble, Tract 89, pp. 119ff.

15. ibid. pp. 38–70.

16. ibid. p. 119.

17. ibid. pp. 128ff.

18. See, for example, E. Mercsh, *Le corps mystique du Christ*, 2 vols (Paris and Brussels 1951), pp. 84–138.

19. Keble, Tract 89, pp. 129ff.

20. See A. Härdelin, 'Pâques et rédemption', *Collectanea Cisterciensia*, 43 (1981), pp. 14–19.

21. Keble, Tract 89, p. 144.

22. John Keble, *Sermons for the Christian Year*, 11 vols (London 1875–80), II, pp. 18ff.

23. Edward Bouverie Pusey, Tract 67, *On Baptism*, p. 308.

24. ibid. p. 116.

25. ibid. p. 272.

26. D. Hurst, ed., *Beda Venerabilis, De tabernaculo et vasis eius* (Turnholti 1969), p. 25.

27. Pusey, Tract 67, pp. 389ff. As Keble and Pusey in their Tracts constantly refer to the Fathers for support, so they constantly oppose 'the modern school', by which they mean not only Calvin, Zwingli and other Protestant classics, but even later English writers, such as Doddridge and Simeon. However without further investigation it is difficult to say more exactly where the line of demarcation has to be drawn between what is distinctively Tractarian and what the doctrine of this 'modern school' is

with regard to our question. The latter was, of course, no uniform phenomenon.

28. See the discussion in B. Leeming, *Principles of Sacramental Theology* (London 1956), esp. pp. 283–345.

29. For example, Pusey, Tract 67, p. 172. See Härdelin, *Tractarian Understanding of the Eucharist*, pp. 72ff. and *passim*.

30. For example, Pusey, Tract 67, p. 276.

31. Edward Bouverie Pusey, in *Plain Sermons by the contributors to the Tracts for the Times*, 10 vols (London 1839–48), III, p. 230.

32. ibid. p. 8.

33. ibid. p. 230.

34. John Henry Newman, *Parochial and Plain Sermons*, new edn, 8 vols (London 1868), VI, p. 242.

35. ibid. III, p. 277.

36. Pusey, Tract 67, pp. 173–5.

37. Keble, *Sermons for the Christian Year*, II, p. 16.

38. Newman, *Parochial and Plain Sermons*, VI, p. 126.

39. Pusey, Tract 67, p. 47.

40. Newman, *Parochial and Plain Sermons*, V, p. 86.

41. Pusey, Tract 67, p. 95; see also p. 171.

42. ibid. p. 176; see also pp. 322ff.

43. Newman, *Parochial and Plain Sermons*, V, p. 118.

44. John Henry Newman, *Lectures on the Doctrine of Justification*, 3rd edn (London 1874), pp. 198ff.

45. John Henry Newman, *Sermons Bearing on Subjects of the Day*, new edn (London 1867), p. 210

46. See for example Newman, *Parochial and Plain Sermons*, VI, p. 136.

47. ibid. p. 151.

48. John Henry Newman, MS, Sermon 456 (The Oratory, Edgbaston, Birmingham: A.50.3), preached on 23 April 1837, pp. 9ff.

49. Newman, *Parochial and Plain Sermons*, VI, p. 3.

50. ibid. V, p. 139.

51. ibid. p. 138. See also Newman's *Lectures on Justification*, pp. 206ff.

52. Newman, *Parochial and Plain Sermons*, V, pp. 140ff. See also III, pp. 299ff.

53. Newman, *Sermons on Subjects of the Day*, p. 161.

54. Newman, *Lectures on Justification*, pp. 174ff.

55. Keble, Tract 89, p. 31.

56. Pusey, in *Plain Sermons*, III, p. 5.

57. Newman, *Lectures on Justification*, p. 174.

58. Pusey, Tract 67, p. 91.

59. ibid. p. 93.

60. ibid. p. 97.

61. ibid. p. 122.

62. Newman, *Sermons on Subjects of the Day*, p. 4.

63. ibid. pp. 113–21.

64. Newman, *Parochial and Plain Sermons*, III, pp. 140ff.; see also II, p. 62; IV, pp. 78, 323ff.

65. ibid. II, p. 211.

66. ibid. I, p. 211.

67. ibid. VI, p. 370.

68. ibid. V, pp. 7–9; see also p. 56.

69. ibid. VII, p. 168.
70. ibid. p. 178.
71. Pusey, Tract 67, pp. 103ff., 171.
72. Keble *Sermons for the Christian Year*, I, pp. 475ff.
73. Keble, in *Plain Sermons*, I, p. 284.
74. I take this opportunity to thank Mr Bruce Johanson, Uppsala, and the Revd Canon Roger Greenacre, Chichester, for their help in improving the English of my manuscript.

6

The Nature of Theological Understanding: some parallels between Newman and Gadamer*

Andrew Louth

It may seem an odd thing to profess to lecture on Newman and Gadamer. If we begin to compare them at first – at least – we shall simply draw out a series of contrasts. Newman was in some ways a typical product of a long-past academic system, not exactly a scholar, not exactly an academic mentor – his greatest influence in Oxford was exercised as vicar of the University Church; Hans-Georg Gadamer ended his academic career as Professor of Philosophy at Heidelberg, born into a German academic family, a very typical product of and representative of German academe, awesomely learned, though exceptional in that he writes in elegant and lucid German. Newman is pretty directly approachable; certainly there are influences on his thought that we should be aware of, but they are the influences on most English minds of the nineteenth century: well-read in English literature, knowledgable in the Greek and Latin classics, influenced in philosophy by such as Butler, Hume, Mill and Coleridge – all this constitutes a very English background, though Coleridge opens the door to other influences. And Newman is *very* English – the profoundest influences on his thought are all English, plus the classics and the Fathers. Gadamer in contrast is not so directly approachable, even to a German. He is formidably learned, and in a very German-focused tradition of learning and culture. Gadamer knows, has studied deeply and pondered on, a tradition reaching (over quite a short span, it is true) from Goethe to Paul Celan through such as Hölderlin and Rilke (and Stefan George, a favourite with him), from Herder to Heidegger, via Hegel and Husserl and Dilthey. And behind these there is deep learning in classical antiquity. The reader is hardly able to keep Gadamer in sight, let alone keep up – especially one who is not German and thus views the intellectual history of mankind from a rather different vantage point. The elegant English philosopher-gentleman of the nineteenth century and the formidably learned mandarin German professor, a nineteenth-century phenomenon which however persists into the present: not an unfair contrast between Newman and Gadamer. But there is worse, if you like. Newman became a Roman

* © 1986 Andrew Louth

Catholic, a cardinal to boot. Gadamer, like Bultmann, is a Protestant: I suppose that is another point of contact – Newman and Gadamer then are both Christians, a point of contact we would not have had, had we taken together Newman and Heidegger. We might finally mention another rather trivial contrast: to understand Newman we must read *lots*, not just the great books, but sermons, essays, letters, and so on, and his thought corresponds to this – searching, tentative, now resolved one way, now another; Gadamer is a man of one book essentially, his *Truth and Method* (*Wahrheit und Methode*), published towards the end of his academic career, the summation of a lifetime's reading and thought – all distilled into a single, coherent statement.[1]

'The nature of theological understanding': even here we have a contrast, for whereas Newman was a theologian and all his thought on the nature of understanding has in view the special case of *theological* understanding, Gadamer is a philosopher, and though he does interest himself in theology it is not really his thoughts there that interest me. With both Newman and Gadamer I want to start by looking at their approach to *understanding* – human understanding in general. And only from there move on to the special case of theological understanding.

But so far we have only contrasts – contrasts that suggest almost a chasm separating two intellectual and cultural traditions. But there are, even at the material level, some interesting points of contact – if we look closely. Let me mention three influences that bear on both Newman and Gadamer, or at least three books they had both read. There is no particular significance in choosing these three: it is just that they suit my purposes.

Both Newman and Gadamer know of the *Logique de Port-Royale*. Newman had read it (in English translation) and was presumably attracted to the spectacle of Jansenist logic applied to the establishment of miracles. Gadamer refers to it very early on in *Truth and Method* as an early ominous example of the application of scientific method to one of the disciplines of the humanities, namely history – an ominous example, for as Gadamer says:

> When the methodological ideal of the natural sciences was applied to the credibility of the historical testimonies of scriptural tradition it inevitably led to results that were catastrophic for Christianity. The distance from the criticism of miracles in the style of the Jansenists to historical criticism of the bible is not far.[2]

Another common source is more interesting, but leads on from the point just made. That common source is Mill's *Logic*: *A System of Logic, Ratiocinative and Deductive* by J. S. Mill.[3] Newman largely disagrees, but at least was interested and stimulated. Gadamer refers to Mill's *Logic* on the very first page of *Truth and Method*, for the German translation of this work (to which he refers) is apparently the source of the distinction, immensely influential in the German intellectual tradition, between *Naturwissenschaft* and *Geisteswissenschaft*, as Schiel translated Mill's *natural science* and *moral science*. That distinction – and the common denominator of *science* – is, as we shall see, of great, almost fateful significance. At its simplest, the distinction between natural and moral science is that between what we know about the physical world and what we know about mankind, both as an individual and as a community: history and ethics, for instance.

One place where Newman makes use of this distinction is towards the beginning of the *Essay on the Development of Doctrine*, where he surveys the 'State of the Evidence', and there he makes reference to another very important common source he has with Gadamer, and that is to Aristotle, in particular to Aristotle's understanding of *phronesis*. In the *Essay* Newman makes but a particular point – about the kind of evidence and argument appropriate in moral, as opposed to natural, proof – and refers to Aristotle's remarks in Book I of the *Nicomachean Ethics*:

> Now our treatment of this subject [namely political science] will be adequate, if it achieves that amount of precision which belongs to its subject matter. The same exactness must not be expected in all departments of philosophy alike ... for it is the mark of an educated mind to expect that amount of exactness in each kind which the nature of the particular subject admits. It is equally unreasonable to accept merely probable conclusions from a mathematician and to demand strict demonstration from an orator.[4]

In the *Grammar of Assent*, when Newman comes to discuss inference and the nature of the illative sense, the influence of Aristotle and in particular the discussion of *phronesis* in Book VI of the *Nicomachean Ethics* is evident.[5] Gadamer too will make much of Aristotle's distinction between practical and theoretical knowledge, between *phronesis* and *sophia*, between knowledge that admits only of probability and that where we expect exactness. Though Gadamer warns us right from the start that this distinction in not tantamount to a distinction between the probable and the true,[6] *phronesis* too is concerned with truth, it is a 'truth-attaining rational quality, concerned with action in relation to things that are good and bad for human beings', to use Rackham's cumbersome, though accurate translation of Aristotle's ἕξιν ἀληθῆ μετὰ λόγου πρακτικὴν περὶ τὰ ἀνθρώπῳ ἀγαθὰ καὶ κακά. And for Newman too the illative sense is certainly a means by which we apprehend *truth*: one of his complaints against Butler (a complaint made, I think, only by the Roman Catholic Newman) is that Butler leaves religious truth in the realm of mere probability and prescinds from truth as such. Gadamer too returns to dwell on Aristotle and Book VI of the *Nichomachean Ethics* in a section of *Truth and Method* entitled '*Die hermeneutische Aktualität des Aristoteles*'.

These three examples show, or at least suggest, that Newman and Gadamer, for all their differences of intellectual style and ambience, draw part of their inspiration from the same wells. But what I want to suggest goes further than that: I want to suggest that Newman and Gadamer are worth comparing and throw light on one another because at the deepest level they view the fundamental challenge to human understanding in very similar terms. 'Throw light on one another': for I think a comparison of the two does suggest areas in which the insights of either are likely to be relevant, areas that might not spring to mind without such a comparison. Gadamer indicates ways in which some of Newman's insights have much wider relevance than might be imagined; and Newman indicates much more natural ways in which Gadamer's insights might be fruitfully pursued in the realm of theology.

As Gadamer himself professes, his work *Truth and Method* 'starts with the resistance within modern science against the universal claim of the scientific method'.[7] The first third of his work is, he proclaims, a 'critique of aesthetic consciousness' intended to 'defend that experience of truth that comes to us through the work of art against an aesthetic theory that lets itself be restricted to a scientific concept of truth'.[8] As Gadamer sees it, the very success of the scientific method as a way of attaining truth in those areas that we in English tend to designate exclusively as 'the sciences' has ensnared the whole effort of human understanding, suggesting that only as any enterprise of human understanding models itself on the procedures of scientific method can it be regarded as an intellectually respectable way of attaining objective truth. In the central section of his book Gadamer traces the way in which historical criticism, or the historical critical method, has been taken to be the equivalent in the humanities to the scientific method and thus rendered the humanities 'intellectually respectable'. Right at the beginning Gadamer states that his aim will be to show 'how little the traditions in which we stand are weakened by modern historical consciousness'.[9]

Gadamer then is concerned to resist, and indeed overcome, a prejudice that has become all but fundamental to our modern intellectual consciousness. It is a prejudice that casts around for procedure, method, and sees the goal to be achieved in terms of objectivity. All these terms – procedure, method, objectivity – have at least one thing in common: they all manifest a concern to reduce the role of the one who knows, who is seeking understanding, in that very process of understanding. The observer, the thinker, is a bit like a rat going through a maze – he does not contribute anything to the process, he just goes through it. This prejudice Gadamer traces back to the Enlightenment with its attempt to break free from inherited wisdom and make a new start: writers like Descartes and Locke saw the key to understanding as the mastery of a method which could be applied to any subject matter and lead in that area to what could be ascertained as true. This method was, as we know, remarkably successful in the natural sciences. The question is whether it can be made successful in what Germans call the *Geisteswissenschaften*, what we used to call the moral sciences and now tend to call the humanities. The general modern prejudice is that it ought to be but is not yet, though the historical critical method offers itself as a candidate; but it is Gadamer's contention that it cannot be made successful without destroying the proper procedures of the humanities and robbing human understanding of a whole dimension. Gadamer's case here is argued at length; all I can do is point to a bit of it.

I have dubbed our modern concern with procedure, method and objectivity a *prejudice* – which is, and is meant to be, paradoxical, as our whole modern concern stemming from the Enlightenment is intended to avoid prejudice. The ideal observer sees what is there, objectively before his eyes, free from any prejudice: the archetypal observer in this sense is Galileo, looking through his telescope at the moons of Jupiter, free from any prejudice suggested by the Ptolemaic system that such moons could not exist. That looks reasonable enough: let us see things as they are, not conditioned by any preconceived ideas. At least it looks reasonable enough when we are concerned with matters that can be brought before our eyes, that can be observed. But in the humanities such is rarely the case: we are either concerned with past events (as in history), or with how things ought to be (as in ethics), or with how things really are, as opposed to how they simply appear to be (as in philosophy), or with someone's personal vision of how things are or something is (when we are reading a poem, for instance, or a novel). But further: in the humanities what we would be doing in studying any subject, except when we are thinking and musing about how people behave, would be reading something, or discussing with someone – and the idea that we can read something, or enter a discussion, without any prejudices or preconceptions is simply absurd. To read or talk we have to know a language; to know a language, how to use it and how it is used, we must have read something of it – the more the better – and cannot read without picking up ideas, notions, conceptions, and cannot begin to read anything new without all these notions and associations being brought to bear on what we are reading. If language is a vehicle for the communication of truth, then that truth cannot be something that we come to by ridding our minds of preconceptions. If we rendered our mind a *tabula rasa*, then we would not be able to read at all.

It is, as Gadamer puts it, precisely the recognition that understanding what somebody says or has written actually involves, as an indispensable presupposition, preconceptions – prejudices – that determines the nature of the problem of understanding in the humanities, the nature of what philosophers like Gadamer are accustomed to call the hermeneutical problem. This does not mean that our prejudices are incorrigible, that no one can learn anything in the humanities, rather it means that we bring to the act of understanding our own prior understandings and that there is an engagement between what we already know and what the other is trying to communicate.

But a prejudice against prejudice is the legacy of the Enlightenment: and this prejudice against prejudice is intended to cut man off from the past, from tradition – it is intended to 'deprive tradition of its power'.[10] Gadamer points out how the pejorative meaning which now primarily attaches to the word 'prejudice' is itself a legacy of the Enlightenment. Prejudice has come to mean an 'unfounded judgment':

> it is only its having a basis, a methodological justification (and not the fact that it may actually be correct) that gives a judgment its dignity. The lack of such a basis does not mean, for the Enlightenment, that there might be other kinds of certainty, but rather that the judgment does not have any foundation in the facts themselves, i.e. that it is 'unfounded'. This is a conclusion only in the spirit of rationalism. It is the reason for the discrediting of prejudices and the claim by scientific knowledge completely to exclude them.[11]

The prejudice against prejudice is then an attempt to make a clean break with tradition, and free the individual to pursue truth objectively, relying simply on correct method and procedure. And it is the same concern that lies behind the growth of what Gadamer calls 'historical consciousness', even though this was in origin an attempt by Romanticism to counteract the Enlightenment's distaste for history and restore to mankind the experience of the past. Briefly, Gadamer argues thus: the Enlightenment dealt with history by applying reason to the records of the past and discarding everything that reason disapproved of – miracles, the supernatural, and suchlike. Or not quite *discarding*: narratives containing such irrational occurrences were to be understood by an attempt to enter into the minds of those men of the past and to reconstruct what must have happened if they described it like that. The 'historical consciousness' that arises with Romanticism, the attempt to see the differences between the ways in which different societies and cultures have understood things, and, respecting such differences, to enter imaginatively into the mind of the past: such historical consciousness only appears to restore the past to present-day men, in fact it involves a radicalisation of the approach of the Enlightenment – 'for the exceptional case of nonsensical tradition has become the general rule for historical consciousness'.[12] *All* past tradition is being treated as if it were nonsense and could only be understood by modern scientific man by an effort of historical imagination. Past tradition has ceased to be tradition, something handed down: the link with the past has been cut. The past is a foreign country: worse, it is a country we can only *pretend* to visit.

But, Gadamer asks:

Does the fact that one is set within various traditions mean really and primarily that one is subject to prejudices and limited in one's freedom? Is not, rather, all human existence, even the freest, limited and qualified in various ways? If this is true, then the idea of an absolute reason is impossible for historical humanity . . .[13]

and with that the idea of a universal science, a *mathesis universalis.* Gadamer presses home his criticism by pointing out how Romanticism is infected by an aesthetic of the genius, who enjoys intense and deeply significant experiences which we lesser mortals can enter into by a process of aesthetic appreciation. Dilthey, for Gadamer the great representative of Romantic hermeneutics, concentrated on autobiography and self-reflection in literature (or put the other way about: he interpreted literature primarily autobiographically: it is the mind of the writer or poet we are seeking to enter, we are not content simply with understanding what he has to say). But:

in fact history does not belong to us, we belong to it. Long before we understand ourselves through the process of self-examination, we understand ourselves in a self-evident way in the family, society and state in which we live. The focus of subjectivity is a distorting mirror. The self-awareness of the individual is only a flickering in the closed circuits of historical life. That is why the prejudices of the individual, far more than his judgments, constitute the historical reality of his being.[14]

From this point Gadamer seeks to rehabilitate, and interpret, prejudices as conditions of understanding. The central question of a truly historical approach to understanding is not, 'How can we rid ourselves of our prejudices?' but 'Where is the ground of the legitimacy of prejudices?' This involves for Gadamer the rehabilitation of authority and tradition, which itself means that there are those from whom we can learn and expect to learn, and thus to whom we strive to attend and understand. Gadamer also seeks to rehabilitate the notion of a 'classic': a work we come to expecting to learn from, expecting it to awaken in us something of the response it has commanded over the centuries. We learn from it what excellence is. Here we are a long way from Empson's giving his pupils poems without saying who they were by, so that they could learn to make an objective judgment of them based on some *method* of appreciation, or criticism. Gadamer defines the meaning of the word 'classical' as consisting in the fact that for such a work 'the duration of the power of the work to speak directly is fundamentally unlimited'.[15] We come to understanding and appreciation by entering into a tradition, by taking much on trust, and thus we come to a mature understanding of our own; but that mature understanding does not detach us from tradition. For any understanding involves bringing to what we are seeking to understand *appropriate* prejudices, or anticipated meanings, that will lead us more deeply into understanding and not trip us up, so to speak. Mature understanding involves the sensitivity to be able to discriminate here. And these prejudices, anticipated meanings, are themselves drawn from, suggested by, our familiarity with tradition, so that 'the anticipation of meaning that governs our understanding is not an act of subjectivity, but proceeds from the communality that binds us to the tradition'.[16]

This sense of continuity between the past and the present – a continuity manifest primarily in our willingness to learn from the past – is put interestingly by Gadamer when he criticises the way in which the Romantic tradition of interpretation speaks in terms of past ages having horizons that are closed to us, but which we enter by, as it were, abandoning our own horizon of understanding and entering, by imagination, into the horizon of the past. To begin with, it presumes that we *can* relinquish our own horizon – that is that we are, in some way, ultimately a-historical beings. But the notion of horizons is useful in that it brings out the genuine difficulty involved in understanding what has been handed down to us from the past. Their horizon was not ours; and unless our horizons can overlap, understanding will be denied us. But it is by letting them overlap, by letting the insights of the past question and inform us in the present, that understanding becomes a possibility.

And such understanding involves action, application: it means being affected in what we do, how we behave, by what we have learnt from others and from the past. It is not a speculative, intellectual act of divining what is in another's mind, it is not an attempt to dominate, but an attempt to understand, to engage with another, and to attain deeper self-understanding.

That is barely a sketch of some salient features of Gadamer's approach to the nature of human understanding in the humanities, but it gives us enough to begin to draw a few parallels with Newman.

We might start by recalling that Newman, like Gadamer, wants to make a sharp distinction between natural and moral science, and while admitting that the experimental method properly holds sway in the former realm, to maintain that it has no competence in the latter. So, for instance, at the beginning of section II of chapter 3 of the *Essay on Development*, after referring to Bacon's being 'celebrated for destroying the credit of a method of reasoning much resembling that which it has been the object of this chapter to recommend', and commending the value of Bacon's ideas in the realm of physical science, Newman goes on:

> But it is otherwise with history, the facts of which are not present; it is otherwise with ethics, in which phenomena are more subtle, closer, and more personal to individuals than other facts, and not referable to any common standard by which all men can decide upon them. In such sciences, we cannot rest upon mere facts, if

we would, because we have not got them. We must do our best with what is given us, and look about for aid from any quarter; and in such circumstances the opinions of others, the traditions of ages, the prescriptions of authority, antecedent auguries, analogies, parallel cases, these and the like, not indeed taken at random, but, like the evidence from the senses, sifted and scrutinized, obviously become of great importance.[17]

It would not be wrong, I think, to emphasise that Newman takes his bearings, as it were, by quoting Bacon and firmly excluding his authority from the realm of moral science: for Bacon is an almost archetypal apologist for the ideals of the Enlightenment, and it is thus these ideals that Newman confronts and rejects in this passage. Both Newman and Gadamer see that it is the claims of the Enlightenment to dispense with tradition and rely on proper procedure that are inimical to the properly *human* way of coming to know human reality: that is precisely Gadamer's concern; for Newman it is, of course, a first step to a defence of theology, seen as a human way of understanding God's dealings with man. There are two ways in particular in which Newman develops his point at this juncture: these are the importance of antecedent understanding, presumption – let us say: prejudice; and the fact that it is a human being who reasons, not some abstract reason that could prescind from the individual, and possibly be reduced to a method or a procedure. These two points are brought out in the *Essay*, where Newman states that 'presumption verified by instances is our ordinary instrument of proof' and remarks that the handling of 'antecedent probability' is not something that all men are equally competent at. He quotes Bacon's remark that 'our method of discovering the sciences does not much depend upon subtlety and strength of genius, but lies level to almost every capacity and understanding', but immediately adds: 'though surely sciences there are, in which genius is everything, and rules all but nothing'.[18]

But first the place of prejudice in human understanding. This is a major theme in Newman's university sermon, 'Love the Safeguard of Faith against Superstition'. There he speaks of the essence of faith as lying in 'its being an antecedent judgment or presumption': as such it can be contrasted with evidence or what is popularly called 'exercises of Reason'. In this latter case 'prejudices and mental peculiarities' are excluded:

nothing can be urged, or made to tell, but what all feel, all comprehend, all can put into words; current language becomes the measure of thought; only such conclusions may be drawn as can produce their reasons; only such reasons are in point as can be exhibited in simple propositions; the multiform and intricate assemblage of considerations, which really lead to judgment and action, must be attenuated or mutilated into a major and a minor premiss.[19]

Various characteristic themes of Newman's cluster together here: that real knowledge, real inference, is not simply theoretical, but bears upon action; that this real knowing and inferring cannot be captured in explicit propositions and sequences of argument; that it is, as it were, active, a creation of the mind itself, the mind reaching forward to facts and not simply passively experiencing them. So faith is 'a judgment about facts in matters of conduct, such, as to be formed, not so much from the impressions legitimately made upon the mind by those facts, as from the reaching forward of the mind itself towards them'.[20] Or again: 'mere evidence would but lead to passive opinions and knowledge; but anticipations and presumptions are the creation of the mind itself; and the faith which exists in them is of an active nature'.[21] Real knowing and inference cannot be reduced to method and procedure, for 'thought is too keen and manifold, its sources too remote and hidden, its faith too personal, delicate and circuitous, its subject matter too various and intricate, to admit of the trammels of any language, of whatever subtlety and of whatever compass', as he puts it in the *Grammar of Assent*.[22]

No method then, for who we are and where we start from – the individual and his prejudices, the individual and the tradition within which he stands, which forms him – are crucial constituents of human knowing. For human knowledge is a person knowing, apprehending truth – not some objective information independent of the human mind that grasps it. 'It is,' as Newman puts it in the *Grammar*, 'the mind that reasons, and that controls its own reasonings, not any technical apparatus of words and propositions'.[23]

So, for Newman, 'egotism is true modesty':

> In religious inquiry each of us can speak only for himself, and for himself he has a right to speak . . . He knows what has satisfied and satisfies himself; if it satisfies him, it is likely to satisfy others; if, as he believes and is sure, it is true, it will approve itself to others also, for there is but one truth.[24]

And a little later on in the *Grammar*, Newman says apropos of Paley's arguments in his *Evidences of Christianity*:

> I say plainly I do not want to be converted by a smart syllogism; if I am asked to convert others by it, I say plainly I do not care to overcome their reason without touching their hearts. . . How, after all, is a man better for Christianity, who has never felt the need of it or the desire?[25]

The clear echo of Coleridge in that last sentence provides an opportunity to notice here a parallel between Newman and the Cambridge theologian of the next generation, F. J. A. Hort, also deeply influenced by Coleridge, a comparison of whose reflections with Gadamer's might prove even more fruitful than the comparison we are engaged on now. Hort had little time for Newman ('I suppose

there is no distinguished theologian in any church or of any school,'
he said in a letter on hearing the news of Newman's death, 'whom
I should find it so hard to think of as having contributed anything
to the support or advance of Christian truth.')[26] Yet in the introduction to his Hulsean Lectures, delivered the year after the publication
of the *Grammar of Assent*, we find Hort echoing Newman closely when
he says:

> the effort to be impersonal affects injuriously the discussion of
> Christian evidences to at least this extent, that it beguiles Chris-
> tians into setting forth the considerations which ought, they think,
> to be convincing to others, with little or no reference to what has
> actually exerted power over their own minds.[27]

(That, incidentally, expresses succinctly one of Karl Barth's objections to the enterprise of natural theology.) And Hort too echoes
Newman's conviction about the inaccessibility of the real springs of
human thought:

> Everything personal – personal thought even more than personal
> feeling, if the distinction is possible – is in a measure absolutely
> inexpressible; and further is relatively inexpressible by reason of the
> complexities and gradations which distinguish vital from artificial
> structure. What can be presented is after all not so much the
> personal conviction itself as a tentative exhibition of some of its
> leading lines, not detached from the evidence but as perceptible
> through the evidence.[28]

'Egotism is true modesty': but does not such a position deliver us
directly into the area of subjectivism, if not solipsism? Is not reason,
and methodical doubt, the safeguard here? This Newman will not
have; the only safeguard here is a 'right state of heart':

> this it is that gives it birth; it also disciplines it . . . It is holiness,
> or dutifulness, or the new creation, or the spiritual mind, however
> we word it, which is the quickening and illuminating principle of
> true Faith, giving it eyes, hands and feet. It is love which forms it
> out of the rude chaos into an image of Christ.[29]

We might here cast an eye back to Gadamer: what for him is the
principle that informs the humanities and ensures that they have to
do with truth and do not simply lapse into subjective opinion, if it
is not reliance on method and objective procedure? Gadamer suggests
that it is the notion of *Bildung* – a word meaning both education and
culture, like the Greek *paideia* – that provides the key here. And he
remarks in an aside that the word *Bildung* is first found in medieval
German mystical writings to refer to the refashioning of the image of
God (the *Bild Gottes*) in man into the true image of God.[30] For
Gadamer the safeguard for the humanities is trust in the process
by which we are fashioned and formed by the tradition of human

understanding that we have inherited. It is almost a secularised form of spirituality: *almost*, for some of these secularised forms of spirituality have actually been rejuvenative of Christian spirituality itself in our own age. With such considerations in mind it is striking to read Newman's own treatment of the reformation of the divine image in man in the *Grammar*, in the section on 'Belief in One God', in chapter 5. It is too long to quote in full, but a brief passage will give some idea:

> . . . the image of God, if duly cherished, may expand, deepen, and be completed, with the growth of their powers and in the course of life, under the varied lessons, within and without them, which are brought home to them concerning the same God, One and Personal, by means of education, social intercourse, experience, and literature.[31]

For Newman one crucial reason why the individual cannot be elided in the process of human understanding, and thus that process is incapable of being reduced to rule and method, is that personal knowledge and inference is concerned with the concrete and particular:

> our most natural mode of reasoning is, not from propositions to propositions, but from things to things, from concrete to concrete, from wholes to wholes . . . This is the mode in which we ordinarily reason, dealing with things directly, and as they stand, one by one, in the concrete, with an intrinsic and personal power, not a conscious adoption of an artificial instrument or expedient.[32]

Which suggests we take a brief glance at least at one of Newman's disciples, the Jesuit and poet Gerard Manley Hopkins, for it is this emphasis on the primacy of the particular and concrete that he interprets in his language of instress and inscape. It is incarnate individuality that he celebrates in the music of Purcell:

> It is the forgèd feature finds me; it is the rehearsal
> Of own, of abrúpt sélf there so thrusts on, so throngs the ear.

And perhaps most significantly, in a follower of Newman, it is the sense of individual rightness in human moral behaviour – something beyond rule and rote – that Hopkins is trying to express when he develops his notion of freedom of *pitch*: pitch – combining suggestions of the exact pitch, or individuality, of a musical note, and the precise thrust, lending to the throw of a ball its exact speed and direction – pitch being, as Hopkins puts it, 'ultimately simple positiveness, that by which being differs from and is more than nothing and not-being', so that 'the thread or chain of such pitches . . . is self, personality'.[33]

Such is barely a beginning of a sketch of the comparisons we might make, and mutual illumination we might expect to find shed, between Newman and Gadamer, when we consider their reflections on the

nature of human understanding. We could easily go on: Gadamer's
notion of the succession and overlap of the horizons of human understanding recalls some of Newman's imagery in the *Essay on Development*
and might suggest ways of engaging with some of the deeper problems
that work raises. But it is hoped that what we have considered here
has suggested lines of thought worth pursuing.

1. H.-G. Gadamer, *Wahrheit und Methode*, 4th edn (Tübingen 1975); English
   tr. from 2nd German edn, *Truth and Method* (2nd English edn with
   corrections, London 1981).
2. *Truth and Method*, p. 19.
3. Newman's notes on this are published in H. M. de Achaval, S. J. and
   J. Derek Holmes, eds, *The Theological Papers of John Henry Newman: on
   Faith and Certainty* (Oxford 1976), pp. 39ff.
4. J. H. Newman, *Essay on the Development of Christian Doctrine*, 8th edn
   (London 1891), ch. 3, sect. II. Newman's reference is to Aristotle, *Eth.
   Nic.* I.3.1,4.
5. J. H. Newman, *An Essay in Aid of a Grammar of Assent*, new imp. (London
   1930), pp. 259ff.
6. *Truth and Method*, p. 19.·
7. ibid. p. xii.
8. ibid. p. xiii.
9. ibid.
10. ibid. p. 238.
11. ibid. p. 240.
12. ibid. p. 244.
13. ibid. p. 245.
14. ibid.
15. ibid. p. 258.
16. ibid. p. 261.
17. Newman, *Essay on Development*, p. 111.
18. ibid. p. 113.
19. John Henry Newman, *Sermons Chiefly on the Theory of Religious Belief,
    Preached before the University of Oxford* (London 1843), p. 223.
20. ibid. pp. 217–18.
21. ibid. p. 219.
22. Newman, *Grammar of Assent*, p. 284.
23. ibid. p. 353.
24. ibid. pp. 384–5.
25. ibid. p. 425.
26. A. F. Hort, *Life and Letters of Fenton John Anthony Hort*, 2 vols (London
    1896), II, p. 423.
27. F. J. A. Hort, *The Way, the Truth, the Life* (London 1897), p. xxx. I am
    not suggesting any influence of Newman on Hort here, which I think
    unlikely.
28. ibid. p. xxxii.
29. Newman, *Sermons on the Theory of Religious Belief*, p. 228.
30. Gadamer, *Wahrheit und Methode*, p. 7; *Truth and Method*, p. 11.
31. Newman, *Grammar of Assent*, p. 116.
32. ibid. pp. 330–1.

33. Christopher Devlin, ed., *The Sermons and Devotional Writings of Gerard Manley Hopkins* (London 1959), p. 151.

7

The Tractarian Liturgical Inheritance Re-assessed*
Louis Weil

During these final decades of the twentieth century a massive restructuring of Catholic sacramental theology is taking place. To sum up a complex question in a few words, the Church is rediscovering the sacramental nature of its own being as the people of God. As a result the particular theology of each individual sacrament is being drawn into a single and unifying focus: all the sacraments are being seen as signs of the presence of the crucified and risen Christ in the midst of his people. This perspective has, of course, far-reaching implications in every aspect of the Church's life, above all for theology, for pastoral practice, and for personal piety.

An assessment of the contribution of the Oxford Movement to this recovery of the ecclesial basis of all sacramental acts obliges us who are the heirs of those crucial days 150 years ago both to be thankful for the insight of the Oxford leaders and at the same time to be honest about the failure of much of their contribution to come to fulfilment. Although there are many factors which contributed to the situation, it is fair to say that much of the best thought of the Tractarians in the area of sacramental theology was sidetracked by their followers into a preoccupation with ceremonial detail. Somehow, in pastoral practice, the substance of the sacramental teaching fostered by the leaders of the Oxford Movement was trivialised by a rupture between theology and liturgy. Liturgy came to be understood in terms of ritual performance rather than as what we might today call the self-realisation of the Church's being. This schism between sacramental theology and ritual practice continues to affect the attitudes of innumerable laity and clergy.

This situation is all the more ironic if we remember that the first leaders of the Oxford Movement demonstrated no great interest in ceremonialism. Their concern was the recovery of the substance of Catholic sacramental teaching. The ritual expressions of that teaching were perceived as a derivative, albeit inevitable, articulation of the more fundamental recovery of the Church's true nature. Even a rudimentary knowledge of liturgical history reveals that the ritual forms through which the Church has signified its faith have, over the

* © 1986 Louis Weil

centuries, varied a great deal with regard to ceremonial simplicity or complexity. There simply is no single ritual pattern which can be designated as 'Catholic' in an ultimate or definitive way. The Church has expressed its faith through a wide range of ritual forms which have been very much shaped by the particularities of the cultural context of each age. In this perspective no single ritual pattern can be absolutised without running the serious risk of alienating the primary sacramental signs from the authentic cultural expressions of a later generation.

The concern of the early Tractarians however was not the imposition of an idealised Catholic ritual pattern. Their concern was what they discerned to be the Church's authentic teaching, and the reaffirmation of that teaching at a time when it had become seriously corroded by a sub-Christian rationalism. In this regard the teaching of Pusey and Newman is not an isolated phenomenon of the nineteenth century. On the Continent such men as Wilhelm Loehe in Germany, Nikolai Grundtvig in Denmark, and Prosper Guéranger in France were all concerned with the same fundamental issue: the rejection of a sterile, rationalist religion in favour of a reaffirmation of orthodox Christian doctrine. For all these men, this reaffirmation of traditional orthodoxy involved the lifting up of the sacramental principle and a concern for the place of corporate worship as fundamental dimensions of the Church's being.

Traditional Christian sacramental doctrine teaches that the sacraments effect what they signify. That simple phrase, 'the sacraments effect what they signify', offers us a groundplan for a reassessment of the Tractarian liturgical inheritance. The early Tractarians were faced with a situation in the Church of England, in the perspective of this sacramental principle, in which the sacraments could be said to effect very little because they signified very little.

The Enlightenment and advances in scientific knowledge had led to an undermining of traditional Christian doctrine. There had developed an increasing emphasis upon the role of reason in human life. Reason alone was held to be the basis for the determination of truth. If faith was operative in any aspect of human life, this was affirmed rather in the realm of the moral life than in belief in specific Christian doctrines. In the Church of England this view is most typically represented by the latitudinarians, who placed a primary importance upon reason in matters of religion. It is obvious that such a view has grave implications for sacramental faith and practice. The emphasis upon reason left no place in the religious life for what we would call the supernatural or the mysterious. God's relation to the created order was to be seen only in his working in and through the natural law of which he was the source, and not through particular instruments.

There were voices within the Church of England which attempted to respond to this essentially deistic form of Christianity, among them

William Law and Joseph Butler, who spoke of the limitations of reason in matters of religious faith. But they were unable to stem the impact of rationalism upon English Church life. The loss of a sense of the supernatural vocation of the Church left it as no more than a department of the State for most English people. Public worship was robbed of its spiritual foundation, and a dry formalism dominated the liturgical practice of the eighteenth century. Obviously in such a context sacramental practice had little importance in a radically de-sacralised institution. The sacraments had come to signify very little indeed.

To a large extent this was the state of the Church on the eve of the Oxford revival, and it was in rejection of this sterile expression of Christianity that the Tractarians began their recovery of the theological underpinnings of the great tradition. The Evangelical movement had made a partial response to the dry rationalism which had come to dominate the Church of England, but because of its emphasis upon the development of what was in effect a highly individualised piety, the Evangelicals did not themselves have an adequately vital sense of the corporate nature of the Christian life. The Oxford Movement complemented the contribution of the Evangelicals by teaching a sacramental understanding of the nature of the Church. Such an understanding emphasises the divine sources of the Church's life. It is not merely a department of State; rather it is itself the instrument of the living God in human history.

The view of the Church as the instrument of God establishes a framework for the role of baptism and Eucharist as instrumental means of redemption. For the Tractarians, God's work of justification is expressed through the instrumentality of these liturgical actions; the sacraments mirror the underlying sacramentality of the Church itself. Grace is not merely God's private gift to the individual Christian. The gifts of grace are to the whole body. On this point Newman writes that Christ

> has lodged His blessings in the body collectively to oblige them to meet *together* if they would gain grace each for himself. The body is the first thing and each member in particular the second. The body is not made up of individual Christians, but each Christian has been made such in his turn by being *taken into the body*.[1]

The sacraments are thus the instruments of God's grace to all the members of the Church. Their corporate nature is fundamental to their meaning, but for the situation which confronted the Tractarians their instrumentality was perhaps a matter of more immediate concern.

Given the general undermining of sacramental worship under the impact of rationalism, it seems inevitable that the Tractarians would give a primary concern to the instrumentality of the sacraments. Although there is a necessary unity in the phrase, 'the sacraments effect what they signify', the contribution of the Tractarians came through an emphasis upon the first aspect, 'the sacraments *effect*'. The traditional teaching of the sacraments as means of grace had been so dangerously eroded in practice that it was imperative that this problem be addressed.

Newman wrote a preface for the second volume of the *Tracts for the Times* in which he discusses the impact of latitudinarian views. He writes:

> we have almost embraced the doctrine that God conveys grace only through the instrumentality of the mental energies ... in contradiction to the primitive view according to which the Church and her Sacraments are the ordained and direct visible means of conveying to the soul what is itself supernatural and unseen.[2]

Newman was concerned to contradict the false rationalism which had 'infected a large mass of men in our communion', and which engendered 'a slowness to believe the possibility of God's having literally blessed ordinances with invisible power'. It is characteristic of Tractarian teaching to emphasise this objective aspect of the sacraments, that 'they effect', that they are true instruments of God's redemptive grace.

The Tractarians were equally emphatic about the gift of faith by which we discern God's presence in his gift. Our salvation depends upon both the reality of God's gift of grace and our response to the gift in faith. Any attitude towards faith which reduces the sacraments to a secondary or derivative role is irreconcilable with Tractarian insistence upon the instrumentality of the sacraments. Faith should not be separated from the gift, but is rather a requirement for the fruitful reception of the grace offered to us by God in the sacraments.

In all this however we see a primacy of concern being placed upon the sacraments as effective instruments precisely because the religious spirit of the time had shaped so contradictory a view. In spite of the concern about the corporate nature of the Church in Tractarian writings, and especially in the work of John Henry Newman, the potent individualism of nineteenth-century culture exerted a critical influence upon the way the theory of sacramental instrumentality was assimilated.

Newman came from an Evangelical family background. His espousal of the principles of the Oxford Movement in a conscious intellectual commitment was added to an underlying, and perhaps often unconscious, commitment to an Evangelical piety in which faith involved an essentially interior nurturing by the Holy Spirit. Evangelical views were generally conditioned by a highly individual-ised piety, and this was not easily put aside in favour of a more corporate piety. We see this in our own time in the negative reactions of many people to the revised rites which have been developed out of a more consciously corporate model of the Church. These new

rites have run head-on into an entrenched individualism to which
the former rites were more easily accommodated. If this is true in
our own time, I would suggest that we need to take the question of
attitudes of piety more seriously as we recognise that many aspects
of Tractarian sacramental teaching were embraced through an intellectual commitment which did not consciously address a deep-rooted
individualistic piety originating from a very different concept of the
Church. The implications of Tractarian ecclesiology for corporate
worship are perhaps only now being assimilated at the pastoral level
of the Church's life.

The whole question is marvellously illuminated in the life and
teaching of Newman. When I undertook a serious reading of the
sermons of Newman I was struck above all by the richness of his
doctrine of the Church. I was amazed by this because there is almost
nothing available in theological literature on Newman's ecclesiology.
What I found in these sermons was a doctrine of the Church which
anticipates the most important work on this subject in our century.
Newman sounded the themes which we are only now beginning to
explore in depth.

In an important article Fr James Tolhurst sets forth the evolution
of Newman's attitude towards the Church from his Evangelical days
and through the period of the Oxford Movement.[3] Tolhurst shows
how Newman at first exemplified the Evangelical ambivalence about
the Church, a tension between the Church as one visible body of all
the baptised and the Calvinist concept of the invisible body of true
believers, made holy through justification. In a sermon on the
Eucharist preached in 1824 Newman emphasises the issues of individual preparation and worthiness. He writes:

> Beware too of a self-righteous spirit. Think not you can ever cleanse
> yourselves so perfectly as to be *worthy* to come; you cannot be
> worthy. Christ is your only worthiness. This holy sacrament is to
> be the *means* of grace and holiness. Come then that you *may* be
> clean: clean from guilt through the blood of Christ, and from sin
> through the inspiration of the Holy Spirit.[4]

At this period Newman viewed the Church 'in terms of the elect
who would be united individually through regeneration by the Holy
Spirit'.[5] Newman himself later reflected upon his Evangelical views
and interpreted his preoccupation with the individual Christian at
the expense of the corporate sense of the Church to an inherited
Evangelical emphasis upon sin. In 1835, some eleven years later,
Newman preached the following words:

> The sight of the sins of Christians has led us to speak of what are
> called the Visible and Invisible Church in what seems an
> unscriptural way. The word 'Church', applied to the body of Chris-
> tians in this world, means but one thing in Scripture, a visible

body invested with invisible privileges. Scripture does not speak of two bodies, one visible, the other invisible, each with its own complement of members.[6]

But this espousal of a corporate and sacramental understanding of the Church did not negate the influence of Evangelical piety upon Newman and many other of the Tractarians. It was possible to defend the instrumental efficacy of the Church's sacraments and yet to view that efficacy through the filter of an individualised piety.

This preoccupation with individual sin which Newman attributed to Evangelical influence finds notable expression in some of the writings of E. B. Pusey. For example, in Tract 81, Pusey treats the questions of eucharistic presence and eucharistic sacrifice as two quite distinct issues. He writes that the Eucharist as a sacramental presence benefits the individual communicant, whereas the eucharistic sacrifice has a collective significance as the sacrifice of the whole Church.[7] Such a distinction between these two aspects of the Eucharist strikes the sacramental theologian of today as artificial because of our strong sense of the ecclesial nature of all sacramental acts. In fact we would insist upon a necessary cohesion between presence and sacrifice as dimensions of an integrated understanding of the Eucharist in the life of the Church.

These dimensions of Evangelical piety seem to have exerted a continuing effect in what we might call the unresolved schism between sacramental theology and liturgical practice. My own interpretation is that there was a failure to discern the impact of individualism in these matters. The ritual practices of western cath-olicism were instituted in a kind of naive archaeologism which was fostered by the nineteenth-century idealisation of all things medieval. There is no question that enormous care was given to the restoration of churches and the preparation of liturgical ceremonial, but the fundamental passivity of the people, their nurturing of individual piety through attendance at essentially clerical rituals, these matters were not effectively addressed at the pastoral level. The pastoral implications of Tractarian ecclesiology could not be fully discerned or implemented given the state of religious understanding in the Church at large at the time.

This indication of the failure of the heirs of the Tractarians to make what we might call the pastoral connections is not intended as a grave faulting of the Tractarians themselves. They lived and worked in a religious situation which was, as we have observed, rather grim. Our reassessment of the Tractarian liturgical inheritance must take into account however a further century and a half of development in the theology and life of the Church. As problematic as is the state of the Church today in many ways, the problems are not the same as those of the 1830s, nor are we living in the same world culturally and socially in which the Tractarians lived. In addition to that, there

are potent signs that we are living in a time of theological development, especially in regard to the doctrine of the Church, which
promises to bear a rich harvest in Christian renewal.

This last point, the development of the doctrine of the Church, is,
I would suggest, a direct result of the more prophetic writings of the
Tractarians. Their restoration to the Church of a sense of sacramental
instrumentality is in itself a contribution of major importance. But
they accomplished far more than that. Newman's teaching on the
doctrine of the Church anticipated many of the major developments
in this area during our own century. It is no casual remark when
contemporary theologians speak of Vatican II as 'Newman's council'.
The conciliar constitution on the Church, *Lumen Gentium*, resounds
with the ecclesiology which we find in Newman's Anglican sermons.
Neither the Anglicans nor the Roman Catholics of the nineteenth
century were prepared to embrace such an ecclesiology, that is,
Newman's idea of the Church as a community. The model of the
Church which Newman lifted up was 'a personal, familial, yet struc-
tured communion'.[8] It is in the more ecumenical situation of the
Church today that this idea can bear its richest fruit.

This renewed ecclesiology will, I believe, prove to be our most
precious inheritance from the Oxford Movement. It is clearly
connected to the Tractarian recovery of a sense of the sacramentality
of the Church and of the particular sacraments as instruments of
grace. But it carries us over into the second aspect of the sacramental
principle with which we began: 'the sacraments effect *what they signify*'.
If this second aspect was not as fully developed by the Tractarians
as we would ask today we must nevertheless remember that it is
strongly implied in their teaching of the sacraments as effective
instruments.

What is it that the sacraments signify? Shaped as we have been
by a privatised piety, we have often tended to think in individualised
terms: 'my communion', 'my mass'. But the great tradition which
the Tractarians sought to restore breathes a different atmosphere, a
corporate atmosphere. This is why Newman's doctrine of the Church
is so prophetic of the rediscovery of the corporate nature of liturgical
worship in our time. In spite of the influences of an individualised
piety, the essential concept of worship among the Tractarians was
corporate. This was inevitable given their vision of the Church. In a
sermon preached by Newman in 1829, he said, 'There is no blessing
on private prayer and study *severed from* public worship.'[9] Private
prayer is thus a derived prayer; the normative expression of Christian
prayer is that of the gathered assembly of believers.

What the sacraments signify is the unity of the mystical body, head
and members, that is, our unity as the people of God in Christ.
From our baptism into the body, we are involved in the corporate
experience of a common faith. Every Eucharist is a celebration of
and a realisation of that unity established through baptism. It is *not*

a sacrament of individual or private salvation; it is salvation through incorporation into the redeemed community. Again Newman, in a sermon preached in 1825, sees the gift of the Holy Spirit as an ecclesial gift, not a private gift to the individual. We become entitled to the gift of the Holy Spirit, he said, 'by belonging to the body of His Church; and we belong to His Church by being baptized into it'.[10] It is thus not surprising that along with the emergence of a theology of the Church as a community there has been a complementary emergence of pastoral imperatives concerning the sacraments of initiation.

When we shift our attention to the Eucharist, the sign of unity is expressed through the common oblation of the whole Church. This was a truth which was firmly grasped in the patristic period, when the Church had a firmer sense of the essential unity of Christ with his Church. This view was movingly expressed by St Augustine in *The City of God* (X, vi):

> The whole redeemed community, that is the congregation and society of the saints, is offered as a universal sacrifice to God through that great Priest, who also offered himself in suffering for us, in the form of a servant that we might be the body of so great a Head . . . This is the sacrifice of Christians: *we being many are one body in Christ.* And this also the Church continually celebrates in the sacrament of the altar, so well known to the faithful, that it may be plain to her that *in that which she offers, she herself is offered.*

Unfortunately late medieval western catholicism lost the insight of this theology and for reasons which were often shaped by non-theological factors had arrived at a point where it was the priest alone who offers Christ in the Eucharist, and the laity were reduced to the role of passive observers. Some of the disciples of the Tractarians, influenced especially by the naive medievalism fostered by the Cambridge Movement, picked up this clericalised distortion supposing it to be the authentic Catholic tradition. But the patristic view was voiced by Robert Isaac Wilberforce, for example, who writes that 'The Eucharistic Sacrifice . . . is the offering up of the collective Church, Christ's mystical Body, but it is also the offering up of Christ himself, by whom that Body is sanctified.'[11] Again, from within the movement itself, we find the sounding of a theme which is coming to fruition in our own time.

This sense of the unity of the whole Church in the Eucharist is one facet of the deeper issue, the ordering of the whole sacramental economy towards the unity of all in Christ and with each other. This is suggestive again of Newman's theology of the Church as a community, not as a theory, but as a daily reality in the daily experience of the local churches throughout the world. Such a vision of the Church as a community, our inheritance from the Tractarians, has far-reaching pastoral implications; implications, certainly, for the nature of the liturgical celebrations as corporate acts, but also implications which extend far beyond the sanctuary or even the church building into every dimension of the human situation. Here too we find that the Tractarians themselves have indicated the path we must follow. In a sermon entitled, 'God With Us', Edward Pusey indicated the connection between sacraments and service in words which may fittingly conclude this reassessment of our Tractarian liturgical inheritance:

> If we would see Him in His Sacraments, we must see Him also, wherever He has declared Himself to be, and especially in His poor. In them also He is 'with us' still. And so our Church has united mercy to His poor with the Sacrament of His Body and Blood . . . Real love to Christ must issue in love to all who are Christ's, and real love to Christ's poor must issue in self-denying acts of love towards them. Casual almsgiving is not Christian charity. Rather, seeing Christ in the poor, the sick, the hungry, the thirsty, the naked, we must . . . seek them out, as we would seek Christ, looking for a blessing from it, far greater than any they can gain from our alms. It was promised of old time, as a blessing, 'the poor shall never cease out of the land', and now we know the mercy of this mysterious blessing, for they are the Presence of our Lord.[12]

That is our inheritance.

1. John Henry Newman, MS, Sermon 213, 'On the Duty of Public Worship' (MSS referred to in these Notes are held at the Oratory, Edgbaston, Birmingham).
2. John Henry Newman, 'Advertisement', in *Tracts for the Times*, II, pp. v–vi.
3. James Tolhurst, 'The Idea of the Church as a Community in the Anglican Sermons of John Henry Newman', *Downside Review*, 101 (1983), pp. 140–64.
4. John Henry Newman, MS, Sermon 42, p. 19; preached 12 December 1824.
5. Tolhurst, 'The Idea of the Church', p. 144.
6. John Henry Newman, *Parochial and Plain Sermons*, new edn, 8 vols (London 1868), III, Sermon 16, p. 221.
7. Edward Bouverie Pusey, Tract 81, *Catena Patrum, No. IV: Testimony of Writers of the Later English Church to the Doctrine of the Eucharistic Sacrifice*, p. 3ff. cf. A. Härdelin, *The Tractarian Understanding of the Eucharist* (Uppsala 1965), pp. 204ff., 290.
8. Tolhurst, 'The Idea of the Church', p. 160.
9. John Henry Newman, MS, Sermon 213, p. 7. cf. Härdelin, *The Tractarian Understanding of the Eucharist*, p. 282.
10. John Henry Newman, MS, Sermon 118, p. 12. cf. Tolhurst, 'The Idea of the Church', p. 148.

11. R. I. Wilberforce, *The Doctrine of the Holy Eucharist*, 2nd edn (London 1853), pp. 390–3.
12. Edward Bouverie Pusey, *Parochial Sermons*, rev. edn, 3 vols (London 1878), I, pp. 58–9.

8

'No Bishop, No Church!'
The Tractarian impact on Anglicanism*

S. W. Sykes and S. W. Gilley

The episcopal churches created by the Church of England now circle the globe, through Africa and southern Asia, Oceania and the Americas. They are in large measure the outcome of the understanding of the episcopate pioneered by the Oxford Movement from the 1830s, by reason of the massive reinforcement which Tractarian theology gave to the existence of an episcopate beyond the boundaries of the English Establishment. It is no accident that Pusey's definition of Puseyism sets in the first three places high estimates of the two sacraments, of episcopacy and of the visible Church,[1] and that the *Tracts for the Times* are full of assertions and arguments about apostolic succession. Yet if that intellectual inheritance has its splendours, it also has its miseries, for in the modern world it scandalously inhibits the ecumenical possibilities of the Anglican communion, by refusing to be honest about the equivocal character of the Anglican appeal to its episcopal foundation.

I

The apostolic character of episcopacy has unquestionably varied in Anglicanism, from the days before and after the great Richard Hooker, in the early and the later Oxford Movement, and in contemporary Anglican ecumenism. But these contexts have varied; and it was one thing for the early Tractarians to advance their theory of episcopacy in polemical argument, and quite another for modern Anglicans to deploy the same theory as *the* Anglican view of episcopacy in the quite different ecumenical circumstances of the modern world.

No one can read the popular, and even the scholarly, literature of the nineteenth century without being struck by the lack of inhibition in religious controversy. Although it must be doubtful whether modern Christians love each other more in any theologically serious meaning of the word 'love', they have grown shy of full-blooded public polemics. In this sense, the nineteenth century appears remote.

* © 1986 S. W. Sykes and S. W. Gilley

It was an age of intense religious vitality and renewal. Yet the period also saw a sharp exacerbation of the party system in the Church of England and the development of a widening gulf between the Church Establishment and continental Protestants, the Free Churches and the Roman Catholics. The Oxford Movement was one of the principal manifestations both of Victorian Christian renewal and of the new intensity of inter-church polemic, in which ecclesiastical institutions flourished in the climate of a fiercer hatred of Christians for one another, as David Newsome and Professor W. R. Ward have superlatively shown.[2] Eighteenth-century Christianity had been generally irenic and latitudinarian, the nineteenth-century Churches were denominational and sectarian; and for that development the Oxford Movement was in part responsible. Moreover the work of Church renewal and revival was in reaction against the secularising and liberalising forces in the wider society, in a deepening division between religion and modern life and thought. The Oxford Movement's new understanding of Church authority and dogma was a product of interdenominational rivalry, of the loosening links between Church and State, and of a fiercer conflict between the Church and the world. Yet these are matters which have often been ignored. John Kent has remarked of the two standard anthologies on the Oxford Movement, by Owen Chadwick and Eugene Fairweather,[3] that they 'might lead the unwary student to suppose that the mind of the Oxford Movement was serene, traditional, lofty and dull, whereas Anglo-Catholic theology was controversial and committed from the first blast of Keble's Assize trumpet'.[4] In fact the Oxford Movement's history was one of battle, and its leaders were soldiers 'marching as to war'.

F. L. Cross has already called attention to the fact that there was little seventeenth-century precedent for the rigidity with which the Tractarians expounded their view of episcopacy.[5] Newman's *Catena patrum* of 1836 stretches from Bishop Wilson to van Mildert and Mant.[6] But like all such compilations the selection was governed by a purpose. Darwell Stone admitted long ago that the claim that such was the only lawful English doctrine could not be supported by history.[7] Newman had written:

> The doctrine in dispute is this: that CHRIST founded a visible Church as an ordinance for ever, and endowed it once for all with spiritual privileges, and set His Apostles over it, as the first in a line of ministers and rulers, like themselves except in their miraculous gifts, and to be continued from them by successive ordination; in consequence, that to adhere to this Church thus distinguished, is among the ordinary duties of a Christian, and is the means of his appropriating the Gospel blessings with an evidence of his doing so not attainable elsewhere.[8]

It must have been obvious to Newman from the study entailed in his recent correspondence with the Abbé Jager that no such doctrine was commonly maintained by Anglicans in the sixteenth century.[9] It was already plain enough to Keble that not merely Jewel, Whitgift and Thomas Cooper, but also Richard Hooker himself had made substantial concessions on this precise question, and it is necessary to note them especially in view of the Tractarian admiration of Hooker.[10]

Hooker's position was that national churches are autonomous institutions with the right to establish their own laws.[11] The Church of God is both a spiritual society and a 'politic society'. Thus while it may not alter the laws of God on doctrine laid down in Scripture, it has the power to lay down laws relating to its own government. These latter, like civil laws, are positive, mutable, binding upon Christians, but subject to their consent. Hooker did not hold that this consent consisted in individual assent; indeed the apologetic purpose of the argument was to urge upon Puritans the duty of conformity to the public consent of the whole people. But it was entirely consistent with the structure of his case that in Book VIII he argues pragmatically in favour of royal supremacy and against the idea that ecclesiastical law could dispense with the laity's assent.

On the question of the episcopal government of the Church, Hooker recorded that he had newly come to accept the historical argument, recently advanced by the Hispano-Flemish divine Hadrian à Saravia, that 'the Apostles themselves left bishops invested with power above other pastors'.[12] But the real basis of his defence of episcopacy was the power of the Church to determine its own positive law. Hence he could consistently argue that episcopal authority might be taken away if it is misused, and that it was the force of custom, not supernatural law, which preserved the Church in continuous observance of that authority.[13] Episcopacy for Hooker, as for many Anglicans before and after, did not belong to what he called 'the essence of Christianity', namely those truths which 'supernaturally appertain' to Christian profession, and are 'necessarily required in every particular Christian man'.[14]

Newman in his *Catena* silently ignored Hooker's qualifications, and Keble referred to them with embarrassment as anomalous. It is in Paget's admirable Introduction to Book V of the *Ecclesiastical Polity* (1899) that there is open acknowledgement of these 'great and serious reserves'.[15] To account for the discrepancy between the old and new views of episcopacy both Keble and Paget urge Hooker's readers to consider the transitional character of the age in which Hooker was writing. But the plea to examine the context of theological views cuts many ways. It was on account of the forceful development by Calvinists and Presbyterians of the view that only a presbyterial government of the Church was sanctioned by Scripture that Anglicans were pushed into the *de iure divino* theory of the episcopate in the 1590s.[16] This attachment was confirmed by the blood of the martyrs Laud and Charles I, who died for it. The revision of the Preface to the Ordinal and the Act of Uniformity visited upon Presbyterians the wrath stored up from the Westminster Assembly of 1643.[17] Yet strict episcopalian theory was not for foreign consumption, as it was not applied with any consistency to non-episcopalian Protestants on the Continent, whose orders were recognised even by sacramental high churchmen like John Cosin. Lutherans and Calvinists had Christian churches, even if second-rate ones; German silver was good, though worth less than episcopal gold. Thus episcopacy was of the *bene esse* of the Church, but not the *esse*: a matter on which Anglicans characteristically felt that they had special cause for self-congratulation.

The political background to these decisions was only reinforced by the growing isolation of the high church party from foreign Prot-estants in the later eighteenth century; so that the rule of the high church divines of the generation before the Oxford Movement, like Archdeacon Daubeny and William van Mildert, was 'no bishop, no church': 'where we find the order of bishops, priests, and deacons regularly appointed, there we find the church of Christ', wrote Daubeny; 'and without these ... it is not called a church'.[18] Dissenters were schismatics outside the Church; their fate was a mystery, but like drunkards and adulterers they had no divine assur-ance of salvation.

The misfortune of nineteenth-century Anglicanism was that the narrowing of ecclesiological theory coincided with the social and political changes which destroyed the basis of Hooker's argument for an episcopal Establishment in the consent of the nation as a whole. For Hooker the Church was more than the clergy: it was the nation in its spiritual aspect, the English people at prayer. Thus the civil magistrate could exercise authority in the Church as truly as any bishop. Indeed the Church's decision to retain the episcopate was one in which the crown had a rightful say, and the more traditionalist Tractarians, Keble and Pusey, remained deeply committed to a mystical view of sacral kingship, as a type of Jesus Christ binding Church and State in one. This power was vested in a Christian polity by that divine law empowering all human corporations to determine their own affairs. But the argument, unlike the Tudor theology of royal supremacy, was pragmatic; it only held good for as long as the English nation was in communion with the Church of England. This was *de facto* the case in the later sixteenth century, apart from the Roman Catholic minority and an inconsiderable number of sectaries; and despite the multitude of new denominations which arose out of the religious ferment of the Interregnum, the non-Anglican proportion of the population remained small until the later eighteenth century.

Moreover in the conservative reaction which followed the French Revolution a more principled churchmanship, that of the non-Erastian

'Hackney Phalanx', dominated ecclesiastical appointments and politics, especially during the fifteen-year ministry of the Tory Prime
Minister Lord Liverpool; so that, as a recent writer puts it, between
1812 and 1827 'the union of Church and State appeared to be working
more in the Church's interests and in accordance with the ideal of
Hooker, than at any time since the reign of Charles II'.[19] The State
actually voted a million and a half pounds for new Anglican churches
in 1818 and 1824, and it was this continuing State support for the
Establishment which made more startling and dramatic the changes
soon to follow.

II

The Tractarian recension of Hooker's episcopacy theory can only be
understood in the light of the Church's new standing in relation to
the consent of the population. The Church's position had in fact been
weakening for more than half a century. The Industrial Revolution
had created the unchurched cities of the north, leaving the great
mass of the parish clergy ministering in the rural south and Midlands.
These social changes lay behind the massive expansion of nonconformity after 1790, inspired by religious rationalism and evangelicalism. In much of Britain the Church of England became a minority
Church, through the spread either of indifference or of religious
dissent. There was also a Roman Catholic population explosion in
Ireland, with an overflow into the industrial towns of mainland
Britain; and the Church of England was linked from 1801 with a
Protestant Church Establishment in Ireland, which was a small
minority of the people. Meanwhile the growing inequalities of clerical
income, exacerbated by the changes of coal revenues and enclosure,
and reflected in the gentrification of the clergy, were an obvious
target for English Whigs and radicals who denounced the Church of
England as the most expensive and pastorally inefficient in the world,
an obvious barrier to the realisation of the self-evident utilitarian
good of the greatest happiness of the greatest number. True, the
Church of England was, from the radical viewpoint, only the corrupt
arm of a corrupt and venal State and crown; but the Church of
England could no longer be considered a truly national institution,
if she was perceived to be, as a later phrase had it, the Tory Party
at prayer.

The outcome in the 1820s was 'a vicious republican anticlericalism
rare in English history. Never it seemed did so many Englishmen
wish to strangle their king with the entrails of the archbishop of
Canterbury.'[20] Indeed the writing for the Church Establishment
appeared to be on the wall, when the repeal of the Test and Corporation Acts in 1828, and Catholic Emancipation in 1829, gave full
rights to dissenters and Roman Catholics to sit in parliament. A

legislature containing non-Episcopalians and non-Protestants was after 1830 the highest voice in the Episcopalian Protestant Church of England; where, in this 1820s 'crisis of the Church', was Hooker's argument now?

From an international perspective these events in England belong to the slow death of the European confessional state; but in the English setting, they took on a special character, and showed up the ambivalence of Hooker's conception of the Church of England as a national and temporal constitution in the natural order, which was also in the supernatural order, the local embodiment of the holy Catholic Church. For if, as Hooker asserted, the Holy Spirit had instituted bishops, then it would be natural to infer (as Hooker had not inferred) that the Church had no power to change what God had ordained;[21] that no merely human legislation could subvert a form of government ordained by divine law, which would stand even if this polity were swept away. It may be readily understood why it seemed that Hooker needed revision, and in what direction. For many high churchmen after 1827, and even more after 1840, the Church Establishment looked less like an eternal embodiment of divine law than a historical compromise which was now being swept away. When the new Whig administration proposed in 1833 the abolition of ten Church of Ireland bishoprics, it did not appear that good churchmen were legislating for the good of the national Church, especially when it was (fruitlessly) proposed to divert some of this money to educating Roman Catholics. The Church of England now seemed to enjoy less freedom and independence than the dissenting bodies, and the choice, as Hurrell Froude put it, was clear, between a national Church and a real one. That circumstance drove the Oxford Movement men back on the other half of Hooker's argument, Christ's commission to the apostles, as the fountainhead of the apostolic succession, as it was that which gave the Church her authority, not the civil power.

Indeed as Newman put it in the first of the Tracts, there was a choice for the English priesthood between worldly and other-worldly power and privilege:

> Should the Government and country so far forget their GOD as to cast off the Church, to deprive it of its temporal honours and substance, *on what* will you rest the claim of respect and attention which you make upon your flocks? Hitherto you have been upheld by your birth, your education, your wealth, your connexions; should these secular advantages cease, on what must CHRIST's Ministers depend?

The answer was their 'APOSTOLICAL DESCENT':

> We have been born, not of blood, nor of the will of the flesh, nor of the will of man [read nation, State, or Whig administration],

but of God. The Lord JESUS CHRIST gave His SPIRIT to His Apostles; they in turn laid their hands on those who should succeed them; and these again on others; and so the sacred gift has been handed down . . . Exalt our Holy Fathers, the Bishops as the Representatives of the Apostles, and the Angels of the Churches; and magnify your office, as being ordained by them to take part in their Ministry.[22]

In short, the State might take the Church's cash; but Christ had created the apostolic order, and the State had no power to take it away.

The doctrine of the apostolic succession was not simply adopted as a weapon against an Erastian State, as we shall see. Yet there is a 'fierceness' about the tone of the early Tracts which Newman honestly recalled in the *Apologia*. The first page of the first tract wished the bishops no 'more blessed termination of their course, than the spoiling of their goods, and martyrdom'; the concluding injunction to readers was to '*choose* your side . . . HE THAT IS NOT WITH ME, IS AGAINST ME, AND HE THAT GATHERETH NOT WITH ME SCATTERETH ABROAD'.[23] Newman also recalled his 'fierce thoughts against the Liberals' in 1833, his refusal to look on the republican tricolour in Algiers harbour or to go sightseeing in the revolutionary sin-city of Paris. He wanted England to be 'vastly more superstitious, more bigoted, more gloomy, more fierce in its religion', and with an unspecific savagery, he argued in his Arian history for 'no mercy' to heretics. 'Again', wrote Newman in the *Apologia*:

> when one of my friends, of liberal and evangelical opinions, wrote to expostulate with me on the course I was taking, I said that we would ride over him and his, as Othniel prevailed over Chushan-rishathaim, king of Mesopotamia. Again, I would have no dealings with my brother [the heretical Francis Newman], and I put my conduct upon a syllogism. I said, 'St Paul bids us avoid those who cause divisions; you cause divisions: therefore I must avoid you'.[24]

Yet this temper of mind was no idiosyncrasy of Newman's. Keble could not bear to be crossed in argument, and Froude's brilliant incisiveness of speech, especially his expressions of hatred for the Reformers, is too well-known to need quotation. There is an element of arrested adolescent immaturity about some of these attitudes, but they were more than a matter of personality. They had to do with the Tractarian defence of the dogmatic principle as the only means of resisting the corrosive power of liberalism in religion. As Newman was to say in *The Tamworth Reading Room*, to hold dogmatic convictions is to be controversial, so that controversy is of the essence of Christianity.[25]

Moreover the Tractarians were not undertaking a mere conservative defence of entrenched high church positions; they were redefining high churchmanship as a highly militant ideology for religious aggression and conquest. Elements of their credo had been heard before: their general repudiation of the Reformation, their alignment of the Anglican middle way as one between popery and protestantism rather than between Rome and Puritanism, their revolutionary understanding of the relations between faith and reason, now linked to their critiques of rationalism, evangelicalism and romanticism, and even in the cases of Newman and Froude at least, their repudiation of the 'Establishmentarian-Erastian' strand in the high church tradition. But in their demand for freedom for the Church, they look very unlike old-fashioned conservative churchmen, and very like their contemporary radicals of the right, the French neo-Ultramontanes, with whom they shared traditionalism, the belief that inherited opinion, not reason, is a proper guide to truth, and that even popular bigotry may enshrine revealed doctrines repudiated by atheist philosophers.[26]

Indeed Hurrell Froude might be called the English patron saint of young right-wing radicals, a type much less common in England than on the Continent. It is perhaps too much to claim that Froude introduced a right-wing continental clericalism into the English Church: Froude's archdeacon father was right-wing and clerical enough already. Yet Froude's admiration for Becket, like his love of the breviary, did impart, to use one of his favourite words, a new clerical 'ethos' to the Anglican ideal of priesthood. The Romans might be 'wretched Tridentines' yet, as Newman put it, 'The spirit of Luther is dead; but Hildebrand and Loyola are alive.'[27] The result was a higher doctrine of ministry and sacrament. A new hostility to the State, a new pride in priesthood, a new sharpness of doctrinal definition, a new hatred of half measures and even zeal for conflict, sharpened the inherited high church insistence on the threefold ministry: leading to Tractarian denunciation of those muddled church-men who belonged to the Church of England for no very good reason, and who believed 'that bishops are a divine ordinance, yet those who have them not are in the same religious condition as those who have'.[28]

None the less the rhetoric of militancy is complex and difficult to interpret. Extremists often rely on the continuing existence both of an opposite extreme and of a stable centre. If the opposition is vanquished or the centre collapses, militant rhetoric immediately changes its function and becomes an elaborately ritualised disguise for pragmatism. Of some importance therefore, as an indication of how the Tractarians' rhetoric is to be construed, is their rejection of the so-called non-episcopal churches and of the Protestant inheritance of the Church of England. At once the problematic character and uncertainty of high Anglican ecclesiology becomes apparent. Newman's anti-protestantism took time to develop, and in Tract 38 he cited not only Calvin's belief in a real eucharistic presence (as Hooker had done before and Paget was to do after him) but also the great Reformer's wish that others should 'submit themselves to truly Christian Bishops, if such could be had'.[29] Newman's enemy at this time was not so much classical protestantism as the modern evangelicalism which had departed from it, as he quite rightly said. The coolest, driest head in the movement was that of William Palmer of Worcester, an old-fashioned 'high and dry' churchman who attracted Newman's gentle satire: Palmer's argument (also developed in Tract 15) was that the non-episcopalian churches of the Continent had been guiltless of heresy and schism in their original act of separation from Rome; their error lay in not afterwards securing for themselves a proper episcopalian church order.[30] Again Pusey, a late-comer to the movement, regarded both the Reformers and Lutherans with more affection than did his confrères; he was astonished by Froude's vehemence against the Reformers in the *Remains*, he was at first willing to subscribe to the Martyrs' Memorial, and his initial response to the notorious plan for a joint Anglo-Prussian bishopric in Jerusalem, which Palmer actually supported, was to see in it a way of reintroducing episcopal orders into the German Church. He later argued, in a work of 1855, that his doctrine of the real presence was Martin Luther's. His knowledge of Germany and German was unique among the movement's original 'Gang of Four' and, in the view of Leighton Frappell, he had an openness to other communions unique among the Tractarians until he tragically succumbed to 'Newmanism'.[31] With the possible exception of Palmer, Pusey was the most learned of the Tractarian scholars, and his irenic leanings as well as his breadth of learning tempered his attitude to foreign Protestants.

But in England, at least, there were 'truly Christian bishops', so that English nonconformists, unlike foreign Protestants, had no excuse. Palmer and Pusey convicted them of heresy and schism;[32] and at a popular level the Oxford Movement's polemical thrust was against the dissenting churches, which, as has already been noted, were undergoing their most rapid expansion in English history. In Cornwall, in Wales, in north-eastern England, they were genuine folk-churches, defining popular religion; nearly everywhere, they were the Establishment's main competitor. High Anglican attitudes toward them were extremely crude: as the learned and otherwise noble-hearted John Mason Neale declared of 'the brave old Church of England':

> Dissenters are like mushrooms,
> That flourish but a day;
> Twelve hundred years through smiles and tears
> She hath lasted on alway! . . .
>
> The true old Church of England
> She alone hath pow'r to teach;
> 'Tis presumption in Dissenters
> When they pretend to preach . . .[33]

The confrontation between Church and Chapel became one of the most fundamental controversies of the nineteenth century, firing the movement to disestablish the Church, to abolish church rate and tithe and to limit Anglican control of education and charity, and the virtual Anglican monopoly over the rites of passage, baptism, marriage and burial. Much of this antagonism was simply social, the consciousness, voiced even by Anglican Evangelicals, that a dissenter was not a gentleman. Yet such unpleasantness was fuelled by the Oxford Movement which, as a recent study shows, destroyed the sympathy of the largest of the dissenting bodies, the Wesleyan Methodist, for the Church Establishment.[34] Tractarian theological arguments divided more deeply Victorian society, which was deeply divided already, reinforcing the tendency to religious conflict implicit in the social gulf between Church and Chapel. This division was eventually embodied in the party political system in late Victorian England, in which, despite the supreme example of William Ewart Gladstone, and a minority of Liberal Anglo-Catholics, most strong high churchmen were Tories, and the great majority of nonconformists voted Liberal.[35]

It has already been said that the apostolic succession was no mere tactical device against the State, but neither was it just a stick for beating dissenters. Indeed it was linked theologically, as Alf Härdelin has shown, with the belief that the sole saving union with Christ was sacramental, 'That the only way of salvation is the partaking of the body and blood of our sacrificed Redeemer' from Christ's properly accredited ministers.[36] The point, as Keble put it in Tract 4, 'ADHERENCE TO THE APOSTOLICAL SUCCESSION THE SAFEST COURSE', was that for dissenters (not excluding Roman Catholics), 'by separating themselves from our communion, they separate themselves not only from a decent, orderly, useful society, but from THE ONLY CHURCH IN THIS REALM WHICH HAS A RIGHT TO BE QUITE SURE THAT SHE HAS THE LORD'S BODY TO GIVE TO HIS PEOPLE'.[37] There was therefore no assurance, security, safety for salvation except in the sacraments of the one apostolic English Church. Härdelin notes that a still stronger statement on this theme by Froude and Keble for the Hadleigh Conference earlier in 1833 was watered down by Palmer, and the Swedish scholar describes this as a 'new ideal of a clerical state and life', one which defined the primary office of the minister as the celebration of the Eucharist.[38] Thus anti-Erastianism, sacramentalism and clericalism come together in Tract 5 by Newman's bosom friend, J. W. Bowden; 'no ordinance of an earthly legislature, could invest us with power over the gifts [sic] of the HOLY GHOST; for such may we well term the power duly to administer the Sacraments which CHRIST has ordained'.[39] Indeed as Keble indicated this was precisely the aspect of the argument for the apostolic succession on which Hooker was deficient, and on which his deficiency has been made good by his theological successors: 'that part of the argument, which they, taught by the primitive Church, regarded as the most vital and decisive: the necessity, namely, of the apostolical commission to the derivation of sacramental grace, and to our mystical communion with Christ'.[40]

The implications of this doctrine were bound, in due course, to bear with unequal severity upon the so-called non-episcopal churches. Although Keble in Tract 4 and Bowden in Tract 30 asserted that in England Roman Catholic bishops were usurpers and intruders and their priests 'unauthorized and schismatical ministers of religion', none the less in foreign lands at least they might be acknowledged to be ministers of the Church.[41] Not so the Presbyterians and those denominations who have no bishop. Of them it has to be asked whether they are 'unchurched'? Keble's answer was that:

> 'Necessary to Salvation', and 'necessary to Church Communion', are not to be used as convertible terms. Neither do we desire to pass sentence on other persons of other countries . . . any more than we should fear to maintain the paramount necessity of Christian belief, because similar difficulties may be raised about virtuous Heathens, Jews, or Mahometans.[42]

But though Keble's explanation is not wholly coherent – he speaks of the salvation of Roman Catholics and Presbyterians in one breath – effectively he places non-episcopalians outside the Church, and assigns their salvation, like that of non-Christians, to a wholly uncovenanted mercy.

Keble had in mind the European countries in which might be found Established churches of Roman, Lutheran, Anglican or Calvinist persuasion, or lands like France where there was a majority Church. What, in his view, was especially serious was gratuitously to choose non-episcopal church ministrations when episcopal ones might be had. What the theory did not account for was the state of the Church in North America, which Newman considered at some length in an article for the *British Critic* in 1839. Newman developed the anti-Protestant implications of the Tractarian episcopal theory in an attack on the title, Protestant-Episcopal Church.[43] One should not speak, expostulated Newman, of Protestant churches having a 'defective form of government'. Their problem was not one of imperfection; they were not part of the Church at all. 'Imperfect! is a mouse an imperfect kind of bat? . . . Did all the swelling of an ambitious heart develop the frog into the bull? Could it "perfect its defective organization"?'[44] Behind this outburst lay Newman's developing conviction that we must dare to be called extravagant in our willingness to draw conclusions consistent with our admitted premises. The idea is advanced that 'Apostolical Order' is an ethical principle, and that churches which lack it are lacking in 'an inward element of truth, in a something mental, moral, spiritual, mystical'.[45] Why Newman did not permit himself the further extravagance of altogether denying to non-episcopalians the 'privileges and grace of Christianity', he does not explain. But the rhetoric, buttressed by organic analogies, had now passed a decisive milestone, and those who follow Newman to this point must needs face the further questions which pressed upon him in the six succeeding years, in his progression to Rome, and upon those later Anglo-Catholics, who in appealing to western Christendom, meant the latest pronouncement by the Holy See.[46]

It was one thing to enunciate the new implications of this episcopal doctrine; it was another to persuade the great mass of Protestant Anglicans of its truth. In the *Lectures on the Prophetical Office*, Newman discusses the Anglo-Catholic *Via Media* as a paper theory, a construction by theologians, still to be realised in a living Church. The theory embodied the Ignatian-Cyprianic vision of the diocesan bishop as the 'God visible', to whom the Christian owed his primary obedience; and though this worked well enough with the high church Bishop Bagot in Oxford – 'My own Bishop was my Pope',[47] Newman later recalled – the theory would obviously not function with Evangelical bishops, or indeed with any bishops hostile to the Tractarians. 'It is everyone's duty', Pusey told Keble in 1842, 'to maintain Catholic truth, even if unhappily opposed by a Bishop'.[48] Even a very moderate high church prelate like Samuel Wilberforce had his problems with obstreperous Anglo-Catholic priests, among them Pusey himself. When Tract 90 and the Tracts themselves succumbed to the united disapproval of the episcopal bench – even the redoubtable Henry Phillpotts voiced his disgust with Tract 90 – it looked as if the Tractarians might fall victim to the very authority they were exalting. The refusal of the Evangelical Charles Sumner, Bishop of Winchester, to ordain Keble's curate Peter Young in 1841 inaugurated a century of guerilla war by high church clergymen who defied their diocesans, on what looked like the congregational principle of maintaining the Catholic faith within one parish. As Keble said, 'If the Church of England were to fail altogether yet it would be found in my parish'.[49] The theory and practice were alike incarnate in John Mason Neale, who had 'a great theoretical admiration for episcopacy with a gift of insulting all embodied Bishops'.[50] You exalted your bishop as an angel, but if the angel called you to order you defied him.

Newman had already seen that his system needed protection against heretical bishops. As Wiseman had shown, there was an appeal in the fourth-century Church from a heretical Donatist episcopate to the Church universal; indeed the patriarchal and papal systems, which Newman regarded as merely human creations, had developed to supply the inadequacies of episcopal rule. There was no such court of appeal in the Anglican system, and the invocation of the faith of the early undivided Church left the high churchmen facing Wiseman's charge that their private judgment was selecting what it wanted from antiquity and ignoring the cardinal principle of the early Church, the united witness of the whole Catholic world. Even the revival of Convocation in the 1850s left the Church of England without a living voice against appeals to the Privy Council, which the Anglo-Catholics regarded as the Erastian protector of liberal or Protestant heresy. The same Privy Council a decade later acted to protect the revenues, if not to defend the doctrines, of the allegedly heretical Bishop of Natal, against the decision of his metropolitan in Cape Town. Indeed Newman and W. G. Ward had made matters easier for all liberals, by driving a coach and horses through the Church's doctrinal standard, the Thirty-Nine articles; and the new broad churchmen of the 1850s profited from their example. The issue for high churchmen was whether the Church of England could show herself to be a living authoritative branch of the Catholic Church against these liberals and Protestants; and for that task, national Establishment was at least as much a hindrance as a help, an aid to the liberal and Protestant enemy.

III

There was therefore an internal complexity, variety and even ambivalence to the Tractarian emphasis upon episcopacy. But taken as a whole it constituted a remarkable reinforcement for the spread of a worldwide episcopal denomination, untrammelled by the State connection so problematic in England. In 1838 there were a mere eighteen overseas bishops;[51] by the date of the first Lambeth Conference in 1867 there were eighty-five overseas dioceses, some with assistant bishops or coadjutors.[52] Not that the Tractarians may be credited with launching the idea of an Anglican fellowship of independent churches. Already Hobart and others in the United States had outlined the principles of a firmly episcopalian body gathered by consensual contract. The example of the United States was vital in the founding of an Episcopal Church in New Zealand.[53] But the idea of a missionary episcopate, romantically sketched by Newman in Tract 33, fired the imagination of high churchmen and led to a remarkable growth in the world-wide spread of bishops in communion with the see of Canterbury: 'the Church is a mother', Newman declared; the Anglican communion is the offspring.[54]

But what was the theory which undergirded it? Henry VIII's and Bishop Gardiner's theory was, like Keble's, quite simply that the Church of England was the Catholic and Apostolic Church of England, that it maintained in all essentials the Catholic faith, the Catholic ministry, the seven Catholic sacraments. That it was not in communion with the see of Rome was no barrier to its catholicity, since communion with Rome was not one of the essentials of the faith. But this theory was of no use in new territories, where two or three episcopates might arrive at much the same time each demanding the exclusive allegiance of the laity. The theory was as a matter of fact already obsolete in the sixteenth century, when English Church people were faced with an episcopate preaching rival versions of the gospel, and must have realised that the wrong choice, indeed any choice, might imply future martyrdom. The rule that the mere possession of a formally valid title to an episcopal see is adequate grounds for affirming the continuity of the Catholic faith makes the Reformation itself unintelligible.

Hooker's theory is at once more subtle and more flexible. The 'great and serious reserves' (Paget) which he made in a watertight *de iure divino* theory are no more than must be made if abandonment of communion with Rome could *ever* be justified. It is also, paradoxically, Hooker's own theory and not the Tractarian recension of it which makes sense of the Episcopal Church in America, or anywhere indeed where the claim to be the church of the nation lacks the popular consent on which Hooker insisted. It was Hooker moreover who insisted on lay participation in Church government; Newman who violently deplored it, specifically in its North American form. For Hooker, as all his generation, plainly understood that Anglicans have to make some sense of the Reformation. There have to be some grounds on which the visible unity, and therefore the continuity of the Church, might be broken if testimony to the gospel is to be maintained. Nor is this merely a matter of the past; there have to be some grounds for maintaining separation if Anglicans are not to be self-condemned as schismatic.

But of course in order to maintain such a judgment there must be a criterion more certain than that of the *iudicium orbis terrarum*. The Anglican reference was to the Scriptures, but to refer to the Scriptures in such a manner as to command reverence for the interpretative activity of the early Church and respect for rational argument. None the less it must be possible for a theological stance to be openly constructed which convicts a contemporary bishop of error, and justifies dissent. The radical Tractarian, in challenging his Evangelical or liberal bishop, was exercising in fact if not in theory precisely the same Christian freedom as the reforming Anglican clergy of the sixteenth century. Bowden's Tract 5, in laying emphasis on the importance of placing the Bible in the hands of every member of the Church, and warning her or him of the importance of Article 6, was utterly Anglican.[55]

The appeal to the Scripture has, however, a corollary, specifically to do with episcopacy. The minority of churchmen in the later years of Elizabeth who expounded a *de iure divino* theory of the episcopate did so on the basis of the *historical* argument that the apostles themselves provided for an episcopal succession. But modern scholarship indicates that the patterns of leadership in the early Church permit no such certainty in reconstruction. The *fact* of apostolical succession, which Newman declared to be 'too notorious to require proof', is no such thing.[56] The modern case for a *de iure divino* theory of episcopacy rests no longer on the first century and the plain testimony of the inspired word of God, but on the second century and a doctrine of divine providence or the direct guidance of the Holy Spirit.[57] But if that is so, as Fr Benedict Green pointed out many years ago,[58] and the ARCIC documents now openly propose, ought not Anglicans to be open to a similar argument in favour of the Roman primacy? This is the natural tendency of the Tractarian position. What indeed in the history of the development of doctrine is not open to the same considerations?

It is perhaps as well to refer back to our remarks about the function of rhetoric. The Tractarian theory was to the core fiercely and intentionally controversial, framed at a time when its supporters could count upon an equally fierce opposition and a languid centrism. In time episcopalianism has been immensely successful, producing in many parts of the world independent episcopal denominations with abundant signs, *pace* Newman in his later years, of Catholic and supernatural life. But the transformation of the Tractarian rhetoric by stages into the smoother language of ecumenical diplomacy is a *metabasis eis allo genos*. The very success of the theory should make us suspicious of its rhetoric in new lands beyond the ocean, in Africa, Asia, the Americas, the Pacific, shorn of its fierceness, indeed of its immediacy, and subserving other ends.

With the destruction of the historical argument for a chain in which every link is known 'from St Peter to our present Metropolitan' goes likewise the strict Presbyterian case which the argument was designed to counteract. Ecumenical circumstances require a greater effort of Catholic imagination and openness of mind than the natural route of the Tractarian success would suggest. The Anglican vocation is to the achievement of reconciliation of *episcope* in a divided Church, and in this the so-called non-episcopal churches must be partners.

Summary

The Oxford Movement restored to the Church of England a consciousness of her place in the Catholic Church of Christ, as a great episcopal communion and not just a national church. Indeed the movement's stress on the necessity of the episcopal office undergirded the nineteenth-century development of an international Anglican communion, in Africa, Asia, the Americas and the Pacific, which occurred despite the Church's loss of its traditional role in the life of the English nation.

Thus the English Church had to surrender something of Richard Hooker's vision of itself as the State and nation at prayer: but the Tractarians also reversed the dominant tradition in Anglican theology, deriving from Hooker, which acknowledged the right of a

Church to decide its own church order, and therefore admitted the orders of non-episcopal churches. Indeed the Oxford Movement renounced its Protestant inheritance and unchurched non-episcopalian English dissenters and foreign non-episcopal Protestants, even while going to war with the bishops of the English Church and exacerbating the Church's own divisions. Thus the movement precipitated a new bitterness in inter-church polemic, in which all the churches expanded on the basis of a fiercer hatred for one another. But if a distinctive Anglican ecclesiology is to be defended in a modern non-polemical setting throughout the world-wide Anglican communion, then Anglicans must come to terms with their Protestant inheritance, by resting their defence of episcopacy on Hooker's argument, acknowledging the existence of apostolic *episcope* in the so-called non-episcopal churches, and admitting what modern scholarship makes clear: that episcopacy is to be valued as a development in Christian history, not as a part of dominical teaching or of the essence of Christianity.

As our Lord set before his disciples the larger vision of a kingdom, but founded a perpetual memorial of his broken body in the world, which was its price, so the very brokenness, the very incompleteness of that Church which is the fragile vessel of love and longing must be the sign of a larger vision and a larger hope.

1. H. P. Liddon, *The Life of Edward Bouverie Pusey*, ed. J. O. Johnston and R. J. Wilson, 4 vols (London 1893–7), II, p. 140.
2. Esp. in David Newsome, *The Parting of Friends* (London 1966); W. R. Ward, *Religion and Society in England 1790–1850* (London and New York 1973).
3. Owen Chadwick, ed., *The Mind of the Oxford Movement* (London 1963); Eugene Fairweather, *The Oxford Movement* (New York 1964), A Library of Protestant Thought.
4. J. Daniélou, A. H. Couratin and John Kent, *The Pelican Guide to Modern Theology*, II, *Historical Theology* (London 1969). p. 320.
5. F. L. Cross, *The Oxford Movement and the Seventeenth Century*, Oxford Movement Centenary Series, No. 3 (London 1933), ch. 7, esp. p. 68.
6. John Henry Newman, Tract 74, *Catena Patrum No. I: Testimony . . . to the Doctrine of the Apostolical Succession*. The claim is specifically made by Newman that the passages quoted are no more than 'tokens and suggestions' of the full testimony contained in the respective works. It is very striking that Newman's *Catena* is specifically endorsed by A. J. Mason, in *The Church of England and Episcopacy* (Cambridge 1914), p. 22. How far Mason's opinion is remote from that of historical scholarship may be seen by comparing his chapter 2, 'Episcopacy and the Elizabethans', with the works cited in note 16 below.
7. In a paper entitled 'Anglo-Catholic Tradition', read on 7 November 1904, and published in F. L. Cross, *Darwell Stone, Churchman and Counsellor* (London 1943), pp. 394–405. Stone admitted that on many of the subjects on which the Tractarians drew up *catenae* it would be possible

to draw up another in a contrary sense. The consequence of this is that 'as to derived and subordinate doctrines there have been more traditions than one, of varying strength and varying popularity', p. 405.

8. Newman, Tract 74, pp. 1–2.

9. See Louis Allen, *John Henry Newman and the Abbé Jager* (London 1975).

10. See John Keble, ed., *The Works of . . . Richard Hooker*, 3 vols (Oxford 1836), I, Editor's Preface, pp. lxxvff.

11. For what follows, see esp. W. D. J. Cargill Thompson, 'The Philosopher of the "Politic Society": Richard Hooker as a Political Thinker', in W. Speed Hill, ed., *Studies on Richard Hooker* (Case Western Reserve University Press 1972), reprinted in W. D. J. Cargill Thompson, *Studies in the Reformation: Luther to Hooker* (London 1980), pp. 131–91.

12. *Of the Laws of Ecclesiastical Polity*, Book VII, xi, 8.

13. The 'whole body of the Church' is said to have 'power to alter, with general consent and upon necessary occasions' even the positive laws of the apostles, 'if there is no command to the contrary'. Thus episcopacy may be said to be *both* instituted by God *and* continued by the judgment of the Church. 'Wherefore lest bishops forget themselves, as if none on earth had authority to touch their states, let them continually bear in mind, that it is rather the force of custom, whereby the Church having so long found it good to continue under the regiment of her virtuous bishops, doth still uphold, maintain, and honour them in that respect, than that any such true and heavenly law can be shewed, by the evidence whereof it may of a truth appear that the Lord himself hath appointed presbyters for ever to be under the regiment of bishops, in what sort soever they behave themselves.' ibid. Book VII, v, 8.

14. Hooker's celebrated treatment of this theme is in ibid., Book III, i, 3–6.

15. Francis Paget, *An Introduction to the Fifth Book of Hooker's Treatise of the Laws of Ecclesiastical Polity* (Oxford 1899), p. 120, and esp. pp. 118ff., specifically referring back to Keble's discussion.

16. This development is recounted in W. D. J. Cargill Thompson, 'Anthony Marten and the Elizabethan Debate on Episcopacy', in G. V. Bennett and J. D. Walsh, eds, *Essays in Modern English Church History, in memory of Norman Sykes* (London 1966). Claire Cross states that the new theories were the opinions of 'a tiny minority' in the Church of England, and that until the late 1580s no Elizabethan churchman had maintained that bishops constituted an inalienable order in a reformed church: 'Churchmen and the Royal Supremacy', in F. Heal and R. O'Day, *Church and Society in England: Henry VIII to James I* (London 1977), pp. 28ff.

17. On the 'abiding resentment' created by the Westminster Assembly, and the subsequent closure of loopholes in ordinations in 1662, see N. Sykes, *Old Priest and New Presbyter* (Cambridge 1956), pp. 114ff.

18. Charles Daubeny, *A Guide to the Church, in several discourses . . .* (London 1798), pp. 34–5. We owe this quotation, and guidance to the theology of this period, to Mrs Elizabeth Varley, who is completing a University of Durham doctoral thesis on the life of William van Mildert.

19. Peter Nockles, 'Pusey and the Question of Church and State', in Perry Butler, ed., *Pusey Rediscovered* (London 1983), pp. 259–60.

20. Sheridan Gilley, 'Nationality and liberty, protestant and catholic: Robert Southey's *Book of the Church*', in Stuart Mews, ed., *Religion and National Identity*, Studies in Church History, 18 (Oxford 1982), pp. 411–12. See

also Sheridan Gilley, 'John Keble and the Victorian Churching of Romanticism', in J. R. Watson, ed., *An Infinite Complexity: essays in Romanticism* (Edinburgh 1983), pp. 226–39.

21. Cargill Thompson has rightly warned against thinking that the concept of 'divine right' (*iure divino*) implied more than that an institution was presumed to have divine sanction, 'Anthony Martin', op. cit. p. 59.

22. John Henry Newman, Tract 1, *Thoughts on the Ministerial Commission*, pp. 1–4.

23. ibid.

24. John Henry Newman, *Apologia pro vita sua: being a history of his religious opinions*, ed. Martin J. Svaglic (Oxford 1967), pp. 42, 52–3.

25. Reprinted in J. H. Newman, *Discussions and Arguments* (London 1872), pp. 254–305; and in Elisabeth Jay, ed., *The Evangelical and Oxford Movements* (Cambridge 1983), esp. p. 173: 'Christianity is faith, faith implies a doctrine, a doctrine propositions, propositions yes or no, yes or no differences. Differences, then, are the natural attendants on Christianity, and you cannot have Christianity, and not have differences. When, then, Sir Robert Peel calls such differences points of "party feeling", what is this but to insult Christianity?'

26. 'Note A', 'Liberalism', *Apologia*, pp. 257–8.

27. ibid. p. 99.

28. ibid.

29. John Henry Newman, Tract 38, *Via Media No. I*, p. 7; see Paget, Introduction, pp. 172–83.

30. We may ask from whom Palmer imagined that Lutherans would secure for themselves a proper episcopalian order. Lutherans may surely be forgiven for not thinking immediately of the Church of England. See William Palmer, *A Treatise on the Church of Christ*, 2 vols (London 1838), I, pp. 382, 388.

31. Leighton Frappell, ' "Science" in the Service of Orthodoxy: the early intellectual development of E. B. Pusey', in Perry Butler, ed., *Pusey Rediscovered*, pp. 26–7.

32. Palmer, *A Treatise on the Church of Christ*, I, pp. 413–17.

33. John Mason Neale, *Songs and Ballads for the People* (London 1843), [p. 3]. We owe this reference to Dr A. L. Sanders, who owns the unique surviving copy of this work.

34. David Hempton, 'Methodism and Anti-Catholic Politics 1800–1846' (unpublished Ph.D. thesis, Univ. St Andrews 1977).

35. D. W. Bebbington, *The Nonconformist Conscience: Chapel and Politics, 1870–1914* (London 1982).

36. One of the four points of the manifesto of the Hadleigh Conference. A. Härdelin, *The Tractarian Understanding of the Eucharist* (Uppsala 1965), p. 116. Härdelin's book is the finest ever written about Tractarian theology.

37. John Keble, Tract 4, *Adherence to the Apostolical Succession the Safest Course*, p. 5.

38. Härdelin, *Tractarian Understanding*, pp. 120, 122.

39. The entire argument of this Tract is concerned with what is termed 'spiritual power', but bears a disturbing similarity to lost status. See Anthony Russell, *The Clerical Profession* (London 1980), p. 109, re. John Kent's query (Daniélou, Couratin and Kent, *Historical Theology*, p. 317),

as to 'how far the growth of Anglo-Catholicism and Evangelicalism was related to the nineteenth-century decline of the social status of the clergy in Britain', perhaps along lines parallel to Roman clerical Ultramontanism.

40. Keble, Preface to *The Works of . . . Richard Hooker*, I, p. lxxvii.
41. J. W. Bowden, Tract 30, *Christian Liberty . . . continued*, p. 6. Bowden extends his argument even to Ireland, where 'the established Church of Ireland alone represents that Church which the labours of St Patrick, in the fifth century, planted in that island'.
42. Keble, Tract 4, p. 6.
43. 'The Anglo-American Church', written for the *British Critic*, and republished in *Essays Critical and Historical* 2 vols (London 1871), I, pp. 308–85). Entirely consistent with this attack is Newman's objection to Bishop Hobart's dictum that the Episcopal Church stands for 'Evangelical Truth and Apostolical Order', p. 363. Here, it may be, we have an indication of the parting of the ways between the American high church movement, of which Hobart was a distinguished protagonist, and the Romanising section of English Tractarianism.
44. ibid. p. 369.
45. ibid.
46. The strange contortions of Anglican papalism are described in M. P. Yelton, *Anglican Papalism and the Rejection of the Revised Prayer Books of 1927-8*, Perowne Prize Essay, Corpus Christi, Cambridge, 1970. On the super-subtle distinctions which kept a brilliant Anglican papalist for a time out of Rome, see R. A. Knox, *A Spiritual Aeneid* (London, 1918).
47. Newman, *Apologia*, p. 56.
48. Cited by Standish Meacham, *Lord Bishop: the life of Samuel Wilberforce 1805-1873* (Harvard 1970), p. 174 et. seq.
49. Georgina Battiscombe, *John Keble: a study in limitations* (London 1963), p. 303.
50. James Bentley, *Ritualism and Politics in Victorian Britain: the attempt to legislate for belief* (Oxford 1978), p. 15.
51. Including the ten American bishops. The others were Nova Scotia (1784), Quebec (1793), Calcutta (1814), Jamaica, Barbados (1824), Madras (1835), Australia (1835), Bombay (1837). Newfoundland and Toronto were to follow in 1839.
52. Alan M. G. Stephenson, *Anglicanism and the Lambeth Conferences* (London 1978), p. 12.
53. cf. the correspondence between Bishop G. W. Doane of New Jersey, and Bishop Selwyn of New Zealand, in G. W. Doane, ed., *Letters from the Bishop of New Zealand*, cited in P. H. E. Thomas, 'The Lambeth Conferences and the Development of Anglican Ecclesiology, 1867–1978' (unpublished Ph.D. thesis, Univ. Durham 1982).
54. 'The Anglo-American Church', *Essays Critical and Historical*, I, p. 312. Having used the vitality of 'our American relatives' as an argument for the vitality of Anglicanism, Newman was constrained (as a Roman Catholic) to observe (in Note VII, 1871) that there are different kinds of liveliness, and that heresy and worldliness also 'live' in a certain sense (p. 381).
55. The Anglican Church eschews the claim of infallibility, but 'puts the Bible into the hand of every member of her communion, and calls upon

him to believe nothing as necessary to salvation which shall not appear, upon mature examination, to be set down therein, or at least to be capable of being proved thereby; but showing, at the same time, her authority as its appointed interpreter, she cautions him not rashly, or without having fully weighed the subject, to dissent from her expositions, the results of the accumulated learning and labour of centuries'. Bowden, Tract 5, pp.13–14.

56. In their important reply to the Congregation for the Doctrine of the Faith's somewhat negative comments upon ARCIC, Heinrich Fries and Karl Rahner specifically cite the Catholic theologian Waltar Kaspar, as follows: 'It is not disputed among historians that we do not find in the New Testament any unitary ordering of ministry. It is also beyond controversy that we cannot trace back the primacy of the bishop of Rome and the threefold ministry (bishops, priests, deacons) to an immediate institution by the earthly Jesus or the risen Christ'. Cited from *Evangelium–Sakramente-Amt und Einheit der Kirche* (Freiburg, Göttingen 1982), pp. 123ff, in Fries and Rahner, 'A Catholic Response to ARCIC', T. Sutcliffe, ed., *Tracts for Our Times* (London 1983), p. 77.

57. See H. Chadwick, 'Episcopacy in the New Testament and early Church', in *Today's Church and Today's World, Preparatory Articles for the Lambeth Conference 1978* (London 1978), pp. 206–14.

58. H. Benedict Green, 'Apostolic Succession and the Anglican Appeal to History', *Church Quarterly Review*, 163 (1961), pp. 293ff.

9

Two Tendencies in Anglo-Catholic Political Theology*

David Nicholls

Just as it was a political event which provoked Karl Barth into questioning the liberal theology of his day and formulating a radical alternative, so it was a political event – the suppression of a number of Irish sees by a Whig government – which led Keble and the Tractarians to attack the practical Erastianism prevalent in early nineteenth-century England.

However, as Barth's work was in substance theological rather than political, the same may be said of the Tractarians. As with Barth, the sovereignty of God's word and the authority of divine revelation were central, so theological concerns – the nature of the Church, the importance of the incarnation, the role of the sacraments, were the principal preoccupation of the Tractarians. How then can we properly speak of a political theology in the context of the Oxford Movement? Is there any sense in which we may speak of it as 'political', other than with respect to the events that initiated it?

In the first place we must agree with Moltmann that 'while there may be a naive and politically unaware theology, there can be no apolitical theology'.[1] What he means is that *all* theologies are formulated and accepted within particular political contexts and that an attempt to understand their meaning ought not to ignore these contexts. There are assumptions made, images and concepts used, implications drawn (or left implicit) which are of a political nature. The first (assumptions, concepts and images) are, it is worth noting, as important as the 'implications'. It is frequently taken for granted that the only significant social or political aspect of the Oxford Movement are its implications or consequences.

Nevertheless the work of the Tractarians was essentially theological rather than political in its explicit concerns. Their writings centred on the holiness and transcendence of God and on the holiness which Christians should manifest in their lives, through prayer, devotion and good works. They wrote of the Church, Catholic and apostolic, of the centrality of the incarnation of the Son of God, and of the sacraments as embodying the saving work of Christ. It is noteworthy that they by no means rejected the strong emphasis upon sin and the fall which was characteristic of Evangelical preaching in their day. One or two of them were in fact raised in this tradition. They assumed and frequently asserted the fact of human sin and the need for personal salvation through the cross of Christ.

The tenor of the explicit political and social teaching of the Tractarians themselves was distinctly conservative. The genuine concern for the poor exhibited by Pusey, Keble and Ward was part of a hierarchical view of civil society in which the aristocracy took a paternal interest in the welfare of the lower classes. This position is reflected clearly in the lay sermons of S. T. Coleridge and explicated at some length in the writings of William Sewell. The Church in particular was said to have a duty to defend the poor against the rapacity of the rich and from the effects of unrestricted competition. Pusey denounced the 'reckless and fraudful competition, whose aim is to cheapen every luxury and vanity, in order that those at ease may spend on fresh accumulated luxuries and vanities what they withhold from the poor'.[2]

Among the fathers of the Oxford Movement the most ambitious attempt to set forth a political theory came from William Sewell. It is curious that his work has largely been ignored by those who have written on the subject of 'Church and Society' in recent years. So far from politicising Christianity Sewell's aim is to christianise politics by deducing a set of political principles from divine revelation. The result is a hierarchically structured community, reflecting both the unity and the plurality of the divine Trinity. Sewell denounced the tendency which he diagnosed in his day to 'systematise, centralise, equalise and harmonise', which he summed up as 'a rationalising thirst for exclusive unity'.[3]

Two Tendencies

It is possible to see two tendencies at work in the social and political theology of the Tractarians and their followers. I shall call these 'incarnationalist' and 'redemptionist'. They are what Max Weber would have called 'ideal types' in the sense that they do not necessarily represent positions which were actually held by anyone in their pure form, but rather are tendencies towards which different positions can be judged to have approximated.

1. With respect to the incarnationalist type the influence of F. D. Maurice is paramount. Within the Anglo-Catholic movement it became particularly powerful towards the end of the nineteenth century with theologians like Charles Gore and Henry Scott Holland. This tendency is however by no means peculiar to Anglo-catholicism and can be seen among liberal Anglicans from the seventeenth-century Cambridge Platonists to the Modern Churchman's Union.

It is normally related to certain forms of philosophical idealism. Maurice regarded himself as a platonist. Scott Holland, Gore, Illingworth and others of the period came under the powerful shadow of Thomas Hill Green of Balliol, who was the leading spirit in the revival of idealism in late-nineteenth century Britain.

This incarnationalist tendency is also idealist in the more popular sense of the term. Life is conceived as an enterprise in which the individual and the group strive to realise ideals, to practice 'Christian values'. It is generally optimistic and gradualist, believing that God's kingdom will come slowly, silently and peacefully and that the mighty will be lowered so gently from their seats as not to feel the bump when they reach the ground.[4] It underestimates the power of sin and the fact of evil. It has little understanding of the fall and of the need for redemption. This is not, of course, a necessary consequence of philosophical idealism; Plato was in certain respects deeply pessimistic while Hegel by no means believed in gradual progress and spoke of 'the slaughter-bench of history'.

The emergence of the positive liberalism of Green as a major force in British intellectual and political life in the 1880s is not, I believe, unconnected with a growing realisation that, unless steps were taken by a reforming State to alleviate some of the harsher consequences of a capitalist economy, violent revolution would ensue.[5] To be sure, most of those who worked for improved social services and who pioneered legislation contributing to the growth of the welfare state did not intend to perpetuate capitalism. But this has been the consequence. In Germany and Italy however harsher methods were found necessary. It is here, among the late-nineteenth century positive liberals, that we may find the roots of present day paternalism and of welfare state ideology: a belief that there are no basic conflicts of interest in the nation (or, as extended by the Brandt Commission, in the world) but that we must all work (and pray, according to the Alternative Service Book) for the common good – a good which may be realised if people would behave a bit more reasonably. It is the Church's job to infuse a spirit of reconciliation which in practice means persuading workers and management to accept minor adjustments in the present arrangements. The role of the Church, in the immortal words of Archbishops Coggan and Blanch, is that of 'influencing society'.

An article in the *Oxford Diocesan Magazine* states that at a recent clergy conference in a large Midland diocese, the SDP-Liberal Alliance had 120 supporters, against 80 for Conservative and 42 for Labour. 'This is not surprising,' comments Sir James Cobban. 'There is much in its policy, much more in its approach to politics and in the outlook of its leaders, that makes it attractive to a Church that is dedicated to reconciliation.'[6] I remember a canon from Christ Church who came to preach at Exeter College, Oxford and claimed that the whole Christian gospel can be summed up in the word 'reconciliation'. There is a sense in which it can, but I felt moved to remind him that the only persons reconciled as a result of the ministry of Jesus were Herod and Pilate. Christians believe in reconciliation, but it is reconciliation through a cross. The incarnationalist tendency fails to take sufficiently seriously the cross and its implications.

Another feature of the incarnationalist position is a rejection of the secular and the desire to christianise everything. 'The state,' wrote F. D. Maurice, 'is as much God's creation as the church.' 'The method of the Incarnation,' wrote A. G. Hebert, 'means that the separation of "sacred" and "secular" is broken down.' 'The task of the Church,' T. S. Eliot told the Malvern Conference of 1941, 'is to christianize the state and society.' 'The distinction between sacred and secular, which has been thrust upon us by the modern world', writes Patrick Curran in a recent issue of a review published by Chichester Theological College, 'is a false one, which no Christian, who believes that God became incarnate in the man Jesus can uphold.'[7] Christianity, we are continually being told, is concerned with the whole of life. Now Christian faith may indeed have implications for any part of our individual or social existence but we ought also to recognise the relative autonomy of important aspects of human life. While we may agree that there is no absolute and ultimate separation between sacred and secular, there is an important distinction to be made between them and a failure to make such a distinction may have disastrous consequences for both Church and State. One need only study the life and writings of Thomas Arnold to appreciate what these consequences might be.[8] Arnold was, of course, no Anglo-Catholic but his ideas, particularly on the Church and the nation, have had an influence on those of the incarnationalist tendency.

The influence of F. D. Maurice on Anglo-catholicism is however much clearer and more explicit. W. G. Peck comments that this influence 'seems to me to have deflected Christian social thought into channels which might have carried it too far from its distinctive origins in a revealed religion of redemption'.[9] The Mauricean legacy may be discerned not only in the thought (if that is the right term) of Scott Holland but also in the ideas of the more radical Stewart Headlam.

Scott Holland in fact comes as near as anyone within the Anglo-Catholic tradition to the ideal type of incarnationlist we are considering. Born in 1847 he was educated at Eton; he then went to Balliol where he was taught by Green. After fourteen years as a senior student of Christ Church he became Canon of St Paul's from 1884 to 1910, when he returned from Amen Court to Tom Quad as Regius Professor of Divinity; he died in 1918. He was, observed George Russel', 'the most agreeable man in London'. 'He was never curt or rude', wrote Edward Lyttelton, 'and it is impossible to imagine him ever giving pain.'[10]

While it is only fair to say that, in his later writings, Scott Holland recognised that the kingdom of heaven would not be realised on earth by a gradual development from within, but 'arrives from afar', his earlier work is characterised by a belief that the kingdom's

> gradual conquest of the world would be marked by the line of its visible success. Step by step it would press that line forward. Slowly, steadily, by the accumulated pressure of the redeemed and ordered material, built up by the unceasing action of the Holy Ghost into a single and solid and massive whole, it was to overbear, by its weight and volume, the kingdom of this world, overturning thrones and empires with the real invincible persistence of actual force.

As part of this gradual christianising process he saw the continued Establishment of the Church of England as 'at once obvious, intelligible, natural, justifiable'.[11] The incarnationalist tendency was perhaps most at home in college quad and cathedral close and manifests many of the characteristics associated with these institutions.

2. The redemptionist tendency, while accepting the vital importance of the incarnation of the Son of God, lays great emphasis upon human sin and the need for salvation. It acknowledges the fundamental goodness of the created order but draws attention to the radical nature of the fall. It sees the purpose of God in Christ as the ultimate reconciliation of all things, yet insists that the death of Christ on the cross represents the mortal battle between the forces of good and evil in the universe: 'We wrestle not against flesh and blood but against principalities and powers . . . against spiritual wickedness in high places'.[21] There can therefore be no easy compromise between the Church and the world, between God and Satan, except of a purely temporary and tactical kind.

Redemptionists have emphasised the 'otherworldly' nature of God's kingdom, not in the sense that it has nothing to do with this earth, but in the sense that its values and principles are opposed to those upon which the kingdoms of this world are built. Christians are 'strangers and pilgrims' in this world and are not to make their home in this order of things:

> Two loves therefore have given origin to these two cities, self-love in contempt of God unto the earthly, love of God in contempt of one's self to the heavenly. The first seeks the glory of men, and the latter desires God only as the testimony of the conscience, the greatest glory . . .[13]

This recognition of two cities or kingdoms has allowed redemptionists to accept the fact of the secular and to be prepared to engage with secular institutions, both by operating within them and at times by confronting them. When working within them, they have insisted that their collaboration is always conditional. They have not however tried to Christianise them, but have accepted the limited good that they are able to achieve and recognised the criteria and rules according to which they work. For redemptionists the message of Christ's kingdom de-sacralises every human institution, whether it be the State, the European Community, private property, the school, the family or the Athenaeum Club. Even the Church must be seen not as an end in itself but as a symbol and means for the realisation of the heavenly city. It is sacred in what it stands for rather than in its present reality: it does however differ radically from the State, whose purposes are strictly mundane.

Within the Anglo-Catholic tradition an example of this redemptionist tendency is John Neville Figgis. Born in 1866, son of a nonconformist minister, Figgis studied history at Cambridge where he came under the influence of Mandell Creighton, Lord Acton and F. W. Maitland. After ordination he worked for several years in the parochial ministry and in 1907 joined the Community of the Resurrection. He died in 1919. While working in a country parish in Dorset he became acutely aware of the bankruptcy of the liberal Christianity which he had assumed up to this point. His radical rejection of liberal protestantism was proclaimed in the Hulsean Lectures of 1908–9, published under the title *The Gospel and Human Needs*.

Based on a supernatural revelation, the Christian faith was proclaimed by Figgis as a religion of redemption having significance for the practical life rather than for the intellect. His lectures were designed to defend the faith of those 'to whom Christ is the one rock, the Cross the one hope, and the Church the abiding home for weak and sin-stained souls'. The gospel is otherworldly, and so far as it appeals to men 'it appeals to them as religious'. Christianity is concerned not simply with social reform, for 'a world wherein everybody is respectable might very well be a world wherein no one is religious'.[14]

Figgis recognised that Christians must accept the fact of a secular State and in a later series of lectures outlined the duties and rights of Christians in the context of a pluralist State. Churchmen ought not to yearn for a past Christendom, nor to attempt to impose upon their fellow citizens the high demands of the gospel. Their ideal must rather be that of a free Church in a free State. The Church may thus maintain its distinct witness to a supernatural gospel which challenges the very foundations upon which the kingdoms of this world are built.[15]

There are two problems associated with this position. One is the practical problem of the Church becoming concerned solely with its own interests and abdicating all responsibility for the affairs of State, other than securing its own freedom. A recent example of this narrow concern would be the reaction of many churchmen to the abortive Police Bill, when criticism was voiced simply about the threat to the confidentiality of information given to clergy in their pastoral capacity, rather than to some of the wider social consequences of the bill. Figgis would certainly have rejected such a narrow approach as misconceived. The Church must work for the creation and maintenance of a State which recognises the freedom of many different groups to exist and to pursue ends chosen by their members. There must of course be limits to this freedom particularly when the activity of one group interferes with that of others and it is a principal job of government to handle such potential conflicts, rather than itself attempting to impose upon its population some substantive common good. What is important is not what a government does but what it allows and encourages to be done.

Related to this is a second, theoretical, problem concerned with the moral basis of such a free secular polity. Figgis would claim that the ultimate basis of such a State is to be found in a Christian doctrine of human nature. From Lord Acton he had learned first that political freedom is important because it allows for human choice and responsibility and secondly that 'power tends to corrupt'.[16] The fact of sin and evil does not justify authoritarian regimes, for they too share in the evil. The only hope is for power to be dispersed and decentralised, which may impede efficiency but also inhibits corruption. Avoiding the worst may, in politics, be more important than attempting to realise the best.

I have taken Figgis to illustrate my redemptionist type; I might have taken A. H. Stanton, Frank Weston, or Conrad Noel. It is perhaps significant that these men wrote from the context of parish, religious community and missionary diocese rather than from a purely academic experience of life. Many Evangelicals and other Protestants might be found holding a position similar to this redemptionist tendency. If held apart from a strong doctrine of creation and incarnation, a belief in the social and indeed cosmic scope of salvation and a robust sacramentalism, it has, however, consequences which may be tragic. A strong belief in the power of evil and sin can be related to an authoritarian politics, for human freedom is thought to be dangerous. Therefore a strong government must hold people in check. This view is clearly present in Luther and in a Catholic form may be seen in a number of French reactionary thinkers of the nineteenth century. 'The executioner,' wrote Joseph de Maistre, 'is the very cornerstone of society.'[17] Sentiments which might indeed have been uttered by our own Prime Minister whose admiration for Victorian values is well known.

There are three further points I wish to make in connection with this distinction between incarnationalist and redemptionist tendencies in Anglo-Catholic Theology. In the first place the distinction by no means coincides with a distinction between left and right in politics. The incarnationalists include those on the left (like Scott Holland or

Stewart Headlam) and those on the right (like Charles Smyth or T. S. Eliot). Redemptionists include those on the left (like Conrad Noel or Figgis) and those on the right (like Enoch Powell).

Secondly the assumption of almost all Anglo-Catholics of both traditions is that we, as Christians, are (and it is natural that in some way we should be) the ones called on to perform acts of caring and concern. We are seen as being in the position of the priest, the Levite, or (hopefully) the good Samaritan, rather than in the position of one in need of help. As a recent author never tires of reminding us, most Anglican writers on these matters, whether on the left or the right, have come from the social élite. Much of their social and political comment is characterised by a consequent odour of condescension. Perhaps Augustine's allegorical interpretation of the parable (revived by Isaac Williams in his poem, 'The Baptistery') was right after all! I almost get the feeling from reading what Pusey says about the poor that God created them so that Pusey and his friends would have an object for their munificence.[18]

A similar spirit seems to inspire much of what Christian agencies write about the question of 'aid' to countries of the third world particularly in response to the Brandt Report. Everything is well when it is a matter of our giving aid to others. I have suggested elsewhere that the more crucial question might be: what will Christians of Europe and North America do when people of the poorer countries start to take what we have often assumed to be ours? There is hardly a case in the history of the world when the condition of an oppressed group has significantly improved as a result of pure altruism on the part of the rich or powerful.[19]

Thirdly there is the almost universal assumption that if only we could get our theology straight we would then be able to deduce our ethics and politics, as if we can somehow get theology straight while working in an ideological and material vacuum. The leaders of the Oxford Movement, particularly Newman and Ward, were aware that belief and practice are dialectically related; religious truth is perceived by acting upon it. The relationship between theology and politics is not, then, a one way affair. Theology is formulated by individuals and groups who are already committed, explicitly or implicitly, to political ideas and practices. This is a point to which I shall return.

Anglo-Catholic Resources

In this section I shall point to a number of important practical and theological resources in Anglo-catholicism from which might be developed a significant political theology. It might seem that I am now about to contradict what I have just said about deducing politics from theology. In answer I should say first that I have not denied that theology may influence political theory or practice and secondly that I am concerned here not simply with Anglo-Catholic theology but also with the practical experience of the movement. We may indeed find that W. G. Ward was right when he suggested the priority of the latter: 'It is', he wrote, 'a far better test of a man's real sentiments that he joins the right party, than that he professes the right opinions.'[20] What then are these resources of Anglo-catholicism?

1. The Tractarians asserted the *catholic* nature of the Church. Certainly the Church of England is also the national Church, but only because and in so far as it is part of an international, a world-wide fellowship. Anglo-Catholics cannot, without betraying a fundamental tenet of the movement, lapse into the kind of chauvinism which has characterised much Anglican religion. Nor should they be guilty of the political heresy of ethnocentrism. I quote from Moltmann who illustrates what he means by ethnocentrism in the following words: 'When Columbus discovered America, the question arose whether the Indians were also human, and a bull of Pope Paul III of 1537 declared that the natives were really men . . .'[21] But what could be more truly ethnocentric than Moltmann's own phrase 'When Columbus discovered America'? The very concept of 'discovery' is ethnocentric; it is taken for granted that America hardly existed in any significant sense before it was 'discovered'. Perhaps we should rather say 'when the Indians of the Caribbean discovered Columbus and his men wandering on their beaches . . .'

On the other hand, however, Anglo-Catholics ought to take the nation seriously, for one implication of their sacramentalism should be a recognition that the general needs to be made concrete and specific. Christians ignore at their peril the natural groups and associations which men and woman recognise as units of their loyalty. Family, civic, regional and functional associations have traditions which must be acknowledged and usually respected. Peter Cornwell's recent book *Church and Nation* sets out the relevant considerations in a stimulating and critical way. Anglo-Catholics have every reason to reject the vapid internationalism or Europeanism of much contemporary liberalism.

Added to the theological principle of catholicity, has been a rich experience in the Church overseas – particularly in the 'mission field' as it was called. This, of course, had its dangers and Anglo-Catholics share responsibility for the way in which Christianity was often used as an ideology of colonial domination. But this has not been the whole story, and their overseas experience may be important for the development of a political theology for the future.[22] The relationship between overseas experience and political theology was brought home in a particularly powerful way by Bishop Frank Weston, but also the names of more recent figures like C. F. Andrews, Ambrose Reeves and Trevor Huddleston come to mind.

2. The Tractarians asserted the apostolicity of the Church and of
the Christian faith – the importance of tradition and of continuity,
even of what is called 'prejudice'. Unbiased judgments on matters in
which a person's feelings are deeply involved are not possible, insisted
Ward. The idea that, in order to decide on questions of religion we
must detach ourselves from Catholic tradition and practice – 'that
we must lie on our oars, as it were, till we have become cool' – was
rejected.[23] This respect for history and tradition is likely to lead
Anglo-Catholics to reject a naive utopianism in politics, to be
suspicious of abstract plans and panaceas, to avoid total solutions.
But respect for history has its dangers. Good and constructive
changes are often brought about in the world by men who are
ignorant of history and who are liberated from a debilitating fatalism
which is an occupational hazard of historians. Hegel was well aware
of this.

3. As many of the Tractarians came to accept some notion of the
development of doctrine and consequently the need for growth and
change even in sacred matters, they could hardly reject change in
the secular world. In fact their whole theology witnessed to the
significance of change. As John Davies has recently reminded us,
their sacramental theology spoke of change. They saw sacraments, in
the words of Lionel Thornton, as 'prophetic symbols of a transformed
creation, as well as the fundamental means through which the process
of transformation is normally effected'.[24]

4. A further aspect of the theology and experience of Anglo-catholicism which has political significance is the importance attached to
authority and obedience in the Church. In a famous passage Isaac
Williams wrote:

> if we were to judge from Holy Scripture, of what were the best
> means of promoting Christianity in the world, we should say obedi-
> ence; and if we were to be asked the second, we should say obedi-
> ence; and if we were to be asked the third, we should say
> obedience.[25]

Obedience to Christ was made concrete for the Tractarians in the
obedience due to the bishop. Yet combined with a deep respect for
the authority of the Church in general and of the episcopate in
particular was the experience of existing as a minority in a largely
hostile Church and community. There are periods when Anglo-Catholics (using the term broadly) have been in a majority situation, but
these are rare. The Laudian Church would, perhaps, be an example.
But generally Anglo-Catholics have been a minority, in the common-
wealth period, as nonjurors, as Puseyites and ritualists. The theoretical respect for authority has thus been combined with a practical
need for liberty. As a minority they were often more concerned to

secure toleration from Anglican authorities, preserving what they regarded as the essentials of the faith, rather than attempting to impose their own pattern of life and worship upon the whole Church of England. They have indeed frequently found common cause with Evangelicals against the desire of the majority of Anglicans to secure a highest common factor of religious belief and practice. In ecclesiastical polity they have been pluralists rather than liberals. Recognising the inevitability of conflict in this world, they have often refused to settle for a quiet life.

Nevertheless respect for authority and hierarchy can easily lead to clericalism both in theory and in practice. Incidentally it is interesting to contrast Newman's relatively enlightened views about the role of the laity with those of Pusey.[26]

5. The doctrine of incarnation, common to Anglo-Catholics of both the incarnationalist and redemptionist tendencies, should also help us to recognise that, just as the Son of God himself became subject to the changes and chances of this fleeting world, so all our ideas and beliefs must be understood and interpreted with reference to the context in which they emerge and flourish. By context I do not simply mean the philosophical atmosphere and the ecclesiastical institutions. Too often the dead hand of 'church history' has descended with a resounding slap on the living body of theology. If we are to understand the development of Christian doctrine it must be in the context of history and not of church history. Political and social experience, together with the images and concepts related to this experience, have vitally affected the liturgical, devotional and theological life of the Church. The very images most frequently used of God are drawn from the world of political rhetoric: king , lord, judge; preachers ascribe might, majesty, dominion and power to God and speak of his government of the universe. Even those images which are not political in their primary reference – father, shepherd, spouse – have frequently had definite political connotations.[27]

May it not indeed be the case that these lively images of God, which the Church employs in prayer, devotion and worship, are much more important than the abstract conceptions of infinity, omnipotence, omniscience, omnipresence, with which philosophers of religion are so concerned? Furthermore can we even understand, in anything more than a notional sense, the idea of God as Trinity – a community in which 'none is afore, or after other: none is greater or less than another' – unless we have had some experience of co-operation and community in our social and political life? If for no other reason, those who are anxious about doctrinal orthodoxy ought to be troubled about political structures. This is a very complex subject, but it is not unreasonable to hope that Anglo-Catholics may be among the vanguard of those who are trying to develop new

images of God based on contemporary social and political experience
– relating received tradition to a changing world.

6. Finally the Anglo-Catholic emphasis upon the holiness and transcendence of God has a very definite political significance, calling
into question the claims of all human institutions. The otherworldly
basis of the gospel challenges all totalitarian institutions, for here, in
this order of things, 'we have no continuing city'. The transcendence
of God is also the only satisfactory guarantee that the kind of relativism implied in what I have been saying about the social context
of doctrine does not lapse into a paradoxical denial of all truth. As
Max Horkheimer observes:

> Truth – eternal truth outlasting human error – cannot as such be
> separated from theism. . . While the latest Protestant theologians
> still permit the desperate to call themselves Christians, they subvert
> the dogma whose truth alone would give their words a meaning.
> The death of God is also the death of eternal truth.[28]

1. J. Moltmann, *Religion and Political Society* (New York 1974), p. 19.
2. *University Sermons*, quoted in W. G. Peck, *The Social Implications of the
   Oxford Movement* (New York 1933), p. 68.
3. William Sewell, *Christian Politics* (Oxford 1848), pp. 19ff and 48–9. See
   also id., *Christian Communism* (Oxford 1848).
4. See Conrad Noel, *Jesus the Heretic* (London 1939), p. 27.
5. See David Nicholls, *The Pluralist State* (London 1975), ch. 1.
6. *Oxford Diocesan Magazine*, 15 (July 1983), p. 13.
7. F. D. Maurice, *The Kingdom of Christ*, 3 vols (London 1838), III, p. 76.
   A. G. Hebert, *Liturgy and Society* (London 1935), p. 191. A few pages
   later he writes 'in Nazi Germany we see a great national movement,
   which it is wrong and foolish to meet with mere condemnation, as it
   would be foolish to ignore the success already achieved' (p. 197). The
   sacralising of politics is one of the principal features of totalitarian
   regimes. T. S. Eliot is quoted in E. R. Norman, *Church and Society in
   England, 1770–1970* (Oxford 1976), p. 398. Patrick Curran, 'Signs of
   Hope', *The Cicestrian*, 55 (Autumn 1983), p. 6.
8. See David Nicholls, 'The Totalitarianism of Thomas Arnold', *Review of
   Politics*, 29:4 (1967), pp. 518f.
9. W. G. Peck, *The Social Implications of the Oxford Movement*, p. 86.
10. E. Lyttelton, *The Mind and Character of Henry Scott Holland* (London 1926),
    p. 11. Writing from Christ Church in 1916 Scott Holland pronounced
    that 'God delights in the loveliness of delicate fabrics', vindicating some
    prophetic words in Matt. 11:8!
11. H. S. Holland, *God's City and the Coming of the Kingdom* (London 1897),
    pp. 39 and 7.
12. Eph 6:12.
13. St Augustine, *The City of God*, 14:28.
14. J. N. Figgis, *The Gospel and Human Needs* (London 1909), pp. 18, 116,
    128.

15. id., *Churches in the Modern State* (London 1913).
16. Lord Acton to Mandell Creighton, in L. Creighton, *Life and Letters of Mandell Creighton*, 2 vols (London 1905), I, p. 372.
17. J. Lively, ed., *The Works of Joseph de Maistre* (London 1965), p. 246; cf. also p. 192.
18. E. B. Pusey, *Parochial Sermons*, 3 vols (London 1852), I, pp. 58–9.
19. See David Nicholls, *Fractions: Christian Reflections on Foreign Aid* (London 1982), originally published as an article in *Crucible* (January–March 1982).
20. W. G. Ward, *The Ideal of a Christian Church* (London 1844), p. 519.
21. J. Moltmann, *Man* (London 1974), p. 8.
22. See John Davies, *The Faith Abroad* (Oxford 1983).
23. W. G. Ward, *The Ideal*, pp. 490–1.
24. L. S. Thornton, 'The Meaning of Christian Sociology', *Christendom*, 1:1 (1931), p. 26.
25. I. Williams, Tract 87, *On Reserve in Communicating Religious Knowledge*, pp. 74–5.
26. J. H. Newman, *On Consulting the Laity in Matters of Doctrine* (New York 1961).
27. See David Nicholls, 'Images of God and the State: political analogy and religious discourse', *Theological Studies*, 42 (1981), p. 195ff; and 'Deity and Domination', *New Blackfriars*, 66 (1985), pp. 21–31, 76–81.
28. M. Horkheimer, *Critique of Instrumental Reason* (New York 1974), pp. 47–8; but see also pp. 61–2.

10

Anglo-Catholicism:
some sociological observations*

W. S. F. Pickering

Introducing the problem

'Anglo-catholicism is now a spent-force.' Such an assertion does not come from sociologists for the simple reason that Anglo-catholicism has so far escaped their close, and some might add, irreverent scrutiny. Rather, it is often uttered by the clergy themselves, and not infrequently by those who would wish to be identified with the movement.[1] Within the Church of England most certainly, and perhaps beyond it, the movement was once a force to be reckoned with: today, it has lost its impetus and strength and has become a relic of the past, a glorious relic none the less.

Our purpose is to examine the alleged change that has taken place and attempt to understand such a change with reference to certain aspects of the social and ideological structure of the movement.

The issue of identification

The immediate and essential task is to identify Anglo-catholicism and to separate it from the Oxford Movement. The difficulty here is that no systematic history of Anglo-catholicism has been written; nothing, that is, in any way comparable to the treatment historians have accorded to the Oxford Movement and to the beginnings of ritualistic innovations that followed in its wake. The two movements can be separated and it is erroneous to treat them as one. Further, unless Anglo-catholicism can be seen as a social reality with fairly well-defined boundaries, generalisations about the movement and an attempt to understand it sociologically become a futile exercise.

No one will deny that from the Oxford Movement came Anglo-catholicism. It was in the manner of a mother giving birth to a daughter. And in a relationship of loyalty, the daughter has proudly acknowledged all the mother provided and stood for; and reciprocally, the mother has always supported the daughter and, despite differences of outlook, has always closed ranks in the face of external threats. But although mother and daughter have acknowledged a close affinity, they are two separate beings and Anglo-catholicism is a different creature from the Oxford Movement. Of course social entities are never clear-cut and are never as obvious as physical objects. Social boundaries are nearly always fuzzy but nevertheless they exist and they have to be drawn as distinctly as possible.

I could spend a great deal of time trying to differentiate the Oxford Movement from nineteenth-century ritualism, and again differentiating both the Oxford Movement and nineteenth-century ritualism from Anglo-catholicism. I wish to obviate what might be an interesting task, but one for another occasion, by simply pointing to Anglo-catholicism in all its fullness and self-confidence, to a period when there could be no doubt about what one was referring to. What I mean by Anglo-catholicism is that which can be found in its hey-day, in the period between the two world wars. As a result of the terrible First World War, Anglo-Catholics found themselves free from the legal harassment and social ostracism of earlier decades and achieved a respected and legitimate place within the national Church of which they were members.[2] This began a period that was crowned by the great effervescent assemblies held in the Albert Hall, which were usually preceded or concluded by well attended services in St Paul's Cathedral or the Wembley Stadium, and conducted with rich Catholic ceremonial. Here were times when powerful theological figures dominated the scene, such as Darwell Stone, N. P. Williams, Edwyn Hoskyns, Charles Gore, A. E. Taylor, A. E. J. Rawlinson, and so on. Priests supported the conventions in abundance, often clad in cassock and biretta, and included such outstanding figures as H. A. Wilson, Marcus Attlay, and above all, Bishop Frank Weston. If Anglo-Catholics today wish to recall a glorious past, then that past was clearly the era of the congresses held in 1920, 1923, 1927, 1930 and 1933. In these Anglo-catholicism could be seen to be firmly established as a party within the Church of England. Adherents were ready to stand up and be counted. They consisted of those who were prepared to identify themselves by being present at the congresses, together with all those who were sympathetic to what the meetings stood for.

This triumphalism can in part be seen by the number of people who registered for the congresses. In 1920 the enrolment was eighteen thousand and it continued to rise steadily to seventy thousand in 1933.[3] The 1923 congress was probably the most impressive. The opening service was held on Monday, 10 July, when a thousand robed clergy assembled in St Paul's Cathedral, which was full to the doors and where the service was a high mass without general communion. There were three days of meetings in the Albert Hall, each morning, afternoon and evening. And there were parallel gatherings at the Queen's Hall, where the cost of admission was lower in order to encourage working-class people to attend. (Most of the lecturers gave their talks in both halls.) Opening services were held not only in St Paul's but in about twenty key Anglo-Catholic parishes in central London, where it was reported that the churches were packed to the doors and where the ceremonial was less restrained than in the cathedral.[4] For various purposes, but mainly for 'the spread of the Catholic Faith in England', twenty-five thousand pounds was raised. What greater note of triumph and success could be sounded than in the telegrams that were sent from the congress to the King, the Archbishop of Canterbury, eastern patriarchs and the Pope. Such messages began: 'sixteen thousand present at the Albert Hall send you greetings ... etc.'[5] Immediately after the congress, conferences and services were held in the provinces, Nottingham being one of the most publicised where Bishop Frank Weston graced it with his presence. This great hero of the 1923 congress had also been present in 1920. Here was a bishop, admittedly of Zanzibar, dressed like a monsignor, who, as chairman of the congress, roused listeners on the last day with a speech that became famous in Anglo-Catholic circles. He called for greater devotion to Christ, devotion to Christ in the sacrament of the altar and also devotion to Christ in the tabernacle. He made a highly emotional appeal that Catholics should go out from the congress and in their devotion to Christ 'fight for their tabernacles!'

Some brief word ought to be said about the congress ten years later. Because it was the largest of all the congresses – and may well have been so because it celebrated the centenary of its mother, the Oxford Movement – the number of devotional commemoration leaflets printed was a hundred thousand.[6] The congress extended over a longer period from Sunday to Sunday (9–16 July). The opening solemn evensong mustered fifteen thousand worshippers and the high mass, a week later, drew forty-five thousand people. Both services were held in Wembley Stadium. There were also pilgrimages and outings to various convents, churches and other places of interest in and around London, including Oxford and Littlemore. The greater following which the congress had compared with previous ones was doubtless due to the commemoration of the Oxford Fathers for whom a high mass of requiem was sung in the Albert Hall. It seems most likely that many joined the celebrations who were not devoted or devout Anglo-Catholics but were admirers and perhaps followers of the Oxford Movement. One thing, beyond all shadow of doubt, was that the Anglo-Catholic congress encouraged the celebration of the Oxford Movement throughout the country, not only within the stronghold of its own supporters but within the Anglican Church at large, both at home and overseas. Thus on 9 July there was a special service from Canterbury Cathedral broadcast on the BBC at which the Archbishop preached. The Archbishop of York also preached on the same subject on the same Sunday at a special service in Westminster Abbey. There were celebrations of the Oxford Movement in every diocese in the country, often in the cathedral. There was also a high mass in the main quadrangle of Keble College, Oxford, for which queues were reported to have started two hours before the service. Processions followed the mass to various points in the city and there were also services at the same time at Lincoln College and St Giles's church.

The congresses, particularly the early ones, exhibited, as we have hinted, a feeling of triumph – triumph over the attacks and even persecution of the early days of the 1860s and 1870s, and even later, when heroic priests not only had to put up with Protestant demonstrations but were also prepared to go to prison rather than to deny the beliefs they held dear to heart. However some doubts still lingered in the congresses about the acceptance of Anglo-Catholics, not least in the 1930 congress, when Protestant extremists renewed their attack on what they considered were the enemies of the Church of England.[7] It was also a triumph against those bishops who tried, and tried in vain, to deny Anglo-Catholics their deeply-held faith to make the Church of England in practice what it was in principle, namely, a Catholic Church. But what created so much hope, both in the early days and in the inter-war period, was the fact that Anglo-catholicism was a movement permeated and stirred by a mission. That mission was not just the catholicising of the Church but a mission aimed at the masses who had nothing to do with any church at all. In the latter half of the nineteenth century it was priests like Lowder, Dolling, Wainwright, Stanton, Adderley, and many others, who were deeply concerned in bringing outsiders into the fold. Their aim was not so much to turn Evangelicals and ordinary Church of England people into Anglo-Catholics but to convert to Christianity people who had little idea what it was all about. Anglo-Catholics believed that they possessed the means heretofore unknown in the Church of England of effectively christianising such areas as the slums of the growing English cities, where heretofore the Established Church had failed in its task. Both the Evangelicals and the Anglo-Catholics wanted to make conversions and in this they had a common purpose of wishing to change people to a specific Christian way of life. Anglo-Catholics started parish missions which were often based on a Roman Catholic model.[8] Bishop Weston said that London was 'terribly in the hands of Satan'.[9] A priest writing to the *Church Times* in connection with the 1923 congress held that Anglo-catholicism was becoming 'more and more a movement of the people'.[10] The assumed reason was quite simply that Anglo-catholicism was an evangelising movement which was bringing the people of England 'back to Christ'. And we might add that it was not only in the slum parishes where Anglo-Catholics appeared to be successful, it was also in the mission field where they created their own missionary societies and appeared to be triumphant in overseas work.[11] Indeed in many respects Anglo-catholicism seemed to work better in Africa or Korea than in English villages. In the Anglo-Catholic congresses the bishops who were present were mainly those from overseas, only one or two were English diocesan bishops – a fact that was often lamented by those who organised the congresses.[12] In another direction 'Evangelical' fervour could be noted among the intellectuals of the movement, some of whom, in words of a *Church Times* leading article, held that 'The world can never be saved except by the Catholic religion.'[13]

But what of the distinctive beliefs of Anglo-Catholics which marked them off from other members of the Church of England? Something of their position can be seen in the appeal for money made at the 1933 congress by Fr H. A. Wilson, vicar of Haggerston in the East End of London:

> I make it [the appeal] because I am a Catholic, I believe that in every place where there is the Blessed Sacrament, there is *ipso facto* Christ our Lord available to all who will look for Him. I believe that the Mass is the same whether it is within St Peter's Rome, or St Paul's London – the showing forth, the representation of the One Perfect Sacrifice of Calvary. I believe that Blessed Mary is my Lady as well as the Lady of her Son, that the saints have much in common even with such a one as I know myself to be.
>
> I believe that I belong to the One True Catholic Church, and that the religion revealed to me is the one and only true religion. And I believe in the Church of England. I am not a Roman Catholic. I, too, do not despise or apologize for my Mother, nor do I think it right to joke at her behind her back . . . It is my duty, my profession to hand on that faith to other people . . . to be missionary-hearted, evangelical.[14]

The decline: some reasons for it

The heady days of the 1920s and 1930s have gone. No more congresses of such a gigantic scale have subsequently taken place. An attempt was made to hold a congress in 1948 but it was not seen as a great success. And in 1983, to celebrate the 150th year of the founding of the Oxford Movement, the second congress of Catholic renewal was held in Loughborough in a university hall of residence where six to seven hundred delegates were assembled. The conference had more than its share of uncertainties and self-criticism. Indeed no better crude indicator of the rise and fall of Anglo-catholicism can be found than in comparing the early and late congresses. Further, nearly all the Anglo-Catholic publishing houses have now disappeared and their output of literature is greatly curtailed. The 'Sign Post' series of books written by up-and-coming Catholic-minded theologians at the beginning of the Second World War has not been succeeded by a series of books of such academic stature. The Anglo-Catholic Summer Schools of Sociology, which valiantly attempted to relate Anglo-Catholic thought to social and political thinking, ceased a decade or so after the Second World War. Many who knew the vitality, vigour and determination of Anglo-catholicism fifty or sixty years ago now behold – would it be too strong to say? – a house in ruins. The system has collapsed. What Anglo-catholicism once stood for scarcely exists. It is now to be found only in certain pockets, notably in London, although admittedly Anglo-Catholic clergy do exert considerable power in the General Synod of the Church of England, as for example in forestalling the attempt to create a scheme of unity with certain Protestant churches based on a covenant principle.[15]

Contemporary Anglo-Catholics might seek comfort for the misfortunes of their movement in the suggestion that most churches over the past century or so have suffered from what might loosely be called secularisation. Declining membership, poor attendances at public worship, a general indifference on the part of society at large towards institutional religion, have been the constant worry of church leaders of all denominations. Mustering considerable resources in manpower, finance, enthusiasm and ideas, not least the heroic efforts of many clergy, the churches have been unable to stem the forces of de-christianisation.[16] Even the Roman Catholic Church, once held to be the bastion against secularising pressures, is now suffering like most other churches. It is easy to point to forces which are believed to be pervading the whole of society and which militate against the traditional churches. It is a lazy and facile way, however, of trying to understand particular religious societies or groups in a society where no one can deny general trends towards agnosticism and the rejection of allegiance to religious institutions. And it is not in accordance with the facts. Although many religious groups are declining, others are on the increase and are showing surprising vitality. Within the Anglican Church one has only to point to the growth of Evangelicals, especially those of a fundamentalist outlook. If we move beyond traditional churches and examines parties, sects, or movements, no simple pattern of decline emerges. Again, just to talk about secularising forces and religious indifference is not in itself an explanation, it is merely a description of what is occurring. Why it is occurring and the consequences of what is happening are of greater importance to the sociologist, and one hopes the theologian, than in outlining what is going on. We must understand each group on its own merits and against the social background in which it is set. And therefore in approaching Anglo-catholicism it is necessary to start with the movement itself and to try to see why the ideals and practices have failed to continue to recruit sufficient members to maintain its momentum in earlier decades.

There were those who, even at the height of Anglo-catholicism, foresaw a decline. They were mainly intellectuals who held that belief was a more important component of religion than devotion and ritual. And in the matter of theology, Anglo-Catholics had in their eyes little to offer. Learned though some scholars such as N. P. Williams, Darwell Stone, and earlier, Charles Gore, were, their contributions to theological issues were on the whole limited and concerned in the main with ecclesiological and liturgical matters. And when theologians such as Gore and R. C. Moberly attempted to relate Anglo-Catholic thought to modern learning with the application of *Lux Mundi* in 1889, there were some, for example H. P. Liddon, who were deeply suspicious of the venture. The emergence of modernism in the Roman Catholic Church also saw Anglo-Catholics in an uncertain and defensive position. Alec Vidler was one who became convinced that traditional Anglo-catholicism could not be espoused, despite his early following of it, just because its theological stance was rigid and backward-looking. The distinctive ideology of Anglo-catholicism was to many intellectuals somewhat trivial in the face of growing scientific thought and a reaction against religion. Commenting on the 1923 congress, the editor of the *Record* wondered whether there was 'enough substance' in the movement 'to give it permanence'.[17] It was implied by the writer that the aims of the movement were nothing more than practical ones, summed up, it might be added, in such a slogan as 'it is the mass that matters'. No movement can endure on such a slim ideological stand. Within their own ranks there were plenty of words of warning, not least that the aims of Anglo-catholicism were too narrow. Once more, at the 1923 congress, which has been noted as perhaps the most outstanding of the congresses, Bishop Gore, whose book, *Belief in God*, had just been published, and who was generally revered as one of the great prophets of Anglo-Catholics as well as an intellectual giant, warned the participants against 'the risk of not making it constantly evident that the sacramental institutions are means, not ends; there is only one end, and that is likeness to God'.[18] And in 1932 Sparrow Simpson, himself a firm Anglo-Catholic, was concerned that the movement was losing the ideal of personal self-sacrifice and was showing signs of disunity.[19] The Catholic renewal movement, dating from the mid-1970s, arose from an awareness that the older movement was in some respects *passé* and was on the point of being burned out.[20]

Throughout the history of Anglo-catholicism there have been many who have been generally sympathetic towards the establishing of a Catholic ethos within the Church of England but who could not identify themselves with some of the doctrines, and more likely a number of the practices propagated by Anglo-Catholics. In this way the movement failed to enlarge its ranks by drawing in people who were broadly sympathetic with the principles propagated by the Oxford Movement. The point of divergence centred on the eternal problem of Anglo-Catholics adopting practices and beliefs which

could be firmly labelled Roman Catholic. The prominence of such
ideology and practice was evident in the 1923 congress, where all
caution was thrown to the wind. It was one thing to sing hymns to
the Blessed Virgin Mary in a small mission church in the slums of
London: it was another to do precisely the same thing in the full
gaze of the public and with the implication that this kind of devotion
was at the heart of Anglo-catholicism. Hudson and Dewar, middle-
of-the-road Catholic-minded supporters, wrote of their unhappiness
about what they saw as changes occurring in the 1923 congress where
there was a great deal of devotion and hymn-singing to our Lady in
the Albert Hall and in other venues of the congress. Great uneasiness
was also shown in the telegram sent to the Pope, who was referred
to as 'the Holy Father', and also to 'the assumption that the extra-
liturgical cultus of the Blessed Sacrament (adoration, exposition and
benediction) was the *esse* of the Catholic position'.[21] And certain
words by Bishop Frank Weston were ambiguous and a source of
criticism when he said: 'Take courage, then, the Eastern Patriarch
smiles on you; the Bishop of the Diocese (of London) loves you; the
Holy Father waits.'[22] And critics might also have drawn attention to
the 'text' which dominated the stage of the Albert Hall (as did the
giant crucifix): 'Blessed and praised for evermore be Jesus Christ on
His Throne of Glory and in the most Holy Sacrament of the Altar'.
The Bishop of London, the much beloved Winnington-Ingram, who
was president of the congress, and who was generally sympathetic to
Anglo-catholicism, was nevertheless critical of the programme and
asked that two hymns to the Blessed Virgin Mary should not be
sung. This is how Bishop Frank Weston publicly replied: 'I appeal
to you who reverence our Lady Mary to remember that she is the
Queen of Courtesy, and, out of courtesy to our President, let us deny
ourselves the joy of singing these hymns. (Cheers).'

It is interesting to note in this connection that the *Church Times*,
which for a long time has had the largest circulation of any Anglican
weekly, tried to defend Anglo-Catholics against those who would
criticise them for assimilating Roman Catholic beliefs and practices.
Admittedly the newspaper was mildly critical, but on the whole it
reported the congresses extensively and favourably. Indeed the *Church
Times* was, though less so now, strongly supportive of the Catholic
position within the Anglican Church, and it remains the favourite
newspaper among Anglo-Catholics. Nevertheless to ward off
attacking blows the paper repeatedly reported of the 1933 congress
that in the services 'the Prayer Book was exactly followed'.[23] Doubtless this was done to draw attention away from those aspects of the
congress which savoured of Roman catholicism.

Any attempt to understand or try to explain the decline in Anglo-
catholicism in recent decades would have to take into account
changing historical circumstances in the culture in which Anglo-
catholicism is set. These changes need to be carefully delineated but

the task is too large to be dealt with adequately in what follows. Any historical analysis must be preceded by looking carefully into the nature of Anglo-catholicism itself, that is, to analyse its structure in terms of belief and practice and in doing this it will be shown that it contains a number of structural or positional ambiguities.

Some ambiguities described

I wish to point briefly to three of several structural ambiguities that are inherent in Anglo-catholicism, which followers may fail to see but which are evident to outsiders, or which, if consciously held by members, have to be contained in some non-national way.

The word 'catholic' and the concept of catholicism, when applied to the Anglican Church take on a popular and unique meaning. Despite the achievements of Anglo-catholicism and Tractarianism – and they were very considerable within the Church of England – the movements have not been able to influence British society at large by shifting its general outlook away from the attitude that to be a Catholic means to be a Roman Catholic. The man in the street still knows little or nothing about the idea that the Church of England is Catholic or that the word catholic has any particular implications for the Established Church. That may go as well for a number of people who call themselves Anglican. We must accept the fact that the word catholic retains the general meaning that is directly associated with the Roman Catholic Church. Another way in which it is frequently used, though far less widely, refers to that which is universal, common or world-wide, especially what might be regarded as universal in Christianity. This is also implied by some in the concept of the Roman Catholic Church. The notion of catholic in the phrase Anglo-Catholic can appeal to neither of these meanings, for neither fits. It is admitted that the word catholic has a long history and is full of complexities. One can of course use the word in an obscure sense. What is emphasised here, however, is common usage – that which is found in society at large and emphasises the problems in trying to use it in an Anglican context. When so used insularity of meaning and ambiguity are inevitable.

The Oxford Movement attempted to demonstrate among other things the inherent Catholic foundation of the Church of England, that it was as much a Catholic Church as was the Roman Catholic Church. To justify the position, many Oxford Fathers and those who followed in their footsteps, adopted what was called the branch theory which, simply stated, is that the Church of England is one of several branches of a stem which is seen to be primitive or early catholicism. The problem that faced all those who held to such a theory was that of explaining the dormant catholic foundation of a Church which over many centuries blatantly declared itself to be Protestant, or at

least accepted and put into practice the 'basic truths' of the Reformation. In the struggles of the sixteenth century England aligned
itself not with Catholic countries against Protestant countries but the
other way round. But given the catholic claims of the Church of
England, how is it possible to have a Catholic Church which, while
it may possess the early creeds at the heart of its declared belief
system, clearly has not had a sacramental or liturgical system over
several hundred years which can in any way be compared with what
one would expect in a Catholic Church? The answer given by Anglo-
Catholics and Tractarians is that the Church of England, while
continuing to possess a validly ordained priesthood according to
apostolic succession and never having promulgated any doctrine that
repudiated what is called fundamental Catholic belief, went through
dark days in forgetting its Catholic heritage. In fundamental matters
it had been miraculously preserved despite internal Protestant pressures to deny them. What was needed in the nineteenth century was
the revival of a Catholic consciousness and the presence of a Catholic-
minded clergy who would put into practice the sacramental system
latent in the Anglican Church. Anglo-Catholic clergy responded
speedily and vigorously to the call. It is important to note that much
was achieved in the face of considerable hostility from members of
the Established Church, both clerical and lay. They maintained that
what Anglo-Catholics were doing was either contrary to ecclesiastical
law or to the tradition of their Church, or was fundamentally wrong
in principle. By the time of the First World War Anglo-Catholics
had shown that no law, ecclesiastical or civil, could be used successfully against them. After that war, as we have seen, there was a great
sense of triumph but the realisation of success contained the seeds of
failure. There were many in the 1920s and 1930s who realised that
it was impossible to catholicise the Church so that it possessed that
degree of uniformity in liturgy and in administration of the sacraments that would make it in any way comparable with the Roman
Catholic Church or some similar body, for example the Orthodox
churches. Evangelicals and middle-of-the-road Anglicans would not
be moved further. By the 1930s it was clearly evident that Anglo-
Catholics would have to settle for being a party within a comprehen-
sive Church: there could never be a take-over. This is not to deny
the enormous influence that they, together with the Tractarians, had
exerted over the Church as a whole. Through that influence there
had been a growth of sacramentalism and ritual which entirely transformed public worship and the interior furnishing of churches.
However the influence was not uniform, and varied according to the
outlook of individual clergy.

But given the party status of Anglo-catholicism and all that the
status and ideology stood for, two problems emerge. Can we really
call a church, the Church of England, a Catholic Church, when after
a hundred years or so of great effort to re-establish its alleged Catholic

heritage, there still remains a large number – one might suggest a majority – of those who are members of the Church but who openly deny or make little of such a heritage and certainly do not wish to follow the specific doctrines and practices promulgated by the Anglo-Catholic party? There is no sense of wholeness or universality in matters of belief and in a sacramental system within the Anglican Church as there is within the Roman Catholic Church. We must search out churches, often by esoteric means, where Catholic privileges, as they are called, are to be found.[24] No such problem faces the Roman Catholic. He knows that in every church the mass is celebrated and confessions are heard as a matter of routine. The other sacraments are also invariably administered. Every church practises the 'essentials'. Can any Catholic church admit to such variability as that which is contained within the Anglican Church? It is not so much the question of variability in essential matters between types of Catholic churches, supposing they exist, but within one alleged Catholic Church.

A dilemma that Anglo-catholicism has always faced, but never more so than in the last half-century, is that of an inability to create a distinctive form of catholicism, together with an inability to reform itself from within. The question arises from the problem of implanting a Catholic system into a Church which has had none for well over three hundred years. How does one proceed to catholicise a Church? One response of course is to restore a medieval ecclesiastical way of life as it was thought to have been practised many hundreds of years ago. In order to produce this, research and time are needed. But even if we are able to restore the cult as it was in the Middle Ages, is it not totally unrealistic to return to the past – a past epitomised by village life and maypole dancing? The Tractarians wanted an even more difficult solution, the restoration of the catholicism of the primitive Church.[25] An alternative, which as everyone knows Anglo-Catholics adopted, was to copy the usage of the Roman Church, as was found to exist in Europe in the nineteenth century. This Romanising policy heaped upon the heads of Anglo-Catholics strong criticism and hostility even to the extent of their being held to be Jesuits! But at least such a policy avoided the charge of obscurantism and of having to wait for years of historico-liturgical scholarship in order to introduce some kind of Catholic ethos. Both the missionary situation in England, which called for immediate action to bring into the Church the masses who had grown up in its industrial cities, and the need to demonstrate to the English people at large that the Anglican Church was indeed Catholic, called for a quick, practical response.

Anglo-catholicism could not produce a coherent and universally accepted liturgical system which was on the one hand Catholic and on the other in some way unique to the British scene. But could any party, real or imaginary, within the Church have been successful in such an aim? There existed no authoritative body, such as the synod of recent times, that could have brought about general change. Anglo-Catholics were initially on the defensive and felt that they had to remain within an acceptable and legal framework, that is, to assume the 1662 Prayer Book as the basis of liturgical and devotional worship. Despite all efforts to squeeze every ounce of catholicity out of the book, it could never in the end provide what was required in the eyes of Catholic-minded priests and would always have to be supplemented by other sources. Prayer-Book Catholics tried to establish a unique path by avoiding a slavish imitation of Roman practice, but they have often been swayed more than they are willing to admit by such an influence. While Anglo-Catholics might appeal to the letter of the Prayer Book, they certainly did not reflect the tradition and usage which had been established for several hundreds of years. Within monasteries and convents established by Anglo-Catholics, at weekday services in parish churches, and in the private devotion of priests, the Roman missal and breviary were often followed by Anglo-Catholic clergy and religious. In reporting on the Anglican monks of Nashdom whom he visited in the early 1960s, Paul Ferris said that they told him that they used the Roman missal and that if they 'became Roman Catholics tomorrow, [they] would only change one word in the service: the name of the bishop'. And then in what was a mere playing with words, they said: 'We're a perfectly normal part of the Church of England. We're not High.'[26]

The movement, just because it was a movement and not a Church, had no means of extending and enforcing a sacramental system on priests who would not accept it. It lacked authority of the kind invested in the pope, in church councils, in a synod of bishops, or in a bishop himself. Uniformity could not be produced because there existed no means of enforcing practice on a group or within the Church at large. All efforts to introduce a Catholic system had to rest with individuals. Justifiably it was said of Anglo-Catholic clergy that every man was his own pope and could therefore do precisely what he wanted to.

Uniformity or reform were well nigh impossible among the Romanisers because, although they acted individually, they accepted with little criticism the practices and devotions of the Roman Church. And when Vatican II took place, such priests found themselves in an extraordinary position. Those who had mirrored Roman catholicism either had to follow some, or as many as possible, of the changes that the council decreed, or else they had to openly deny the reforms and continue in their old ways. If they adopted the first policy they would without hesitation play into the hands of those critics who said that they had always studiously accepted everything that Rome taught and practised, irrespective of what it actually was. 'When the pope said jump, they all jumped.' They were suddenly thrust into the embarrassing position of having to argue, in line with Vatican

II, against old practices which they had so slavishly sacralised. If, on the other hand, they rejected the changes demanded by Vatican II and continued in the Counter-Reformation ethos, they would in their own eyes alienate themselves from contemporary Roman catholicism and would be charged with even greater sectarianism by being in the 'Lefebvre wing' of Anglo-catholicism. They would thus become a sect within a sect and supporters of a dying form of catholicism.

The ambiguity over sectarianism

We have just hinted that Anglo-catholicism has qualities which are sectarian. This charge has often been made, but it should be noted that not every party within a larger body is a sect or has sectarian qualities. Anglo-Catholics, however, constitute a group which is indeed sect-like. Most important to note is that Anglo-Catholics often seem to rejoice in their sectarianism and this in many respects under-lines their true quality. They are keen to create lines of demarcation between themselves and others, to speak of 'we' and 'they' even with reference to those within the Anglican Church. The lines are made particularly sharp by Anglo-Catholics establishing their own 'cath-olic' language – 'saying mass', 'Catholic doctrine teaches . . .', 'work in the box', 'fulfilling one's religious obligations', and so on. And the use of titles is just as important. Indeed, if any Anglican calls a priest father, it is as clear an indication as anything else – at least it used to be the case a decade ago – that the person is an Anglo-Catholic. The development of a particular language places Anglo-Catholics in a different category from 'ordinary C. of E. people'. By this means they established their own sub-culture which, to both insiders and outsiders, is seen as being foreign to the general culture which the Church of England has nurtured and in which it is set.

To maintain a sectarian outlook, or to join a sect, however, is not in itself an illogical or ambiguous thing to do. Today, in a highly secular society, anyone who seriously attempts to be a Christian, who professes the creeds and regularly takes part in worship, will be participating in sect-like activities, or even operating within a sect. The churches themselves, by the meagreness of their following, and this includes the Established Church, have much about them that is sect-like. But sects are not to be condemned because they are just sects. Sects of various kinds have always existed. And sects, as Ernst Troeltsch stated decades ago, can become churches. What is ambiguous is to adopt a sect-like position in the name of catholicism. The notion of universality, of being world-wide and embracing people of widely different cultural, social and national backgrounds, is contrary to the notion of adopting a sectarian stance. In one sense, Catholic sects have existed all down the ages, witness the Cathars, the Waldensians, the Old Catholics of the 1870s. In most cases these groups tended to deny Catholic principles and beliefs. Such was the position of the continental Reformers of the sixteenth century. They had no wish to be associated theologically with the Roman Catholic Church. The dilemma of the Anglo-Catholics has been their wish to maintain their own Catholic identity as a party within the Anglican Church, as being the branch of the Catholic Church. They were caught in a trap in that, while claiming to be Catholic, they were forced to adopt sectarian characteristics. Perhaps many of those who have left Anglo-catholicism for Roman catholicism have been very well aware of such ambiguity. Can there be a stronger ecclesiastical dichotomy than Catholic/sect? In short, a Catholic sect is a contradiction in terms.

There is another problem concerning sectarianism which can only be touched on briefly. It is this: sectarianism can often be used as a legitimate means of expressing anger – legitimate at least in the eyes of the actor. What I want to suggest is that there is still at the parish level a particular form of aggression evident among some Anglo-Catholic priests and old-time Anglo-Catholics in which they unleash aggression against the very Church of which they are members, and not surprisingly against protestantism, which is considered next. Sometimes Anglo-Catholics deny the fact that they are members of the Church of England and they wish to denigrate all that is generally associated with that Church. For evidence of this, read some of the novels of Compton Mackenzie, and it can also be found more genteelly expressed in the novels of Barbara Pym.

The ambiguity over the Roman Catholic Church

A third ambiguity within Anglo-catholicism is centred on the presence on its very doorstep of a Church that practises the ideals some Anglicans try to realise but only partially achieve. Over and against Anglo-catholicism stands the formidable Roman Catholic Church. Here *is* the ideal, not found in the recesses of the mind or in the imagination, but as a reality around the corner as it were, with its cathedrals, especially Westminster Cathedral with its new abbeys and convents, with its religiously-based schools, and with its direct links with the Church in Europe, and indeed all around the world. It is Catholic in every sense of the word.

The physical nearness of Roman Catholic churches has seldom been openly recognised by Anglo-Catholics to be a threat, or to put them in an ambiguous position, despite the fact that they represent ideals which Anglo-Catholics can never emulate. Anglo-Catholics might, sometimes seriously, at other times in jest, talk about the 'Italian mission' to England, implying that catholicism is already in the country and that the Church of England, a truly national Church if ever there was one, has, through the efforts of Anglo-catholicism, the responsibility for the nurture of the Catholic faith in England. The quip about the 'Italian mission' makes those who use the phrase a laughing stock rather than those who are the object of ridicule. The phrase can never be taken seriously, and although it points to a love-hate relationship, the amount of hate on the part of Anglo-Catholics has been minimal. Rather, it indicates a love-jealousy relationship.

Anglo-Catholics, in contrast to Evangelicals, have never vigorously attacked the Roman Church. How could they, when that Church embodies so many of their ideals? Of course, it was sometimes criticised for its Petrine claims, for papal infallibility, for belief in the Assumption of the Blessed Virgin Mary. Here were the only differences between 'them' and 'us'. 'And don't let us emphasize these too much!' This overall attitude towards the Church of Rome is evident in the popular book by W. L. Knox, *The Catholic Movement in the Church of England*, published in 1923. Wilfred Knox was never as attracted to Rome as his younger brother Ronald, but, interestingly enough, in this book which is an apologetic for Anglo-catholicism, his criticism of strongly Romanising tendencies in Anglo-catholicism is put in small print in a footnote.[27] In a gentlemanly kind of way, Knox appears to say, 'I'm very sorry but I have to make a minor point of criticism of those Anglo-Catholics who slavishly follow Roman Catholic doctrines and practices.'

But there was another reason for silence where there might have been criticism. In the general hope for the reunion of Christendom which began to emerge in the Church of England and Free churches in the late nineteenth century, many Anglo-Catholics, who were great supporters of reunion, yearned for one thing only – unity with the Roman Church. The yearning was seen by some to be obsessive.[28] Such hopes, voiced in the 1920 congress, were heightened by the successful instigation of the Malines Conversations, which were held between 1921 and 1925. It was politically undesirable, even if there was the slightest wish to do so, to attack with determination the very people one hoped to join hands with.

Not only did Anglo-Catholics fail to criticise the Roman Church on matters of basic doctrine, they never considered critically and extensively the question of persecution, the practices of missionaries overseas, as in the case of Mexico, the Index, papal measures against liberalism, democracy and modernism, birth-control, mixed marriages, and so on. In reading Anglo-Catholic literature one gains the general impression that nearly everything the Roman Catholic Church did at every level of its structure was right, and that by contrast Anglicans had done much that was wrong. In comparing themselves with Roman Catholics, Anglo-Catholics were always apologetic when they referred to their Church, conceding points in a rather masochistic way, rather than underlining the advantage and superiority of their own position. Thus Wilfred Knox could write:

> Anglicans have always been handicapped by the fact that they make no claim to the exclusion of all other religious bodies in the one true Church . . . against this claim Romans have the advantage of a clear-cut logical system . . . They are thus able to point to a visible centre of Christian unity: and at the same time the modern developments of Papal authority make it apparently easy to supply an authoritative answer to any question of controversy that may be raised at any given moment.[29]

Anglo-Catholics thus saw in the Roman Catholic Church, at worst, a Church that needed some slight reform but no more than what we might call today 'a cosmetic change'.

The only 'anti-feelings' that Anglo-Catholics showed were those directed, often with considerable vehemence, against protestantism, and so often that form of protestantism found in the Church of England. Unlike the Oxford Fathers, Anglo-Catholics wished to distance themselves as far as possible from Protestants and, indeed, one of the hallmarks which distinguishes Anglo-Catholics from Tractarianism is their attitude towards protestantism. Thus Fr Andrew, the saintly Anglican religious who never, it appears, was attracted by the Roman Catholic Church, wrote: 'I was, as you know, once a Protestant.'[30] Yet he had been born and nurtured in the Anglican Church! Thus the heritage of the Reformation Fathers was the *bête noire* of Anglo-Catholics. Any stick was used to beat it and they readily marshalled arguments to show the failure of Protestant doctrine, its lack of liturgy, and its feeble pastoral concern.[31] And protestantism was seen not only as religious infidelity but the cause of many social evils, the break-up of Christendom, the rise of the secular State, in short the root of secularisation itself. Part of such an attitude might be attributed to the English and Anglican disease of showing very little interest in church affairs on the Continent. Apart from one or two exceptions, few English theologians had any contacts at all with theologians in France or Germany. And the English knew very little about what was going on in the Roman Catholic Church in, say, France during the nineteenth century and in its relation to the State. Nor were they aware of what went on behind the scenes in Catholic parish life, so that it was very easy to take the arm-chair attitude and to examine doctrines on paper without seeing how they were put into practice.

A lack of criticism against the Roman Church on the one hand, and an onslaught on Protestant churches on the other, meant that the boundaries around Anglo-catholicism were strongly defined on one flank but were very flabby on the other. Anglo-catholicism failed to create socially adequate lines of demarcation. Social boundaries are generally upheld by positive and negative sanctions, by promulgating a strong, positive ideology and at the same time projecting a negative ideology against a potential rival. Groups most successful in maintaining their position, like the Roman Catholic Church, are those which have strenuously utilised both approaches. Other factors may be important but unless there exists some process by which a potential rival is contained, social identity is considerably weakened.

One might briefly mention at this point conversions to Roman catholicism of those who, before 'going over', were Anglo-Catholics. This is an important and extensive topic and needs to be fully explored, not least because it directly relates to the structural ambiguity of Anglo-catholicism. Suffice it to say that large numbers of conversions – large in Anglican eyes at least – of those who trod the well-worn path from high Anglicanism to Roman catholicism greatly debilitated the Oxford and Catholic movements. Sparrow Simpson called the losses 'an indescribable calamity'.[32] Beginning in the mid-1840s with Newman and a few of his disciples before him, the path has been largely trodden by clergy, some of whom rose to great prominence in the Roman Church, such as Manning, Newman, Ronald Knox, C. C. Martindale and B. C. Butler. It has been estimated that between 1833 and 1933 alone a thousand clergy crossed the divide.[33] And there were a number of influential or intellectual laymen such as Chesterton, the Sitwells, Sir H. Slessor, Compton Mackenzie, and so on. The Roman Catholic Church in England thus found a valuable vein of recruitment which they had never anticipated or sought to discover. For the Church of England, and particularly the Anglo-Catholic party, the effect was totally negative in three ways. One, there was the loss of important leaders and thinkers at a time when the Church was facing the forces of secularisation and was in great need of as much manpower in terms of clergy and intellectuals as it could muster. Two, the result meant that the opponents of Anglo-catholicism had the pleasure of seeing their prophecies fulfilled. The logical outcome of Anglo-catholicism was there for all to see! What further need is there of argument? Three, it spread fear and uncertainty within the ranks of Anglo-Catholics as members wondered whether or not they should follow suit, or as they speculated about whether their friends and heroes would be crossing what they saw as the thin line of the Roman divide. Hostility from Protestant-roused mobs, censure by bishops, even the prospect of prison, were sufferings to be welcomed for the sake of truth and opportunities for identification with the martyrs. But people taking a short-cut to the ideal, deserting a sinking ship, gave rise to insecurity and to an undermining of morale.[34] This was all the more evident when conversions meant denying before God the errors of one's ways within a Church formerly held to be Catholic and an instrument of God's grace.

Conclusion

In what has been said, some evidence has been given to support the contention that Anglo-catholicism as a party within the Anglican Church has undergone a serious decline from a peak which occurred in the 1920s and 1930s. In order to set the stage to understand such a decline, attention has been drawn, not so much to particular historical factors operating in the ecclesiastical and social world surrounding Anglo-catholicism, as to the positional or structural factors within Anglo-catholicism itself. It is precisely here that one has to begin the process of moving towards an explanation.

By pointing to certain structural aspects of a social entity, the parameters of movement in which an individual can operate are disclosed. Such aspects reveal the possibilities of change both to the structure itself and also changes in the direction an individual may take. Structure implies logic and rationality. Nevertheless all social structures contain elements of illogicality or irrationality. One of the tasks of the sociologist is to show the presence of such jagged and ambiguous elements. Certain structures contain more inner stress than others and by pointing to some of the positions deliberately adopted by a group, one can observe how such positions may give rise to tension and intellectual difficulty. Tension appears just because a position may contain elements that conflict with others. Some individuals may find that the tensions cannot be solved in themselves or contained within themselves and therefore have no option but to leave the group, where that is possible. Again, the existence of ambiguity visible to an outsider may prevent him or her joining the group. Seldom do people willingly embrace ambiguity and tension, unless they can see advantages of another order.

In one sense structure is well nigh timeless; certainly it refers to large periods of time. Clearly a more exact explanation of changes within a group comes with the introduction of historical factors, of particular events and occasions, but these only make sense when they are related to the structure of the group itself. Such factors do not imply determinism. Rather, a structural explanation offers a framework in which other factors operate. Individuals are subject to these factors but the structure marks out limitations which surround people and demonstrates the potential courses of action that are open to them.

Beyond the three positional ambiguities that have just been posited, namely, that the concept of Anglo-catholicism, the sectarianism of the movement, and the immediate presence of the Roman Catholic Church, stands an overriding ambiguity which dominates them all. The Oxford Movement attempted to establish a theological position that the Church of England was Catholic in nature and origin. Given that, the next thing was to translate the theology into practice, to work it out in the parish situation. It was precisely this problem that the Anglo-Catholics responded to with such great vigour, and in which they, together with the Tractarians, completely changed the face of the Established Church. Their answer gave rise to a number of ambiguities. The level of catholicisation that they introduced was both uneven and in many cases unacceptable to much of the population. But are Anglo-Catholics really to be blamed or criticised for what they did? Is not the issue much deeper than they realised, caught up as they were in such enthusiasm? Might it not be argued that they failed not so much in the answer that they gave but by reason of the very problem set by the Oxford Movement which they embraced? Was it not an insoluble problem? Can a Church with approximately four hundred years of history in which protestantism has played such a prominent, decisive, but not exclusive part – can a Church which is a veritable *mélange* – ever be catholicised in a genuine or widely accepted sense?

1. See A. Wilkinson, 'Requiem for Anglo-Catholicism', *Theology*, 81 (1978), pp. 40–5.
2. See A. R. Vidler, *Scenes from a Clerical Life: an autobiography* (London 1977), p. 18; A. Wilkinson, *The Church of England and the First World War* (London 1978), pp. 175ff.
3. *Church Times*, 21 July 1933.
4. See ibid. 13 July 1923.
5. ibid.
6. For details of the congress, see ibid. 21 July 1933.
7. See ibid. 4 July 1930, 11 July 1930.
8. J. Kent, *Holding the Fort: studies in Victorian revivalism* (London 1978), ch. 7.
9. *Church Times*, 12 July 1923.
10. ibid.
11. See E. R. Morgan, ed., *Essays, Catholic and Missionary* (London 1928).
12. See *Church Times*, 11 July 1930.
13. ibid. 14 July 1933; see also A. H. Rees, *The Faith in England* (London 1941), pp. 184–5.
14. *Church Times*, 21 July 1933.
15. For other ways of documenting the decline, see Wilkinson, 'Requiem for Anglo-Catholicism'.
16. See W. S. F. Pickering, ed., *A Social History of the Diocese of Newcastle 1882–1982* (Stocksfield and London 1981), ch. 7.
17. Quoted in *Church Times*, 20 July 1923.
18. ibid. 13 July 1923.
19. W. J. Sparrow Simpson, *The History of the Anglo-Catholic Revival from 1845* (London 1932), pp. 289ff.
20. *The Times*, 9 March 1983.
21. *Church Times*, 20 July 1923.
22. ibid. 13 July 1923.
23. ibid. 21 July 1933.
24. Sir Henry Slessor, *Through Anglicanism to the Church* (London 1948), p. 12.
25. Sparrow Simpson, *History of the Anglo-Catholic Revival*, p. 11.

26. P. Ferris, *The Church of England* (London 1964), pp. 196–7.
27. W. B. Knox, *The Catholic Movement in the Church of England* (London 1923), pp. 238–9 n.1.
28. P. Fitzgerald, *The Knox Brothers* (London 1977), p. 159.
29. Knox, *The Catholic Movement*, p. 194.
30. K. E. Burne, *The Life and Letters of Father Andrew*, SDC (London 1948), p. 143.
31. See A. H. Rees, *The Faith in England* (London 1941).
32. Sparrow Simpson, *History of the Anglo-Catholic Revival*, p. 289.
33. S. Leslie, *The Oxford Movement, 1833–1933* (London 1933), p. 154.
34. W. Carey, *Conversion, Catholicism, and the English Church* (London 1923), p. 80.

11

Anglicanism in Popish Dress*

Peter Toon

In *Evangelical Theology: a response to Tractarianism* (1979) I gave an account of nineteenth-century Evangelical attitudes towards Tractarianism/Anglo-catholicism. This led me to think deeply about such concepts as 'Evangelical' and 'Catholic' and 'Catholic Evangelical'. In a popular book, *The Anglican Way: Evangelical and Catholic*, I presented the following thesis. Anglicans are called to be wholly Evangelical and wholly Catholic all the time. Not Catholic in order and Evangelical in doctrine, or some other half-and-half combination; and not symbiosis – Catholic and Evangelical living off each other: but wholly Evangelical and wholly Catholic in all that we are and do. For example, a bishop is to be both in the apostolic succession and to embody the gospel in his life and preach it in his sermons, addresses and talks.

Today within the Anglican communion there is a spirit of friendliness and co-operation between those who belong to the Evangelical and Anglo-Catholic schools of churchmanship/doctrine. Because both schools agree on so much that is fundamental – for example trinitarian and christological dogma – then they may be seen as two closely related, yet different groupings. From the inside we know that while there is so much that is shared – a high view of the sacred Scriptures, the truth in the Catholic creeds, the importance of liturgy – and so much that needs to be opposed – heresy and immorality in Church and society – there are certain doctrines and principles that do distinguish and separate the two schools of churchmanship. What divides includes doctrines of soteriology and ecclesiology, and aspects of ceremonial and ritual.

My first task is to highlight the Evangelical response to the birth and growth of the Tractarian Movement, remembering that in 1840 about a fifth of the clergy of the Church of England and Ireland could be described as Evangelical. When this is done, I shall ask: 'What is at the heart of the Evangelical criticism of the Tractarian doctrine and ceremony?' And: 'Is the movement from Evangelical faith to Anglo-Catholic faith simply a growth in spirituality or does it involve a major change of emphasis (a paradigm change)?'

Evangelical criticism

By the end of 1833 the editors of the two most important Evangelical publications – the twice-weekly newspaper, the *Record*, and the monthly magazine, the *Christian Observer* – were suspicious of the Oxford Tract writers and their views. Four months were enough to discern the character of the new movement. The *Record* had this to say on 5 December:

> We must confess the surprise was extreme and the sorrow poignant with which we read the tracts of the Apostolical Society at Oxford, extracts from which appeared in our last number. Had we not read them with our own eyes it would have been difficult to persuade us that such effusions could have escaped, at any time, from the pens of Protestant clergymen, more especially at such a time as the present, and with the professed object, and that most sincerely entertained, of defending the Church in her great peril.

A strong doctrine of apostolic succession worried the editorial staff of this newspaper, for they were Calvinists. The *Christian Observer* stated: 'We see a Society formed at Oxford, the members of which, professing themselves to be the most orthodox upholders of the Church, have begun to scatter throughout the land publications which, for bigotry, Popery, and intolerance surpass the writings even of Laud and Sacheverell.'[1]

In response to these and later comments in the *Christian Observer*, a magazine that had been founded in the days when the Clapham sect was such an important force in English religion, Newman told the editor, Mr Wilks, 'the general conduct of your magazine towards the Tracts has been an exception to its mildness and urbanity'.[2]

Not all Evangelicals were against the Tracts between 1833 and 1835. Some who read them were impressed or pleased; others however suspected that they were moving in the direction of Rome, the products of the devil as he appeared as an angel of light. And for short periods in these early days common enemies brought together all those who had high views of Scripture, the Catholic creeds, the Prayer Book and the Articles of Religion. On two Oxford occasions – the controversy over subscription to the Articles at matriculation in 1834–5, and the appointment of Dr Hampden as Regius Professor of Divinity in 1836 – the differences were forgotten as the Tractarians and Evangelicals (with others) fought for what they saw as the biblical and Catholic heritage of the Church of England. So there was little controversy in 1834–5.

But 1836 saw the fears of December 1833 revived. One of the distinguished leaders of the Evangelicals, Edward Bickersteth, secretary of the Church Missionary Society, let it be known in January 1836 that he was a firm opponent of Tractarianism, even though he was also known as a great reader and lover of the early

Fathers. In his *Remarks on the Progress of Popery* (1836) he had this to say:

> A highly respectable, learned and devout class of men has arisen up at one of our Universities, the tendency of whose writings is departure from Protestantism, and approach to papal doctrine. They publish 'tracts for the times' and while they oppose the most glaring part of popery – the infallibility of the Pope, the worship of images, transubstantiation and the like – yet, though the spirit of the times is marked by the opposite fault, the very principles of popery are brought forward by them under deference to human authority, especially that of the Fathers: overvaluing the Christian ministry and sacraments and undervaluing Justification by faith. With much learning and study of the Fathers, with great apparent, and in some cases real, devotion and a devotedness ascetic and peculiar, they seem . . . to open another door to the land of darkness and shadow of death, where the Man of Sin reigns.[3]

It is important to notice the association of ideas: in a book that is primarily about Roman catholicism he refers to Tractarianism. If we try to understand the way in which Protestants in Northern Ireland (or in the Bible Belt, USA, or in strict Afrikaaner 'Calvinism') think and talk about Roman catholicism, then we have some indication of how Protestants in England – respectable Anglicans and dissenters – talked and thought about 'popery'. Anything which appeared to be contributing to the cause of the pope, that 'Man of Sin', was opposed with a deep sense that God, for Christ's sake, required such opposition.

From 1836 onwards Evangelicals paid careful attention to all publications from the Tract writers and their friends, and they began to see the old medieval Roman doctrines (discarded, as they believed, at the Reformation by the Church of England) being revived in slightly different dress, but certainly being revived in the 1830s. For example, the reviewer of Newman's *Prophetical Office* (1837) had this to say:

> There is so much zeal for the prosperity of that Church of which Mr Newman is himself a member and a minister, that it is impossible not to lament the failure of his enterprise in its defence. The chief error, ingrained, interwoven, incorporated with his whole treatise is the deference to be paid to the authority of *human* writings and the disparagement of the *sacred* records. Far as this last may be from the intentions, and even from the contemplations of the author, it meets us in every page of his volume, and unless we are greatly deceived, will prove noxious to his own spiritual health.[4]

'The deference to be paid to the authority of human writings' was a theme taken up in printed sermons and books. The two most significant publications were the lengthy *Ancient Christianity* by Isaac

Taylor, author of the *History of Enthusiasm* and a nonconformist who became an Anglican layman, and *The Divine Rule of Faith and Practice* by William Goode the younger, rector of St Antholin, Watling Street.

Taylor attempted to take the lid off the ancient Church to reveal all its weaknesses and corruption and to show that it was just as bad as the medieval Latin Church. Recognising that he had to confine himself to a specific yet central subject which 'must be well adapted to the general purpose of bringing into view, vividly and distinctly, the general, and the specific merits and faults of the time in question', he chose the practices of celibacy and virginity. He attempted to prove that they were found from early times in eastern, African and western churches and so came within the general application of the rule of Vincent of Lérins. It was his argument:

> That the notions and practices connected with the doctrine of the superlative merit of religious celibacy, were at once the causes and the effects of errors in theology, of perverted moral sentiments, of superstitious usages, of hierarchical usurpations; and that they furnish us with a criterion for estimating the GENERAL VALUE OF ANCIENT CHRISTIANITY; and, in a word, afford reason enough for regarding, if not with jealousy, at least with extreme caution, any attempt to induce the modern church to imitate the ancient church.[5]

He was convinced that the medieval practices of celibacy and virginity were no worse than, and could even have been an improvement on, the system of the age of the Council of Nicea. Certainly Taylor overstated his case but it was not without substance.

Goode was a first-rate scholar and, among other important areas, he sought to show that the Rule of St Vincent – *quod semper, ubique et ab omnibus* – could not be used as the Tractarians claimed. There was just not enough information available to use it fruitfully of the first three centuries. The only infallible rule of faith is the sacred Scripture, he maintained, and the best interpreter of Scripture is Scripture.

What, then, is the value of tradition? Goode asserted that 'the testimony of the early Fathers respecting facts and practices of which their sense were cognizant, is sufficient to assure us, that such facts and practices took place in their time in the Primitive Church'. And he continued by maintaining that

> the usage of the Primitive Orthodox Church from the Apostolical times (as far as it can be ascertained) may justly be taken as a guide to show us, how rites and practices enjoined in Scripture are to be carried into effect; and also, to a certain extent, in its general rites and practices, that is, so far as to recommend them to our attention, and perhaps to justify modern Churches in following them, inasmuch as it is not probable, that, from the very first, the

Orthodox Church should have adopted a superstitious or improper usage.

Developing this he agreed that in such matters as the keeping of the Lord's day, the practice of infant baptism, the regular Eucharist and the threefold order of the ministry, the value of tradition was to confirm what a careful study of Scripture reveals. In other areas where there is no specific scriptural warrant – such as the sign of the cross in baptism – each national Church, having the authority to decree what rites and ceremonies are to be in use, may follow primitive practice as long as any such practice is not required as necessary to salvation.[6]

Having entered into a debate over the question of tradition it is not surprising that there was also a debate over justification. It came about in this way. The contents of Pusey's Tracts *On Baptism* (1836–7) were described in the *Christian Observer* as based upon 'the darkest ages of Popery when man had debased Christianity from a spiritual system'. Indeed such were Pusey's views that it was suggested that 'the learned Professor ought to lecture at Maynooth or the Vatican', rather than in Protestant Oxford. Mr Wilks asked: 'How could Pusey remain a C. of E. clergyman and hold views at variance with the Articles and Homilies?'[7]

Newman responded to the challenge from the editor and published two letters in the *Christian Observer*, which later appeared as Tract 82. Commenting, the editor referred to the 'character and evils of the system inculcated in the Tracts' and confessed that they were 'anti-evangelical, anti-Protestant, and a snare of our ghostly enemy to impede the progress of the pure Gospel of Christ and to endanger the souls of men'.[8] He proceeded to issue a challenge to Newman to come clean on justification. Newman responded, not by sending a third letter but by beginning a series of lectures in St Mary's Church, Oxford. They were published as *Lectures on the Doctrine of Justification*.[9] Newman recognised that within the Protestant tradition there was the strong conviction that the Church stands or falls by its adherence to the biblical doctrine of righteousness and faith. So, using his patristic knowledge and skill, he lectured and wrote on the biblical doctrine of justification.

Having read the *Lectures* the editorial writer of the *Record* lamented:

Who has read *Newman on Justification*, himself having been given of God to receive the doctrine in its Scriptural simplicity and fulness, without lamenting over the dark conceptions of the man, and being led afresh to confess that till God teaches, darkness broods over the human mind, whether Greek or barbarian, in relation to the essentials of Gospel truth.[10]

And of course the old western doctrine of justification as presented by Newman in patristic and biblical dress was attacked in printed sermons and books.

It is reasonable to call it 'old' and 'western' because, despite Newman's creative use of the teaching of the Greek Fathers, he still maintained that the *formal* cause of justification is the presence of the Holy Spirit in the soul, and that the meaning of justification is primarily (not solely) 'to make righteous'. In contrast, the Protestant tradition spoke with one voice to state that the formal cause of justification is the external righteousness of the exalted mediator, Jesus Christ. Newman rightly desired to unite the declaration of God in heaven concerning the placing of a sinner in a right relationship with himself and the impartation of the divine life to the soul of that sinner. In practice however his emphasis was on the latter, and therefore to his contemporaries it appeared that he was merely presenting, in another form, the Tridentine doctrine. It will be interesting to see whether the present Anglican/Roman Catholic commission finds Newman's presentation of justification a viable point for unified thinking.

From 1837 onwards there was also growing suspicion in Evangelical ranks, often informed by exaggerated reports of what was happening at Littlemore or in Oxford college chapels, as to Tractarian decorations of chapels, use of vestments and ritual/ceremonial. In August 1837 the *Christian Observer* carried a heading: 'Unauthorised Innovations at Oxford'. The contest, it was made clear, was not about mere externals but against anti-Protestant principles: The editor explained as follows:

> We are not over-scrupulous about ecclesiastical ceremonies, provided all things be done decently and in order; but ceremonies unusual or unauthorised ought to be discountenanced were it only upon the ground of irregularity; and the particular observances [described by Peter Maurice] are peculiarly to be deprecated because they are part and parcel of a doctrinal and ecclesiastical system which tends to subvert the pure Gospel of Christ and the foundations of the Protestant Church. We cannot hear without just alarm of Fellows of Colleges crossing themselves at particular parts of the service, as if they were in a mass-house, instead of a Protestant academical chapel; of the ostentatious display, inside and outside of the churches, of crosses, triangles, doves and other decorations, in a manner unusual in Protestant places of worship . . . of side tables introduced into chancels for the attendants to place the bread and wine upon . . . and even in the University Church itself . . . of Mr Newman's accompanying the administration of the Lord's Supper with unprescribed bowings, approachings and retirings.[11]

So worried was John Sumner, the Evangelical bishop of Chester, that he advised his nephew not to attend the University Church where Newman was!

Of course, the Evangelical criticism was sometimes directed at the excesses of the younger and wilder members of the Tractarian movement. Every cause has its cranks and the Tractarian had its select number. But, this said, the Tractarians were not careful enough in the way they described the Protestant Reformation of the sixteenth century. That Newman and Keble as editors allowed the immature comments of Froude on the Reformation to be printed in his *Remains* (1838–9) was a piece of naivety or stupidity, for such comments could only inflame the feelings of the majority of Church of England members, lay and clerical. Let it not be forgotten that the Martyrs Memorial of Oxford stands as a monument, not only to Evangelical commitment to the principles of the English Reformation but also to the commitment of many high churchmen and others of no particular churchmanship to the same principles. So also the publications of the Parker Society.[12] While Evangelicals were disgusted by the apparent rejection by the Tractarians of the principles of the Reformation and by the refusal to see anything wrong with late medieval Catholic doctrine and practice, they were not alone in their disgust. Indeed it was in 1840–2 when high churchman and Evangelical churchman firmly joined hands that new designations began to appear like 'Evangelical high churchmen' and 'high-church Evangelicals'.[13] The fact is that most remaining traditional high churchmen felt nearer to the doctrines of the Evangelicals than to the developed Tractarian teaching. And it was William Goode, the leading Evangelical scholar, who republished in 1843 the treatises on the doctrine of the Church by the 'Standard' high church divines, Bishop Sanderson and Dr Thomas Jackson.

We move on to Tract 90, which aimed to show the 'Catholic' principles of the Thirty-Nine Articles. Evangelicals joined in the cries of horror and added to them in sermons, tracts and books. One notable Evangelical lady, Charlotte Elizabeth, considered that Tract 90 contained 'the development of that foul conspiracy, against our church, our Bible and our souls'. A year later the new Professor of Poetry, James Garbett (who had defeated the Tractarian Isaac Williams in the vote in Convocation) gave the Bampton Lectures. He surveyed the Tractarian publications and declared:

> The system is Romanism; not partially, but essentially; not *yet* Romanism, indeed, as historical recollections have expressed it to be; not Romanism in *all* its palpable and revolting incongruities to the heart and understanding. But – Romanism, as it has, in all ages, represented itself to the young and to the devout – Romanism, as it is when purified by elevated feelings, and minds originally trained in Scripture truth – Romanism, as it combines with itself all that is grand and beautiful in art, specious in reason and

seductive in sentiment – Romanism, which may be safe in those scripturally-trained minds who have presented it to themselves and to the world in this beautified shape – but Romanism, still perverting the truth of the Gospel while it decorates it – Romanism, which though it looks paternally and benignly in the amiable spirits of its present advocates, involves principles ever fatal to human liberty and progression – Romanism, with the establishment of whose theory the Articles of the Church of England cannot co-exist, and whose unseen and unavowed operations in *practice* will paralyse her spiritual power and destroy the Church of Christ, by substituting human forms for her Prophet, Priest and King.[14]

Garbett held that the key to Tractarianism was in Tract 90 and the unfolding of the system was to be found in the *British Critic*, which conveyed Tractarian ideas.

By the time that Newman had left the Church of England in 1845 Evangelicals were in controversy with Tractarians in these areas:

1. The relationship of the Bible and tradition.
2. The doctrine of justification and its relation to baptism.
3. The nature of the Church of God.
4. The validity of non-episcopal ordination to the presbyterate.
5. The relation of regeneration to the sacrament of baptism.
6. The presence of Christ in the Eucharist.
7. The interpretation of the formularies and canons of the Church with respect to both doctrine and ritual.

Further doctrinal controversies were to come over the 'sacrifice of the Eucharist' and the nature of the ordained priesthood. Then of course there were the later famous ritualistic controversies and lawsuits in which five Tractarian clergy preferred to go to prison rather than obey the law and give up their 'Catholic practices'.

Take the case of Bishop Ryle, the Church Association, and James Bell-Cox of St Margaret's, Liverpool. Bishop Ryle did not really know how to handle Bell-Cox and was under powerful pressure from a local doctor, James Hake, a well-known Protestant, and the Church Association to allow prosecution. In the end the prosecution went ahead and the story behind it, and of it, was told in detail by the Liverpool papers.[15] Here is the list of complaints that James Hake made, and they may be taken as the regular things of which Evangelicals made complaint in the late Victorian period:

1. Lighted candles in church when not required.
2. Elevation of the paten in Holy Communion.
3. Mixing water and wine in the chalice.
4. Prostration of the priest during the prayer of consecration.
5. Bowing towards the crucifix on the communion table.
6. Making the sign of the cross while giving the elements to the communicants.

7. Wearing vestments.
8. Singing or saying the 'Agnus Dei' after the prayer of consecration.
9. Standing with the back to the people during the administration of Holy Communion.
10. Obscuring the manual acts.
11. Ceremonial washing of the cup.
12. Kissing the Gospel.

Many of these things are now common features in Anglican eucharistic worship but only a few of them would be found in Evangelical churches today.

Facing questions

What is at the heart of this Evangelical criticism? To say it is mere bigotry is to speak without knowledge or wisdom. Evangelicals of the Victorian period knew that they were encountering teaching and practices in the Church of England which were, to say the least, novel. They looked at this teaching and practice through spectacles that were manufactured within the Protestant tradition – a tradition moulded by the sixteenth-century formularies of the Church, by Foxe's *Book of Martyrs*, by seventeenth-century Puritans and by eighteenth-century evangelicals (William Romaine, Thomas Scott, and others). They believed that the English Church of the Elizabethan Settlement was truly the embodiment of a reformed catholicity and they regretted the expulsion of the nonconformists in 1660–2. Nevertheless they believed that the post-1662 Church of England was a Protestant church, with a confession of faith, a prayer-book and an ordinal which embodied genuine reformed faith. They were wholly opposed to the system of belief and practice known as popery or Romanism and thus they were also opposed to all attempts to encourage or abett it.

So what was at the root of the strong, critical, Evangelical response to Tractarianism/Anglo-catholicism? Was it a basic, inbred fear of popery and Romanism? Was it fear lest the good old Church of England would lose its character as a reformed Catholic Church? Was it fear lest the new, growing party would prevent the growth of the Evangelical party within the national Church? Was it the result of a basic refusal to think again about the purpose of the Church and of the will of God for it? Were the Evangelicals so set in their ways that they did not want to be disturbed? Was it that they did not want the Lord to give more light from his holy Word? Did they seriously undervalue the meaning and place of tradition in the Church? To these and to similar questions the answer is a qualified 'yes'. But the truth of the matter is rather deeper than saying a modified 'yes' to these questions.

Deep in the Evangelical ethos and at the heart of the Evangelical experience lies the theme of salvation by grace through faith. In other words justification by faith – a right relationship with God in and through faith and by Christ – whether articulated in precise theological terms or in the imprecise style of the popular language of Zion, is the basis for the Evangelical approach. And as a corollary there goes the doctrine of regeneration by the Holy Spirit – new birth, being born again/from above. John Wesley held that:

> if any doctrines within the whole compass of Christianity may be properly termed 'fundamental' they are doubtless these two – the doctrine of justification and that of the new birth: the former relating to the great work which God does for us, in forgiving our sins; the latter, to the great work which God does in us, in renewing our fallen nature.[16]

This is why it was in reaction to Pusey's Tract *On Baptism*, with its teaching on baptismal (= sacramental) regeneration, that the editor of the *Christian Observer* made the challenge concerning justification by faith. The new birth and justification by faith were seen as the two sides of the one coin of salvation. Newman, with his Evangelical upbringing, recognised this and produced his *Lectures on Justification*, which are as much about regeneration as justification. Regrettably in this important publication Newman showed that he only knew Luther in a second-hand way. Had he mastered Luther as he mastered Athanasius, who can tell what would have been the history of the Church of England in the Victorian era.

The Evangelical understanding of justification meant that all approaches to God which suggested salvation by effort or by merit, or which suggested that there were other mediators (Mary, saints and priests) than Jesus Christ, and which suggested that non-Episcopalians could not be sure that they had salvation and were in the one Church of God, were anathema. Because of justification by faith and new birth by the Spirit, Evangelicals believed that by faith a believer entered into the 'invisible' holy Catholic and apostolic Church of God and also entered into privileges and duties in the visible local church. In nineteenth-century terms, this approach tended to be somewhat individualistic in tone and, further, it was usually expressed in dependence upon scholastic categories (formal and meritorious cause, and so on), but these faults do not in any way change the basic fact that this commitment to justification by faith was fundamental to Victorian Evangelicals. To become a Tractarian or Anglo-Catholic involved ditching this fundamental.

Today, because of the influence of the biblical theology movement, the liturgical movement and the charismatic movement, and in the context of fighting the new radical liberalism with its negative theological input, it is not so easy to say that the basic dividing line between Evangelicals and Anglo-Catholics is the doctrine of justification by faith. In the 1980s we find that Evangelicals emphasise attendance at the weekly Eucharist, use gowned choirs, see their preachers in surplices, deacons ordained wearing stoles, and happily subscribe to buy a pastoral staff for one of their number who is consecrated a bishop. Some of them share with Anglo-Catholics a deep commitment to informed social and political action. Such activities and positions would have been heavily criticised by Evangelicals in the Victorian era. Over in the USA there is the very interesting phenomenon of Evangelicals, influenced by writers such as C. S. Lewis, retaining an Evangelical faith but adopting an Anglo-Catholic way of worship. Nashotah House now welcomes such people as students. Turning to Anglo-Catholics we find that they, too have changed. In traditional 'spikey' churches we now find prayer groups, praying in an extempore way, and Bible-study groups as keen as any Evangelical groups. There is talk of mission and evangelism and of converting people to Christ. So we seem to be into a situation in which, while some Evangelicals retain justification by faith and embrace 'western catholicity', some Anglo-Catholics retain 'western catholicity' and embrace justification by faith. This leads, especially in charismatic groups, to the exclamation, 'We cannot see where we are different!' This is an interesting phenomenon and we shall watch it with interest. But to complete the picture we need to recall that there are determined attempts from both the Evangelical and Anglo-Catholic sides to revive the old style of doctrine and practice, and to maintain party lines.

To return to the nineteenth century, I give the final word to Bishop Moule of Durham who had this comment to make on the rise and progress of the Oxford Movement:

> With all readiness I admit that this epoch and its results brought contributions of good to English Christianity. An exaggeration is sometimes used to correct its opposite, and the extreme prominence given by the Tractarians to the sacraments, and to the corporate idea, and to the greatness of worship, had a work to do in that way and did it. But this cannot overcome in me the conviction that the root principles of the Oxford Movement were widely other than those of the Reformation, and out of scale with the authentic theology of the Scriptures. I do not wonder that from nearly the first the new teaching was regarded with suspicion and that earnest efforts were made to counteract it.[17]

From my perspective, I think that Bishop Moule is right.

1. *Christian Observer*, Preface to the bound vol. for 1833.
2. ibid. (1837), p. 115.
3. E. Bickersteth, *Remarks on the Progress of Popery* (London 1836), p. 17.
4. *Christian Observer* (1838), p. 312.

5. I. Taylor, *Ancient Christianity* (London 1842), I, Introduction.
6. W. Goode, *The Divine Rule of Faith* (London 1842), I, p. 193.
7. *Christian Observer* (1836), editorial for December.
8. ibid. (1837), February-March.
9. There is a chapter on Newman's doctrine of justification in P. Toon, *Justification and Sanctification* (Westchester, Ill. and Basingstoke 1983).
10. *Record*, 15 April 1839.
11. *Christian Observer* (August 1837).
12. See further P. Toon, 'The Parker Society', *Historical Magazine of the Protestant Episcopal Church*, xlvi, 3 (1977).
13. See further, id., 'Evangelical Tractarians', *Churchman*, 93, No. 1.
14. For details, see J. Garbett, *Christ as Prophet, Priest and King* (London 1842), II.
15. See M. Smout and P. Toon, 'Bishop Ryle: ritualism and reaction in Protestant Liverpool' (typescript 1972, Liverpool Public Library).
16. J. Wesley, *Forty-four Sermons* (London, 1944), Sermon 39.
17. H. C. G. Moule, *The Evangelical School in the Church of England* (London 1901), pp. 31–2.

12

'A Mystical Substitute for the Glorious Gospel'?
A Methodist critique of Tractarianism*

Gordon S. Wakefield

I will begin by stating several well known facts about Wesley and Methodism; then dilate on certain clear contrasts between Methodism and the Oxford Movement, which were bound to be productive of mutual criticism if not hostility; and will then examine the strictures of a redoubtable Methodist antagonist, the Victorian theologian Dr J. H. Rigg. Finally to continue to the present day by briefly noting the effect the Oxford Movement has had on Methodism and making some assessment of the present position and prospect.

Every schoolboy – every schoolgirl – knows that Wesley was a high churchman, one of the few survivors of the many children of a penurious Lincolnshire rector and his remarkable and very beautiful wife, the son and daughter of dissenting ministers who independently of each other had turned to the Church of England in their youth in opposition to the Unitarianism into which the dissenting bodies were fast lapsing. Wesley was early influenced by the spirituality of the Carolines and the nonjurors and his first published work in 1733 was a collection of prayers, which heavily plagiarised nonjuring sources. On the importance of discipline, of prayer and fasting, regular offices, a central, indeed daily, Eucharist, and an admiration for the Fathers and some rather eccentric characters of the Catholic Reformation, the Tractarians could have taught him nothing. And all this he never repudiated but constantly republished for the edification of men and women drawn from the common way, converted colliers, gin drinkers and the like, to whom the spires of Oxford were as remote as the Indies.

It is also fascinating to recall that Wesley was a friend and spiritual mentor of the young Irishman Alexander Knox, who, writing from his semi-invalid seclusion, not only anticipated the Tractarian teaching, not least of the English Church as the *via media*, but declared – he died in 1831:

> I trust the time will come and that it is not at any great distance (though I confess as yet I see no sign of its approach) when the

providential deposit which distinguishes the Church of England will be rightly appreciated; and Mr Wesley's designation as the precursive announcer of its hitherto undeveloped excellences, will be fully understood and adequately recognised.[1]

But there was more to Wesley than this noble tradition, and other influences played on his life, notably German pietism. Both Wesley and Newman had two conversions, were men of what recent spirituality has called the 'second journey'; but their conversions were in reverse order. Newman was evangelically converted at the age of fifteen, then came his Catholic conversion which took two decades to lead him at last to his hard lodging in the Roman obedience. Wesley dedicated all his life to God as a young Oxford don in 1725, influenced by Thomas à Kempis and Jeremy Taylor, and then, after a time nearly as long and years as restless, found peace on 24 May 1738 in a little society in Aldersgate Street, as may be read from Luther's commmentary on the Epistle to the Romans. A Methodist scholar, for whom the great anniversary in 1983 is not Keble's Assize Sermon but Luther's birth, said to the Methodist Conference, 'If John is our father, Martin is our grandfather'. This is a lineage which some Lutherans have been embarrassed to recognise, and it is acceptable only if it is remembered that, important as grandfathers are, theirs is rarely a predominant influence on the developing child. And there is much in Wesley and in Methodism which belongs to other sources and which is not content, for instance, with the great Reformer's description of the Christian as 'always a sinner, always penitent, always justified'. But after 1738 Wesley could assert that fundamental to our formation in Christ are justification and the new birth. But Wesley was never a Calvinist; indeed the Calvinists were his fiercest foes, which is why Anglican Evangelicals and Methodists have never been the congenial companions that the undiscerning may have thought. If you want to label him in this aspect, you could say that he was an Evangelical Arminian. And this, rather than his high churchmanship, has had the greatest influence on Methodism.

What cannot be too often reiterated is the remarkable confluence between the spiritual pilgrimage of the Oxford don John Wesley and the folk religion of those of the new industrial towns for whom the Anglican parochial system failed to provide. The Methodist was a popular movement, reaching down to the poor, the ignorant and the deprived, as the Tractarian, until it broke out from its academic confines, was not. True, Hurrell Froude was antagonistic to the religion of gentlemen and believed that the strength of the Church had always lain in the poorest classes, while Keble longed for the privileges of Oxford University to be open to every child of every parent. But the Methodist 'style' was different from the Tractarian and the Oxford Fathers were repelled by it. Pusey, in his preface to the English edition of Surin's *Fondements de la vie spirituelle*, pays tribute

to the preaching of the Evangelical revival, which brought the dull
torpid age of deism back to the realities of human sin and the
centrality of the cross, but he deplores Wesleyanism, which 'threatens
to be one of the most dreadful scourges with which the Church was
ever afflicted, the great antagonist of penitence'.[2] Later he admits the
validity of Methodist conversions.

> If a Wesleyan minister preaches his naked Gospel that 'we are all
> sinners', that 'Christ died to save sinners', that he bids all sinners
> come to him and saith whoso cometh unto me, I will in no way
> cast out; this is, of course, fundamental gospel truth; and when
> God blesses through it those who know no more, He blesseth
> through faithful reception of His truth.[3]

But the Wesleyan's is a 'naked gospel' denuded of the sacramental
robe of the apostolic order which clothes and protects and graces the
soul. It is only fair to add that, unknown to Pusey, Methodist
preachers at this time were bemoaning the fact that Methodism had
'achieved much by conquest, little by nurture'. But there was no
point of contact. The very mention of 'Puseyism' would throw the
Methodist Conference into a rage, and it is rumoured that Methodist
parents subdued recalcitrant offspring with the threat: 'Be good, or
Dr Pusey'll get you!'[4]

Newman was more aware of the treasures of Methodism, though
he did not like Wesley: 'putting aside his exceeding self-confidence,
he seems to me to have a black self-will, a bitterness of religious
passion, which is very unamiable. Whitfield seems far better'.[5] Is this
a manifestation of Newman's erstwhile Calvinism and an example
of the Calvinist-Methodist mutual antipathy we have noted? It is
important to observe that John Wesley and John Henry Newman,
by any standards the two outstanding English Christians since the
Reformation – and the Church of England could contain neither of
them – would have profoundly irritated and annoyed each other. How
Wesley would have distrusted and condemned Newman's intellectual
subtlety; how incompatible he would have found it with his desire
of 'plain truth for plain people'! And Methodist worship is surely
condemned in much Tractarian teaching, most notably in Newman's
sermon, 'Religious Worship, a Remedy for Excitements'.

In Charlotte Brontë's novel *Shirley*, there is a description of Yorkshire Methodist worship:

> Briarfield chapel, a large, new, raw, Wesleyan place of worship,
> rose but a hundred yards distant; and, as there was even now a
> prayer-meeeting being held within its walls, the illumination of
> its windows cast a bright reflection on the road, while a hymn of
> a most extraordinary description, such as a very Quaker might
> feel himself moved by the spirit to dance to, roused cheerily all
> the echoes of the vicinage. The words were distinctly audible by

snatches: here is a quotation or two from different strains; for the
singers passed jauntily from hymn to hymn and from tune to tune,
with an ease and buoyancy all their own.

> Oh! who can explain
> This struggle for life,
> This travail and pain,
> This trembling and strife?
> Plague, earthquake, and famine
> And tumult and war,
> The wonderful coming
> Of Jesus declare! . . .

Here followed an interval of clamorous prayer, accompanied by
fearful groans. A shout of 'I've found liberty!' 'Doad o'Bill's has
fun' liberty!' rung from the chapel, and out all the assembly broke
again . . .

> Oh the goodness of God
> In employing a clod
> His tribute of glory to raise;
> His standard to bear,
> And with triumph declare
> His unspeakable riches of grace!

. . . The stanza which followed . . . after another and longer interregnum of shouts, yells, ejaculations, frantic cries, agonized groans,
seemed to cap the climax of noise and zeal.

> Sleeping on the brink of sin,
> Tophet gaped to take us in;
> Mercy to our rescue flew, –
> Broke the snare, and brought us through.
>
> Here, as in a lion's den,
> Undevour'd we still remain;
> Pass secure the watery flood,
> Hanging on the arm of God.
>
> Here –

(Terrible, most distracting to the ear was the strained shout in
which the last stanza was given).

> Here we raise our voices higher,
> Shout in the refiner's fire;
> Clap our hands amidst the flame,
> Glory give to Jesus' name!

The roof of the chapel did *not* fly off; which speaks volumes in
praise of its solid slating.[6]

That is not quite the style of the Tractarians!

The whole principle of 'reserve', which extends far beyond the two tracts of Isaac Williams and is found also in Keble and Newman, is alien to Methodism. Williams discovered it by a selective reading of the New Testament, which is how much doctrine is established. He was particularly distressed by the clamant preaching of the cross and the profanation of 'the highest and most sacred of all Christian doctrines' by its being 'pressed before and pressed home to all persons indiscriminately, and most especially to those who are leading unChristian lives'.[7] Paul's preaching of Christ crucified means 'the necessity of our being crucified to the world', and this is not something you can shout at street corners. Keble as Professor of Poetry delivered his lectures in Latin that they might not be caviare to the general and declared: 'Religion and Poetry are akin because each is marked by a pure reserve, a kind of modesty or reverence . . . Beauty is shy, is not like a man rushing out in front of a crowd'.[8] This enables the expression of what, if not so concealed, is so tremendous that it would drive to insanity.

Keble once preached a University Sermon which so overwhelmed Newman and Froude that they walked back to Oriel in silence and it was some time before they could trust themselves to speak. Keble got to hear of this and of others' praises, and so he deliberately made his next sermon a disappointment to his hearers, a tedious and turgid harangue without unity or effectiveness: so fearful was he that his audience had thought more of him than of his subject. This is totally the antithesis of the spirit of Methodism, where it has been the custom for preachers to wish one another 'a good time' in the pulpit – a piece of homiletic hedonism one could not imagine on the lips of a Tractarian.

More seriously, the Wesleys' conversion hymn seems to challenge the notion of 'reserve':

> And shall I slight my Father's love
> And basely fear his gifts to own?
> Unmindful of his favours prove
> Shall I the hallowed Cross to shun
> Refuse his righteousness to impart
> By hiding it within my heart?

Contrast Newman: 'true life is a hidden life in the heart; and though it cannot exist without deeds, yet these are for the most part secret deeds, secret charities, secret prayers, secret self-denials, secret struggles, secret victories'.[9]

The contrast is not precise because the two writers are not talking about exactly the same thing and Wesley would not deny the importance of the hidden life and that our outward witness must spring from hidden streams which are not exhausted by what flows out into the world. But Methodist and Evangelical piety is always fearful of not speaking when opportunity offers, of not telling out the deeds of the Lord in one's own experience. It is interesting though, that in a later time, what I was almost tempted to call 'our own day' (though it is not that) Dietrich Bonhoeffer also counselled a *disciplina arcani* and believed that there were occasions when the desire to talk about the things of Christ was mistaken and might prove abortive and obscure the real meaning of the gospel.[10] (He was one of those Lutherans who did not rejoice to own Methodism as a blood relation, and when he wanted to be rude to psychologists talked of 'secularised methodism'.) Methodists would also feel that the Tractarian ethos inhibited the universalism of the gospel, denied the gift of assurance and taught a different view of holiness from theirs.

Methodism proclaimed with rapturous stridency that – as a raw young preacher of the 1850s put it when expounding John 3:16 – when God loves, he loves the world, when God gives, he gives his Son, and when he saves, he saves to the uttermost.

> For all my Lord was crucified,
> For all, for all, my Saviour died.
>
> Thy undistinguishing regard
> Was cast on Adam's fallen race
> For all thou hast in Christ prepared,
> Sufficient, sovereign, saving grace.

The Tractarians could never claim to be so confident. Newman's cradle Calvinism made him cautious, sure though he is that God's tender mercies are over all his works; yet many are called and few chosen. The way of salvation is straight and narrow and not over-crowded. Assurance which the Methodists regarded as a gift of the Spirit was deemed by the Tractarians to be very dangerous. 'There is no safety brethren, but never to think ourselves safe.' So Pusey. Brilioth writes of 'the anxious precision, the fear of every excess of joy, or confidence, the trait of Puritanical severity which at times seems to form the fundamental tone of the Tractarian temper'.[11] Methodists have not so learned Christ. 'We have not received the spirit of bondage again unto fear but the spirit of adoption whereby we cry "Abba Father".'[12] There is much fear in Tractarian piety. 'Holiness rather than peace' was a slogan Newman learned from his Evangelical mentor Thomas Scott. 'Holiness is happiness' was the conviction of Wesley.

Methodists found Tractarians gloomy and depressing. Newman was so by nature. Baron von Hügel, the Roman Catholic lay theo-logian who knew him at the end of his long life, thought that this would preclude his canonisation.[13] He rather enjoyed the solemn and the sombre. (There is an Advent sermon which begins with a poetic passage in which he remarks how appropriate to the season of judgment are the outward conditions. 'The very frost and cold, rain and gloom . . . The season is chill and dark, and the breath of the morning is damp, and worshippers are few . . .'[14] For Newman the 'kindly light' always shone 'amid the encircling gloom'. He did preach joy, yet admitted it rather as a Christian duty. 'Gloom is no Christian temper; that repentance is not real which has not love in it; that self-chastisement is not acceptable which is not sweetened by faith and cheerfulness; we must live in sunshine even when we sorrow; we must live in God's presence'.

There is also a verse in *Lyra Apostolica*:

> Meekness, love, patience, faith's serene repose
>   And the soul's tutored mirth
> Bidding the slow heart dance, to prove her power
>   O'er self in its proud hour.

That is a stately minuet, as if learned from a manual on how to dance, with a diagram of the steps in mind. How spontaneous in comparison is Wesley, as in the hymn quoted by Charlotte Brontë, or 'My heart it doth dance at the sound of his name'.

There is no doubt also that Pusey's great sense of sin and mortification seemed to Methodists to betoken a heart still in thrall to sin, which had never known Evangelical joy.

> He breaks the power of cancelled sin
> He sets the prisoner free!

That is not tailored to a hair shirt or a need for flagellation. Pusey had known deep personal sorrow, which he felt might be God's judgment on him. Wesley would have thought his grief excessive. We know that there was another side to it all, and in the end I believe that these differences are personal and temperamental and necessary to the catholicity of the Church. But they *are* differences.

And for the Tractarians holiness appeared first as obedience and then as a sense of the *mysterium tremendum et fascinans*, the awfulness of things unseen. The notions of mystery and awe are found over and over again in their writings. For the Methodist too there was mystery:

> 'Tis mystery all! The immortal dies
> Who can explore his strange design
> In vain the first born seraph tries
> To sound the depths of love divine.
> 'Tis mercy all! Let faith adore
> Let angel minds enquire no more!

Notice the change. The mystery is the mercy of God's love for sinners. 'The vilest offender may turn and find grace.' And the response is perhaps not so much 'awe' as 'wonder'. 'The wonder why such love

to me.' And if it passes into awe it is not before the terrifying majesty
of the divine holiness but in amazement at the divine love for sinners:

> The o'erwhelming power of saving grace
> The sight which veils the seraph's face
> The speechless awe that dares not move
> And all the silent heaven of love!

For Wesley holiness was perfect love – the keeping of the two great
commandments. This is by no means absent from Pusey but has not
the same emphasis. Wesley would have made an excellent sociologist
– he had almost a social scientist's approach to Christian perfection,
devising a questionnaire to discover how far his people had cast away
anger, resentment and jealousy. This was dangerous and deserved
Tractarian strictures.

Let me now turn to a critique of Tractarianism, James H. Rigg's
Oxford High Anglicanism. Rigg was Principal of Westminster College,
now in Oxford, for thirty-five years. His portrait hangs in the college
hall and a study of it tells a great deal. He was an able and eloquent
theologian, though his mind, as Gordon Rupp has said, was no
Wilkinson sword blade. When he set about him, he did so with a
bludgeon.

His book is a curious blend of antipathies, valid judgments, and
some not ungrudging admiration. It may be said – to put it mildly
– that he did not like the Church of England and was always asserting
in a way which we would call 'triumphalist' the world-wide
supremacy of Methodism. As a young man he had written an attack
on what he regarded as the muddled Coleridgean neo-Platonism of
F. D. Maurice. One of the things that annoyed Rigg about the
Tractarians was that in spite of 'the feeble threnody' of Keble's Assize
Sermon they sought to endow a Church which was really a political
creation with mystical efficacy, and were rigid about succession and
sacraments. There he lays his finger on a real weakness of the Tractarian position. He also declared that the teaching of Hooker and
Barrow is completely irreconcilable with the views which Keble
learned from his father and brother and which he and Froude and
Newman embraced as the basis of Tractarian teaching.

Rigg was a muscular Christian, though he disapproved of cricket
on Sundays at Newman's oratory, and he was forever harping on the
femininity of the Tractarians. Of Keble he writes: 'His feminine
genius clung like ivy to the forms of the Church which he so often apos-
trophises as his "Mother" '; though he does go on to assert that
'day by day his morning hymn seems to gather depth and beauty'.[15]
As for Newman, 'he was lacking in manly strength and we cannot
easily accept as a great man anyone who is not a truly manly man'.[16]
But if Rigg disliked the Church of England, his fear of the Church

of Rome was of Kensitite proportions. For his second edition he devoured with much licking of his rather sensual lips Walsh's *Secret History of the Oxford Movement*. The way of the Tractarians is the road to the scarlet woman of the seven hills. Newman was dishonest in that he appeared to hesitate so long before going over; but he finally took the logical course, went where he belonged, and much good did it do him: condemned to the life of sleepy hollow, as Rigg called the Birmingham Oratory. Pusey however was the most dangerous of the three leaders. He was responsible for the strange hybrid monster, Anglo-catholicism. Rigg concedes that Pusey was the most manly of the Tractarians, and that 'he was a good man, however lamentably in error; and though his life and influence have wrought terrible mischief, they have also been in some respects an inspiration for good'.[17] His working faith was better than his teaching. But Puseyism is popery, 'not revived from its embers as by Laud in a nation not yet truly reformed, but revived in Protestant England'.[18]

The two plague-spots of Puseyism are its high sacramental perversions whereby the holy seals of Christian faith and profession are turned into superstitions; and its dehumanising doctrine of the confessional. Papal infallibility is a less revolting tenet than that which invests the priest with the prerogative of the confessor. One aspect of this which disturbed the aged Rigg was that 'poor, frail and fallible young mortals fresh from college' should be made confessors.

There was a genuine fear expressed by other Methodists and many Anglicans, and not allayed by reports of Pusey's severe penances and asceticism nor by his recognition of the dangers: 'you may pervert the sacrament [of confession] from its legitimate end into a subtle means of feeding evil passions and sin in your own mind'.[19]

Rigg believed that the confessional had been supplanted by Wesleyanism's doctrine of present salvation. His successor as Principal of Westminster College, H. B. Workman, quoting an earlier Wesleyan, W. F. Slater, declared: 'The confessional is an instrument of priestcraft; the class-meeting is the bulwark of spiritual freedom.' Rigg seems to have forgotten that 'present salvation' did not do away in early Methodism with the need for helps to growth in grace, and that Wesley's classes and bands were suspected of popery because they were a form of group confessional.[20] They did contribute to the evolution of British democracy, as the Roman Catholic system did not, but our time has shown that groups may be more tyrannical and manipulative than priests and even more sinister. And a wiser Wesleyan and more brilliant scholar than Rigg, James Hope Moulton, preached a synod sermon in the very year of Rigg's second edition. It was on the foot-washing, which he called 'A Neglected Sacrament'. For him, the class-meeting was the equivalent of the pedilavium, the true means by which Christ's command to do as he did may be carried out, but he recognises that not everyone can bare his soul in a group, and that some need the personal counsellor, if not confessor. This controversy is now surely at an end.[21]

But we have not yet considered the criticism which has given our title. Rigg's full text speaks of 'that system of theurgic mysticism which our modern High Anglicans have substituted for the glorious gospel of the Blessed God'.

Here we come, not to an 'either/or' as Rigg and others would have us, but to one more difference of temperament and spiritual experience, which results in two different types of Christian spirituality, which should co-exist in juxtaposition in the Church and sometimes within individuals themselves. Charles Wesley could interpret, and rhapsodise about both; but Rigg would not respond to his mystical strain; neither did John Wesley.

The gospel is of a deliverance through a work not our own. The initiative is God's. He takes responsibility for his own creation and loves us from the foundations of the world, though there is often no beauty that he should desire us. Through his act, in the life, death and resurrection of Jesus Christ, he redeems the whole world out of his own free grace and irrespective of any virtue or merit. As F. D. Maurice saw in a very Wesleyan way, *pace* Rigg, this act claims every human soul for God and is in some sense the world's baptism. And the implication, as far as the individual soul is concerned, is that if he or she turns to God in penitence and trust, God does not say 'Welcome! but you have a long passage to work.' He receives him as the father did the prodigal and treats him as though he were already righteous. There is profound psychology in the Pauline doctrine of justification by faith, rediscovered by Luther. But God does not leave the soul naked any more than the father did the prodigal. He bids him put on Christ, so that he may grow into Christ's likeness by, so to speak, wearing his clothes, or as Max Beerbohm's 'happy hypocrite' became handsome and worthy of his mistress by covering his own ugly features with the mask of a handsome man. That is the gospel and it is no fiction. The imputed righteousness is real, effects a change of heart and life and soul because there is a new disposition and a new regime within the fellowship of the Church and with the aid of the means of grace and all the saints. True it may be made not a matter of faith, which is God's gift of a new relation to him, but of feeling, and perhaps Brilioth's reference to the 'exaggeratedly subjective and individualistic method of the Methodist teaching of conversion' is not unfair.[22]

But there are those who have by nature a longing for God, a capacity for love of him, which though it is perverted and diminished by sin cannot rest content either with the normal responses of faith in acceptance of forgiveness and practical dedication, or even with the acknowledgement of Jesus as personal Saviour in the Evangelical phrase so much restored to common use. Perhaps love rather than faith is the true description of their state. They long for union and for the holiness which alone makes this possible. For them also, there is an awareness of the world beyond this, of the reality behind the things of sense, which is seen as through a veil in the mundane concerns and duties of daily life. Newman was such a one; Keble too, with his understanding of poetry and his tract, *On the Mysticism attributed to the Early Fathers of the Church*; but perhaps above all Pusey, for such devotion is not a flight of the alone to the alone, as in some mysticism, even western Catholic; it demands liturgy and the sacraments because in them Christ mystically re-enacts in his people the events of his life. So far from being a substitute for the gospel they bring it into the immediacy of our lives here and now, and more, they raise us by anticipation into the heavenly places. We are caught up into what was done once for all on earth and is eternal in the heavens. Our salvation becomes present, not because of our pious feelings but because we are there united with Christ and worshipping with angels and archangels and all the company of heaven.

Ironically, no one in English spirituality until the Tractarians expressed this so powerfully as Wesley in his eucharistic hymns, and in his remarkable paraphrase of Song of Songs 1:20:

> Thou Shepherd of Israel and mine
> The joy and desire of my heart
> For closer communion I pine,
> I long to reside where thou art.
> The pasture I languish to find
> Where all who their Shepherd obey
> Are fed on thy bosom reclined
> And screened from the heat of the day.
>
> Ah! show me that happiest place
> The place of thy people's abode
> Where saints in an ecstasy gaze
> And hang on a crucified God.
> Thy love for a sinner declare
> Thy passion and death on the tree
> My spirit to Calvary bear
> To suffer and triumph with thee.
>
> 'Tis there with the lambs of thy flock
> There only I covet to rest,
> To lie at the foot of the rock
> Or rise to be hid in thy breast;
> 'Tis there I would always abide,
> And never a moment depart,
> Concealed in the cleft of thy side,
> Eternally held in thy heart.

Pusey could have prayed that. But not everyone. Twice in the exposition to the Methodist Conference of 1983, referred to earlier,

Professor Kingsley Barrett, who pointed his hearers to Jesus in Paul and John, confessed that he was an earthy, non-mystical person; and we must recognise that there are many such, perhaps the majority. But the spirituality of Wesley's hymn, so beautifully characteristic of the Tractarians, is not a theurgic substitute for the gospel. It is one of its manifestations. And it is found in Methodism.

In the spring of 1843 Nicolai Grundtvig from Denmark stayed in the Queen's College, Oxford. He had come to meet the Tractarians and to assess the Oxford Movement. He found its sacramentalism congenial but felt that Pusey and Newman were in 'dangerous' popish ways, though he appreciated their concern with the real appropriation of grace and holiness. The Evangelicals knew little of real Christianity but the Wesleyans had the power of preaching and religious fervour, and he wrote of them and the Tractarians: 'Could these two movements find each other and coalesce, have their eyes open for the importance of the word of faith in the Christian congregation [he wanted a Lutheran dimension too] then the conditions of a rich Church life would be in existence in England.'[23]

The tragedy of English Christianity is that after a hundred and fifty years of hide and seek, and some seasons of hope, the two movements have not found each other except on occasional encounters and in some personal friendships. The Tractarians have influenced Methodism greatly; to its detriment in that under Rigg's leadership the Wesleyans revised their Baptismal Service in 1880 to exclude baptismal regeneration; and also to drive it further from the rich sacramentalism of its origins. But it is the Tractarians who have given English Christianity the vision of the one united Church so magnificently described in the Lambeth Appeal of 1920, and have persuaded Methodism to be willing to regard episcopal government as a *sine qua non* of a reconciled Christendom.

And yet it is their successors who in the end have felt, many of them, unable to accept practical proposals towards visible unity, which have been brought forward in 1969, 1972 and 1982. It looks sometimes as though these rejections have been the virtual suicide of Anglo-catholicism. The Anglican-Methodist *Scheme* of 1972 was probably the last chance of the union of non-Roman Catholic churches on Catholic principles. And Anglicans have forfeited the possibility of being the *via media* or 'bridge Church'. The ARCIC discussions will continue but churches of the Reformed and Methodist traditions will pursue their own separate ways with Rome. And you would be surprised to hear what Roman Catholics and Methodists say to one another when there are no Anglicans present. A Roman Catholic bishop once said to me, 'Of course, there are structural resemblances between the Anglicans and ourselves, but spiritually I find more in common with the Free Churches, and especially the Baptist Area

Superintendent.' And I know a Roman Catholic theologian who feels that the Methodist Eucharist may have greater validity than the Anglican because it is authorised by one central Church authority – the Methodist Conference, the corporate pope – whereas in the Church of England there are forty or more different bishops with varied theologies ordaining its ministers. Meanwhile the new generation is less ecumenical than the last. The liveliest Christian manifestations are not inspired by the vision of the Church and all that the Tractarians stood for by their affirmation of the mystical body. And all the great historic confessions are in decline.

The only way forward is an ever more dedicated and disciplined quest for catholicity – a Christianity which is authentic, which reaffirms its fidelity to the historic creeds and is able to recognise legitimate development. Theology is important here, though Bishop Huddleston[24] is too optimistic in seeming to think that a theology of creation is within our grasp, or that it can stand alone. It must be accompanied by a theology of redemption and an eschatology. I feel that Andrew Louth's essay, *Discerning the Mystery*, with its understanding of the true nature of tradition, is worthy of the most serious discussion and debate. Nor must the search be a colloquy of western Christians.

But to be Catholic means more than this. It is in the Orthodox term 'Sobornost' – togetherness – or as a Methodist would say 'fellowship'. Let not our friendships be sundered in spite of controversies, disagreements and disappointments. Wesley found in William Law the nonjuror, who also had profound influence on the Tractarians, the definition of the Catholic spirit:

> There is therefore a catholic spirit, a communion of saints in the love of God and all goodness, which no one can learn from what is called orthodoxy in particular churches, but is only to be had by a total dying to all worldly views, by a pure love of God and by such unction from above, as delivers the mind from all selfishness and makes it love truth and goodness with an equality of affection in every man, whether he be Christian, Jew or Gentile . . .
>
> We must enter into a catholic affection for all men, love the spirit of the Gospel wherever we see it, not work ourselves up into an abhorrence of a George Fox, or an Ignatius Loyola, but be equally glad of the light of the Gospel wherever it shines . . .[25]

But let me end with Pusey:

> As we love him who is our head with a more burning self-devoted love, we must in him love his members. And love understands thoughts of love, although ill-expressed, and catches at thoughts of truth though conveyed in broken words and but half-uttered, and reads the heart with which it sympathises and can even open to its undeveloped meaning, or what it should mean instead of

being repelled by rude or imperfect speech. As we love our Lord
more, we shall love more all whom he loves; as we love more we
shall understand one another better. One grain of love avails more
than many pounds of controversy.[26]

A mystical substitute? No, the holy of holies!

1. Alexander Knox, *Remains* (London 1836), IV, p. 308.
2. J. J. Surin, *Foundations of the Spiritual Life*, ed. E. B. Pusey (London 1844).
3. E. B. Pusey, *An Eirenicon* (Oxford 1865), p. 272.
4. S. Coley, *Life of Thomas Collins* (London 1869[2]), pp. 8–9.
5. J. H. Newman, Letter to Mrs John Mozley, 19 January 1837, included
   in Joyce Sugg, ed., *A Packet of Letters* (Oxford 1983), pp. 38ff. Newman
   did say in an essay on 'Selina Countess of Huntingdon' that he preferred
   Wesley to the sixteenth-century Reformers, 'a serious inquirer would
   have greater reason for saying *Sit anima mea Wesleio* than *Cum Luthero* or
   Cum Calvino'; but this does not imply personal affinity.
6. Charlotte Brontë, *Shirley* (1849), Pelican English Library edn (London
   1974), pp. 163–5.
7. Isaac Williams, Tract 87, *On Reserve in Communicating Religious Knowledge*
   (1840); see Elisabeth Jay, ed., *The Evangelical and Oxford Movements*
   (Cambridge 1983), pp. 106ff.
8. John Keble, *Prælectiones Academicae*, pp. 813–15, tr. Owen Chadwick, *The
   Mind of the Oxford Movement* (London 1960), pp. 69ff.
9. J. H. Newman, *Parochial and Plain Sermons* (London 1879), V, p. 243.
10. D. Bonhoeffer, *Letters and Papers from Prison* (London 1953), p. 146.
11. Y. Brilioth, *Evangelicalism and the Oxford Movement* (Oxford 1934), p. 9.
12. Rom. 8:15.
13. F. von Hügel, *Essays and Addresses*, 2nd ser. (London 1930), p. 242.
14. J. H. Newman, *Parochial and Plain Sermons*, V, p. 271.
15. J. H. Rigg, *Oxford High Anglicanism* (1895, 2nd edn rev., London 1899),
    pp. 30, 31.
16. ibid. p. 132.
17. ibid. p. 298.
18. ibid. p. 234.
19. E. B. Pusey, *Nine Sermons preached before the University of Oxford*, quoted in
    O. Chadwick, op. cit. pp. 200ff.
20. W. F. Slater, *Methodism in the Light of the Early Church* (London and
    Edinburgh 1885).
21. J. H. Moulton, *A Neglected Sacrament* (London 1919), pp. 98ff.
22. Y. Brilioth, op. cit. p. 22.
23. ibid. p. 55.
24. In a sermon commemorating Keble's Assize Sermon, 14 July 1983,
    University Church, Oxford.
25. William Law, *Works* (1762 edn, repr. Setley and Canterbury 1892–3),
    VI, pp. 183–4, 188.
26. E. B. Pusey, *Parochial Sermons*, rev. edn (1878), II, p. 74.

13

The Bible and the Call:
the biblical roots of the monastic life in history and today*

Barnabas Lindars, SSF

The Oxford Movement is generally reckoned to have started with John Keble's Assize Sermon on *National Apostasy*, preached in the University Church at Oxford on 14 July 1833.[1] One of the results of the movement was the revival of religious and monastic orders in the Church of England. It seems fitting therefore that one who has entered into this particular aspect of the Tractarian inheritance should mark the occasion by giving some consideration to the religious life, and I shall do this in terms of my own discipline as a biblical scholar.

To begin with, the central isssue of Keble's sermon has a direct bearing on the call to the religious life, which has been a feature of Christianity through many centuries, however unfamiliar it may be to western protestantism. Whatever we make of the issue of the suppression of the Irish bishoprics, it was certainly perceived by Keble in terms of 'national apostasy', an act of the nation's secular government in defiance of the claims of the spiritual institution of the Church. Thus the point at issue was the sovereign claim of God over against the secular State. This had a wider relevance in relation to the Erastian tendencies of the theological liberalism of the day. The movement which followed Keble's sermon found a ready response among those who were influenced by the contemporary romantic revival, well known to us from pre-Victorian Gothic architecture and the novels of Sir Walter Scott. Thus the movement tended to look back to the medieval period. But it would be a mistake to suppose that the revival of the religious life in the English Church was simply motivated by a nostalgic turning to the so-called 'ages of faith'. The medieval past was valued seriously as an expression of the primacy of the spiritual order over the secular. The Oxford Movement is first and foremost a holiness movement, and it sees the Church as the divinely appointed institution to maintain the primacy of God in national life. This continuing task requires the constant renewal of the Church in holiness. With such aims and ideals before them, it is not surprising – indeed it was inevitable – that some of those influenced by the Oxford Movement should seek to restore the religious life in the Church of England, and that some among them should feel called personally to the pursuit of holiness in this way.[2]

It is not my purpose to tell again how these hopes and desires were fulfilled, beginning with the taking of vows by Marian Rebecca Hughes in the presence of Dr Pusey in 1841, only eight years after the Oxford Movement started.[3] What is more relevant is to point out the parallel between this revival of the religious life and the original impetus in the third and fourth centuries, when men fled from the corrupting influence of the cities to the deserts of Egypt and Palestine.[4] It was a zeal for holiness which inspired the first tentative forms of the religious life, and this has been true ever since. Many people today think that the religious life is morally justified only if it is the framework for dedicated service to mankind. Otherwise it is felt to be self-regarding. The pursuit of holiness is regarded as a luxury, parasitic on society because it is dependent upon charity, and contributing nothing in return. But it has to be pointed out that, though the religious orders have a tremendous record of service to mankind, sometimes heroic by any standards, professional agencies do it much better. The call to dedicated service is not identical with the call to the religious life, although they are often intertwined. This is why the religious life has a distinct *form*, which can be summarised in two words, withdrawal and celibacy. These conditions are misunderstood if they are regarded as a kind of stripping for action in social service. In fact withdrawal limits the scope of social action, and no one would suggest today that all social workers ought to be celibate. But the religious call can be expressed only as the longing for God, which demands satisfaction in a form of life that is geared towards this end. Those who have this calling necessarily 'leave the world' (as the saying goes). Even if they actually live and work in the midst of the city and are deeply involved in social caring, there will always be an element of detachment which marks them off from the rest of society.

The monastic life is not peculiarly Christian. Buddhist monasteries in Thailand and Tibet show an astonishingly similar phenomenon. But this raises the question whether monasticism is not only specifically Christian, but may also be an aberration. Historically there is a gap of two and a half centuries between Christian origins and the beginnings of monasticism. It is thus a serious question whether the religious life has its roots in the Bible. In what follows I shall attempt to tackle this question first, and so in the first section we shall be concerned with the biblical basis of the *form* of the religious life. I shall then turn to the way in which the Bible is fundamental to the self-understanding of those who live this form of life, and of course this will vindicate the Christian manifestations of the religious life, whatever their origins. So the second section will be concerned with the *spirit* of the religious life. Finally I shall try to show how some modern developments in the interpretation of Scripture can contribute to the renewal of the religious life today.

I

The form of the religious life

The problem involved in the form of the religious life is that it is an ascetical way, which seems far removed from the teaching of the Son of Man who 'came eating and drinking . . . a friend of tax-collectors and sinners' (Matt. 11:19). The flight to the desert is not merely an escape from the world, like John Bunyan's Pilgrim leaving the City of Destruction. It is also a matter of celibacy, and this must surely be seen in relation to the idealisation of virginity in the second century, possibly under non-Christian influences. Some of the writings of the Gnostic sects (now better known as a result of the discoveries at Nag Hammadi) represent salvation in terms of the transcending of sexuality.[5] This normally goes with Encratite views, which often include rejection of marriage. Such views were widespread at the time, and certainly affected Catholic Christianity. Tatian, the Syrian who came to Rome about AD 160 and made the Diatessaron, or harmony, of the gospels, was banished because of his Encratite[6] teaching. The lost Gospel of the Egyptians, known from quotations in Clement of Alexandria, shows a similar insistence on the transcending of sex, and must be dated about the same time. Moreover we can see hints of the same tendency in the New Testament itself. 1 Timothy 4:3 condemns those who 'forbid marriage and enjoin abstinence from foods'. It is widely held that the people referred to are Gnostic teachers of some kind.[7] The fact that this teaching is repudiated might suggest that the Bible is not favourable to the form of the religious life.

However we must be careful to distinguish between voluntary and compulsory asceticism. Christianity has never given official approval to compulsory celibacy, except in so far as certain offices (e.g. the episcopate in eastern Orthodox churches and the priesthood in the Roman Catholic Church) have been reserved to celibates, and even in these cases it is probable that it is due to an extension of the ideals of the religious life into the sphere of secular ecclesiastical administration. On the other hand there are ample indications, both in the Bible and in the Jewish world of New Testament times, that voluntary celibacy, or at least temporary abstinence from sexual relations, was undertaken for religious reasons, so that there was nothing alien to Christianity when the religious life began. In fact, as we shall see, the monastic movement regarded itself as a reform movement, and this way of life was chosen out of a concern for the very centre of the gospel message.

Voluntary celibacy in the Bible and in New Testament times has two principal motives, and both are important for the later emergence of the religious life. In primitive times sexual functions were felt to entail ceremonial uncleanness, requiring elaborate cleansing rites to restore the situation, and making it impossible to enter the sphere of the holy until these had been duly performed. In Exodus 19:15 Moses requires the people to abstain from sex for three days before the solemn assembly on Mount Sinai. There is also the famous story of David and the shewbread (bread of the presence) in I Samuel 21:1–6, which the priest at Shiloh will not give him unless he can be sure that David's men 'have kept themselves from women'. These taboos were codified in the law, so that they remained operative in New Testament times.[8] But the relevance of this to our present concern is that for this reason sexual abstinence was felt to be necessary for the privilege of the vision of God. In 1 Enoch 83–90, written shortly after the Maccabean revolt, Enoch describes two visions which he had before he married his wife Edna. The same point is made in Jubilees 4:19 (*c.* 100 BC). That is, of course, fiction, but it appears to be put into practice in the case of the Qumran sect. It seems virtually certain that the full members of the community remained unmarried, so as to be always fit for the study of the law.[9] Theirs was a very different approach from that of the Pharisees, whose handling of the law was mainly legalistic, using it as the basis of guiding popular religion. The Qumran sect had a more mystical approach, aimed at providing entry into the heavenly secrets, as can be seen in the spirituality of the Thanksgiving Hymns. The relationship between the community in the monastery at Qumran and the numerous small branches, certainly consisting of married people, which are provided for in the Damascus Document, seems to have been rather similar to that of Franciscan tertiaries in relation to a first order of celibates. Besides these precedents there is evidence for Jewish hermits in the desert in New Testament times, notably Josephus's teacher Bannus, who apparently lived a kind of back-to-nature existence in the Judaean desert, and was much sought after for his spiritual advice (*Vita* 11).

These facts need to be borne in mind as we approach the New Testament. The First Epistle to Timothy, besides condemning those who forbid marriage, also happens to be the earliest evidence for an order of widows (1 Tim. 5:9ff.). It is clear from the context that it is a voluntary order, and that the members are not free to marry again, so that we must presume that they have taken some sort of vow of celibacy. It is unlikely that the order existed merely for philanthropic work. Rather, if we may adduce the description of a widow just given in verse 5, that she 'has set her hope in God and continues in supplications and prayers night and day' (like the prophetess Anna in Luke 2:36ff., who 'did not depart from the temple, worshipping with fasting and prayer night and day'), it would seem that these women, having *previously* been notable for their charitable activity, are now seeking closer union with God and access to the heavenly mysteries as well as continuing in works of mercy.[10]

A little earlier in time we have the evidence of Paul in 1 Corinthians 7:5, where Paul tells the married among his readers not to abstain from sexual relations 'except perhaps by agreement for a season, that you may devote yourselves to prayer'. He then immediately expresses his 'wish that all were as I myself am' (verse 7). The context indicates that the reason for such total sexual abstinence is to make possible continual devotion to prayer. We know from other evidence that Paul 'was caught up to the third heaven' and that he 'heard things that cannot be told, which man may not utter' (2 Cor. 12:1–4). This suggests that one reason why Paul was a celibate was his desire for what he calls in the same context 'visions and revelations'. But his vision of the risen Christ on the Damascus road had also specified his calling to be the apostle to the Gentiles (Gal. 1:16). Thus Paul splendidly illustrates the two sides of voluntary celibacy, the vision of God and consecration to his service. His celibacy has nothing whatever to do with neurotic inhibitions about sex.[11]

Having worked back to Paul, it is obvious that we must consider the celibacy of Jesus himself. Jesus' baptismal experience (Mark 1:10ff.) can be compared with the conversion of Paul, because the tradition clearly preserves an authentic incident, even though it has been overlaid with christological interpretation, and this incident is both a vision of God and a call to service. There is absolutely no evidence that Jesus was ever married, and it is a reasonable, and not merely speculative, conclusion that he, like Paul after him, was deliberately unmarried. On the other hand Jesus did not require his disciples to be celibate, and we know from Corinthians 9:5 that 'the other apostles and the brothers of the Lord and Cephas (Peter)' were accompanied by their wives in their apostolic work in Paul's day. This gives weight to the evidence of the saying about eunuchs, which is found only in Matthew 19:10–12. Matthew has slipped this in after a paragraph derived from Mark about divorce. He has effected the transition by means of an editorial verse, in which he makes the disciples complain that Jesus has given such an impossible ideal for marriage that it might be better not to marry at all.[12] The saying itself distinguishes between those incapable of marriage from birth, those rendered incapable by men (presumably by mutilation) and those 'who have made themselves eunuchs for the sake of the kingdom of heaven'. Matthew is careful to point out that this last group is not intended to be all the disciples, but only those who are 'able to receive this'. Opinion is divided about the purpose of this voluntary celibacy, whether it is to free the disciples from encumbrances for the sake of the mission, or to enable them to attend without distraction to their own preparation for the kingdom because time is short (as suggested by Paul in 1 Corinthians 7:25ff.). But what is more important is that, if the saying is authentic, it is likely to be Jesus'

explanation of his own abstention from marriage.[13] For it is characteristic of the irony of Jesus to talk about himself in such a general and
allusive way.[14]

Two further points need to be made before we leave this section.
First, it is obvious that, with the precedents for celibacy which I have
mentioned, the pioneers of the religious life should look primarily to
the example of Jesus himself. But the idea of consecration to God's
service which this entails is in his case immeasurably deepened by
his self-sacrifice on the cross. Both John and Hebrews incorporate
this idea in their christologies: 'For their sake I consecrate myself'
(John 17:19); 'By that will we have been sanctified through the
offering of the body of Jesus Christ once for all' (Heb. 10:10). There
is a basis here for the notion of consecrated virginity which is entirely
independent of unhealthy ideas of sexual taboos.[15]

The other point is that the characteristic life-style of the Christian
tradition of the religious life is based on the example of Jesus and
the disciples. Though we really know very little about the Twelve as
a group, the picture of them in company with Jesus, and particularly
at the Last Supper, is sufficient to provide the model for the cenobitic
life, in which the religious community seeks to reproduce the fellowship of the disciples with Jesus. Moreover the poverty and hardship
of Jesus and the Twelve are indicated in the gospels in various ways,
partly because Jesus addressed his message primarily to the poor and
called them 'blessed', and partly because of his famous reply to a
would-be follower that 'The foxes have holes and the birds of the air
have their nests, but the Son of man has nowhere to lay his head'
(Matt. 8:20). These indications are carried over into the idealised
picture of the primitive Church in Acts, where it appears as a sort
of commune with pooling of possessions.

With such examples before them, it is not surprising that the
pioneers of the religious life claimed that they had the gospel on their
side. According to Cassian's *Conferences* 18, Abba Piamun insisted
that there was historical continuity with the primitive Church. He
claimed that the apostles themselves formed a religious community,
but it proved to be too rigorous for the younger converts.[16] So various
mitigations were permitted. But then the older Christians themselves
became slack and insisted on having the same privileges. However
there were some who tried hard to maintain the old rigour, and these
eventually formed themselves into separate communities. Out of these
communities the first hermits, St Antony and Abba Paul, withdrew
further into the desert for the sake of greater spiritual combat. Of
course this description is largely wishful thinking, but it does show
very clearly that the monastic movement of the late third century
regarded itself as a reform movement, a protest against the corruption
of the Church by the world. The aim was to reproduce the original
zeal of the apostles. It was a pursuit of perfection, an attempt to put

into practice the apostolic call in the fullest possible way and with the utmost integrity.

II

The spirit of the religious life

We have now reached the point where our thought is moving from the biblical basis of the *form* of the religious life to consideration of its *spirit*. The monastic way is response to the call to perfection contained in the gospel. According to the Life of St Antony, attributed to St Athanasius, the young Antony, who is generally held to be the founder of Christian monasticism, was decisively influenced by the words of Jesus in Matthew 19:21: 'If you would be perfect, go, sell what you possess and give to the poor, and you will have treasure in heaven; and come, follow me' (*Vita Ant.* 2). This was in the year AD 271, or thereabouts, but he did not withdraw into solitude for another fifteen years. In the meantime he pursued his vocation by study of the Scriptures and by a simple mode of life with manual work.

The point which is important for us here is that the mainspring of Antony's new life (if the *Vita* is to be trusted) is the *literal* following of the gospel. So he made the study of Scripture his chief mental occupation in order to fulfil his vocation and attain its object in a life lived in union with Christ. This means that Bible study, for Antony and for all his followers in the monastic tradition, is undertaken not for the sake of acquiring information, nor as the basis for theological arguments, but in order to know Christ, who is 'the way and the truth and the life' (John 14:6). This explains why the teachings of the Desert Fathers, collected by Cassian in his *Conferences* and continued by later writers in the *Philokalia*, are taken up with the *heart*.[17] The heart is of course understood in the biblical sense as the centre of mental impressions and the source of intentions and the springs of action. This has a direct basis in the teaching of Jesus, that 'out of the heart of man come evil thoughts, etc.' (Mark 7:21) and 'the good man out of the good treasure of his heart produces good' (Luke 6:45). Thus the life of the monk, like the life of the disciple, is concerned with maintaining the heart in such a way that Christ is always at the centre. As the passions too easily take over control, they must be carefully guarded. The great ascetic struggles of Antony in the desert are concerned with exploring what is involved in this maintenance of the heart before God. He and his followers thereby reached depths of psychological understanding which have not been surpassed until the rise of modern analytic psychology.

So the study of Scripture is undertaken to know Christ and to keep him in the centre of the heart before God. This might seem to confine attention to the gospels and epistles, but in fact the whole of the Bible, both Old and New Testaments, could be drawn into this single aim through the well established process of allegorical interpretation. This is an aspect of the Christian spiritual tradition which needs to be taken seriously. Too often it is dismissed as nothing but fantasy, in which the Bible is deprived of its true meaning and made to fit whatever the interpreter wants it to mean. Nevertheless it was the dominant method of interpretation from New Testament times right until the Reformation in the sixteenth century. Inevitably the revival of interest in the ancient Church associated with the Oxford Movement drew attention to it. One of the first people to defend the traditional exegesis was John Keble himself in his lengthy and learned Tract 89, *On the Mysticism attributed to the Early Fathers of the Church* (1840–1). By mysticism he meant the allegorical interpretation. Significantly, from our point of view, Keble records the contemptuous attitude of the opponents of it on the grounds that the Fathers are 'dwelling too much on counsels of perfection, tending (it is affirmed) to contemplation rather than action, to monastic rather than social and practical virtue' (repr. 1868, p. 7). Obviously 'perfection', 'contemplation' and 'monastic' are bad words, but those who actually live the religious life, and indeed all who, whatever their state of life, practise contemplation, will not be put off by such sneers.

Allegorical interpretation is of more than one kind. Òrigen, who died at just about the same time as Antony was born, defined three senses of Scripture, the literal, the moral and the allegorical (*De Principiis*, IV. 1.11). The literal sense is of course the plain meaning of the text, which may often be simply historical in the Old Testament. The moral sense may often be the literal sense (e.g. the Ten Commandments are generally taken literally), but it may be a matter of seeking moral lessons from material which primarily has a different purpose. The allegorical sense finds correspondences between particular passages of Scripture and the central truths of salvation. But although Origen lumped together all varieties of the allegorical sense as the 'spirit' (the literal and moral senses being the 'body' and the 'soul'),. his own practice in his commentaries shows that he was well aware of important subdivisions. In fact the variety of allegorical interpretation is already visible within the New Testament itself (as Keble pointed out), and stems from different facets of the Jewish background. Allegorical interpretation is not a Christian invention, but part of Christianity's inheritance. We can distinguish two main forms of it. There is first the method of *typology*, which sees the whole of the Old Testament as prophetic, and finds the fulfilment in the present or immediate future. Christianity finds the fulfilment in the Christ-event, but we can see exactly the same thing in the Dead Sea Scrolls, in which the Scriptures are expounded in relation to the Qumran sect's own history and expectations, and the updating technique of the Targumim attests the same process in mainstream

Judaism.[18] Secondly there is what is sometimes called the *anagogical* sense, characteristic of Philo and derived from Hellenistic interpretations of Homer, in which historical texts are interpreted in terms of the virtues of the soul, and of course this is applied in a Christian setting to the progress towards final salvation of those who belong to Christ by faith.[19] Thus the monk who seeks to keep Christ at the centre of the heart has more than the literal sense of Scripture at his disposal. He can range more widely through the Bible, both Old and New Testaments, finding moral lessons, which of course are evaluated in relation to the direct moral teaching of Christ, pondering the acts of God and the prophecies which point forward to Christ typologically, and seeing his own spiritual journey, as one who moves by faith in Christ towards the promised land of union with God, in terms of the whole history of God's people. This is recommended by Abba Nesteros, one of the monks consulted by Cassian (*Conferences* 14), who is an early witness to the fourfold sense of Scripture, literal, moral, typological and anagogical, which remained dominant until the end of the Middle Ages.[20]

The legitimacy of allegorical interpretation is still a matter of debate. Keble was successful in showing the inspirational value of reading the whole Bible with the mind trained on Christ, and, as I have just indicated, this is just what the monk, seeking perfection by way of contemplation, is concerned to do. Keble was less successful in claiming that it is 'a part of *theology*' (p. 9, Keble's italics), intended by God himself as an aspect of divine revelation.[21] Historical typology had a fresh vogue in the 1950s in connection with the Biblical Theology movement, when it was sharply distinguished from other forms of allegorical interpretation.[22] But again the inspirational value of it alone survived criticism. A. C. Charity, in his rather neglected book, *Events and their Afterlife* (1966), pointed to the dialectic interaction, whereby the antitype (e.g. Christ's act of redemption) is illuminated by the type (e.g. the Exodus) in relation to an existential approach to Scripture (my own response as one to whom God speaks).[23] This helps us to see why, in spite of its problematical character, the allegorical approach to Scripture does enrich the understanding. Now, very recently, Andrew Louth has taken up the question again in his *Discerning the Mystery* (1983), in which he relates this enrichment of understanding to current developments in the theory of knowledge. If this turns out to be successful it will vindicate Keble's claim that allegorical interpretation is a genuine aspect of theology, and not merely a matter of spiritual edification.[24]

III

The bible and the religious life today

We seem to have strayed away from the religious life, but I have felt it necessary to labour the question of biblical interpretation because of the way in which it relates to the spirit of the religious life. Just as the form of the religious life has precedents in the Bible, so its spirit is Christ-centred, and the scriptural diet of the monk, in liturgy and *divina lectio*, is aimed at maintaining Christ at the centre of the heart before God. And, as Keble again pointed out, the reading of the Bible in this way enables one to understand the whole of life in the same Christ-centred way, so that all activity, including the works of mercy, can be integrated in the pursuit of perfection which Jesus enjoined upon his disciples.

As a result of critical study, we are now in a better position to appreciate the essential message of Jesus and the life-style of the gospel, which, as we have seen, are central to the religious vocation. One feature of this renewal of vision is that the tendency to think in terms of a double standard, which led to the rejection of monasticism in the Reformation, has been decisively repudiated in the face of the universality of the gospel and the lack of any distinction between levels of discipleship in the teaching of Jesus, when critically appraised.

Consequently the religious life has to be seen in a different relationship with the rest of Christian society. The saying about those who make themselves eunuchs for the sake of the kingdom of heaven, however it is interpreted, is directed, not to all, but to 'those who can receive it'. Thus the religious life is the exception rather than the rule. But it is a valid exception, and for those who feel called to it it may well be the only way. It is, then, a particular form of discipleship. Its particularity consists in its being geared to a form of life which is, as far as possible, a literal following of the gospel. From this point of view it is a sign to the rest of the Church of the discipleship which is incumbent upon all.

No doubt sociological factors are at work, and it would be rash to claim that new trends in the religious life are derived entirely from clearer perception of the meaning of the gospel. But two current tendencies do seem to correspond with this recovery of vision. One is the tendency of active monks and nuns to go for small non-institutional situations in which they can identify with local people by living the life of the gospel in their midst. The other is the pull towards the withdrawn life of contemplation, including a remarkable revival of the hermit life, like that of Antony seventeen hundred years ago.

Those who are called to either of these two ways will need to maintain the integrity of their aim in the literal following of the gospel. But their spirituality needs to be based equally on the endeavour to maintain Christ in the heart. For this purpose the Bible remains central, because all derivative Christian literature carries with it the tendency to distortion at the same time as it stimulates new thought. For this purpose the Christ-centred interpretation of Scripture, exemplified in the tradition of allegorical exegesis, has its proper part to play. But it will be held in check, and kept free from its own kind of distortions, by a thorough grounding in the literal sense of the gospels, established by critical procedures, in which the real Christ is found.

According to the ideals of the Oxford Movement, the Church exists to maintain the primacy of God in national life, or it would be better to say in human life. The religious life, both in form and in spirit, is a witness to this aim, even in its most hidden forms, because withdrawal is itself a part of the witness. Those of us who belong to the Church of England may be deeply thankful for the Oxford Movement, which made possible the revival of the religious life in our Church. But we also view with gratitude the development of religious orders to some extent in both Lutheran and Reformed churches. The call to religious life not only has its roots in the Bible, but also finds response in many parts of Christendom both east and west.

1. John Keble, *National Apostasy Considered in a Sermon Preached in St Mary's Oxford, before His Majesty's Judges of Assize on Sunday, July 14, 1833* (Oxford 1833); repr. in John Keble, *Sermons Academical and Occasional*, 2nd edn (Oxford 1848).

2. A favourable climate of opinion had already begun to be formed by the immigrant priests and religious, especially sisters, from France during the French Revolution and the Napoleonic wars. A. M. Allchin, *The Silent Rebellion* (see n. 3) draws attention to pleas for English Sisters of Charity made by R. Southey in his *Sir Thomas More; or Colloquies on the Progress and Prospects of Society* (1829), II, pp. 304ff; and by A. R. C. Dallas, *Protestant Sisters of Charity: a letter addressed to the Lord Bishop of London* (1826).

3. cf. A. M. Allchin, *The Silent Rebellion: Anglican religious communities, 1845–1900* (London 1958); P. Anson, *The Call of the Cloister* (London 1955).

4. For a popular description of the movement, see D. J. Chitty, *The Desert a City* (Oxford 1966).

5. Logion 114 of the *Gospel of Thomas* may be quoted as an example of Gnostic views: 'Simon Peter said to them, "Let Mary leave us, for women are not worthy of life." Jesus said, "I myself shall lead her in order to make her male, so that she too may become a living spirit resembling you males. For every woman who will make herself male will enter the Kingdom of Heaven." ' Tr. in J. M. Robinson, ed., *The Nag Hammadi Library in English* (San Francisco 1977), p. 130.

6. 'Encratite' (= self-controlled) is a designation applied to various sects by Irenaeus (*Adv. Haer.*, I.28) and Hippolytus (*Ref.* VIII.13). The second

century *Acts of Paul and Thecla*, 3.11, attributes to Paul the idea that virginity is necessary to salvation. The earlier writers of the Syrian church of Edessa almost unanimously idealise celibacy: cf. R. Murray, *Symbols of Church and Kingdom: a study in early Syriac tradition* (Cambridge 1975), pp. 11–18). It is seen in terms of consecration to the holy war against the enemies of God. Murray traces this emphasis to the Jewish Christian origin of the Syrian Church, influenced by the Essenes (see below). If this is correct, it permits the conclusion that the idealisation of virginity has two different origins. The Jewish tradition is a matter of purity in relation to the holy, as we shall see. The Greek Platonic tradition is a matter of dualism of matter and spirit, in which sexuality belongs to matter and is inherently evil. The perversion of asceticism into libertinism, characteristic of the Carpocratians in Egypt in the second century, depends on the latter influence, because the members of the sect regard themselves as superior to the body, which they despise at the same time as indulging it. The diverse origins of the ascetical ideal explain the ambiguity of Christian writers on the subject at this time, e.g. Clement of Alexandria in the *Stromateis*.

7. Gnosticism (the belief that evil in human experience can be overcome by possession of the true knowledge) certainly antedates the rise of Christianity, but the date when it began to influence Christianity, and to be influenced by Christianity, is still a matter of dispute. Many of the Nag Hammadi texts (cf. note 5) are pagan writings with a Christian veneer. The authentic letters of Paul show no certain contact with Gnosticism. The Pastoral Epistles, probably written pseudonymously around the end of the first century, seem to attest the first contacts. None of the Christian Gnostic sects of the second century can be proved to have come into existence as early as this. See the brief outline by R. McL. Wilson in *A New Dictionary of Christian Theology* (London 1983), pp. 226–30, including a useful short bibliography.

8. Lev. 15:18; 22:1–6.

9. cf. G. Vermes, *The Dead Sea Scrolls: Qumran in Perspective* (London 1977), pp. 96f., 106ff., 217ff. On the need for celibacy for the vision of God, cf. Philo, *Vita Moysis*, II.68f.

10. The story of Martha and Mary (Luke 10:38–42) may perhaps be relevant here, though it is not in any way concerned with the question of celibacy. The traditional exegesis in terms of the active life and the contemplative life is of course anachronistic. But it may be taken to support the primacy of contemplation in the Christian life. I. H. Marshall, *The Gospel of Luke* (Exeter 1978), ad loc., summarising the work of other scholars, points out that the position of the story, following the parable of the Good Samaritan (Luke 10:25–37), which was concerned with the love of neighbour, suggests that the present story is concerned with the love of God (Grundmann). Hence it inculcates the duty of listening to Jesus as the teacher of the word of God (Klostermann). Martha (the name means 'lady'), being mistress of the household, may have been a widow (Easton). Marshall says: 'Thus the story is not meant to exalt the contemplative life above the life of action, but to indicate the proper way to serve Jesus; one serves him by listening to his word rather than by providing excessively for his needs' (p. 451). As women were not normally taught by rabbis, the story may have arisen in connection with

the more liberal attitude of the Church towards the despised classes, derived from Jesus himself. But the interpretation of the story remains problematical because of the textual confusion of Jesus' reply in v. 41ff. The reading which has the best claim to originality on text-critical grounds yields the following sense (P^{45} P^{75} C* W Θ lat sy^{cph} sa bo^{ms}): 'Martha, Martha, you are troubled about many things, but there is [still] need of one thing [more]; for Mary has chosen the good (i.e. the best) share [of the duties], which will not be taken away from her' (so RSV, NEB). Thus the service of Jesus includes hearing his word as its most important feature. The motif, which was clearly dear to Luke, is echoed in Luke 11:27ff. where Jesus' saying 'Blessed are those who hear the word of God and keep it' is contrasted with the cry of a woman, 'Blessed is the womb which bore you and the paps which you have sucked.'

11. The popular opinion that Paul was a widower has no evidential basis in his writings, but is a deduction from the rabbinic evidence for marriage as an obligation for men, collected in Strack-Billerbeck, ii, 372ff. But the passages show that this was not something that could be taken for granted, and the more recent recovery of the Qumran literature confirms the evidence of Paul himself that voluntary celibacy was by no means unknown in Judaism of New Testament times.

12. The redactional character of verse 10 is recognised by most scholars, cf. F. W. Beare, *The Gospel According to Matthew* (Oxford 1982), ad loc. This strongly suggests that the following verses on eunuchs come from a source, and are not the work of Matthew himself (against R. H. Gundry, *Matthew* [Grand Rapids, Michigan 1982], ad loc.). It should now be clear that the recommendation of voluntary celibacy which they embody is at home in a Jewish Christian setting, from which Matthew's special material seems to be derived.

13. This was hinted at by A. H. McNeile, *The Gospel According to St Matthew* (London 1915), p. 276, but the suggestion has not received the attention it deserves: 'If they are genuine, the Lord may be referring to the fact that some of the disciples had given up thoughts of marriage in order to follow him . . . For Jesus Himself also self-dedication to His Father's business may possibly have involved a conscious act of abnegation.'

14. See Barnabas Lindars, *Jesus Son of Man* (London 1983), in which this trait is a recurring feature of the Son of Man sayings isolated on linguistic grounds as capable of being authentic sayings of Jesus.

15. It may also be mentioned in this connection that the taking of the vow with shaving of the head in the tradition of the religious life is derived from the Nazirite vow (Numbers 6), though that does not entail celibacy, and (in spite of the annunciation stories of Samson in Judges 13 and John the Baptist in Luke 1) was normally a matter of limited duration. Thus Paul in Acts 18:18 had his hair cut at Cenchreae in fulfilment of a vow, no doubt intending to complete the appropriate sacrifices on arrival in Jerusalem. Similarly Josephus (*Jewish War*, II.313) describes how a woman called Berenice took a thirty-day vow requiring abstinence from wine, and shaved her head at the conclusion of the period.

16. The description is deduced from Acts 2:45; 4:32–5. For the work of Cassian, cf. W. O. Chadwick, *John Cassian*, 2nd edn (Cambridge 1968).

17. The *Philokalia* is a collection of excerpts from spiritual writers from the

Desert Fathers to the fifteenth century, compiled by St Nikodimos of the
Holy Mountain and St Makarios of Corinth. Selections from the Russian
version, tr. E. Kadloubovsky and G. E. H. Palmer, in *Writings from the
Philokalia on the Prayer of the Heart* (London 1951); and *Early Fathers from
the Philokalia* (London 1954). A complete translation, based on a critical
text of the original Greek, is in process of publication by G. E. H. Palmer,
Philip Sherrard and Kallistos Ware, *The Philokalia*, 5 vols projected; I,
II, (London 1979, 1981).

18. For Qumran interpretation, see G. Vermes, *Post-Biblical Jewish Studies*
(London 1975), pp. 37–49; for the Targums, ibid., pp. 59–146; B. D.
Chilton, *The Glory of Israel: the Theology and Provenance of the Isaiah Targum*
(Sheffield 1983).

19. There is no direct debt to Philo in the New Testament, but features of
the Philonic style of exegesis can be seen in Paul's allegory in Gal.
5:21–31. In the second century the Alexandrian school of exegesis
founded by Pantaenus, and known chiefly from the works of Clement
and Origen, based their principles of exegesis on the work of Philo. For
Philo, cf. H. E. Ryle, *Philo and Holy Scripture* (London 1895); J. Daniélou,
Philon d'Alexandrie (Paris 1958). For the use of Philo by Origen, cf. R. P.
C. Hanson, *Allegory and Event* (London 1959).

20. In fact Nesteros refers to the moral sense as tropological and the typo-
logical sense as allegorical. These, with the literal (or historical) and
anagogical sense, remain the customary designations in medieval usage.
The standard work on the Middle Ages is H. de Lubac, *Exégèse Médiévale.
Les quatre sens de l'Ecriture*, 2 parts in 4 vols (Paris 1959–64). See also B.
Smalley, *The Study of the Bible in the Middle Ages*, 3rd edn (Oxford 1983).

21. Keble's emphasis on theology may perhaps be justified (see n.24), but
the claim of divine intention is more difficult. He was of course dependent
on the patristic tradition, for which this is axiomatic. The Alexandrian
school, following Philo, had an oracular concept of the inspiration of
Scripture. Difficulties, discrepancies and barbarities in the sacred text
were there for a purpose, and therefore must contain a hidden meaning,
seeing that they could not be taken at face-value. The same principle is
found in rabbinic exegesis. Augustine, *De Doctrina Christiana*, IV, maintained that God's self-revelation is too bright for the eyes of fallen man,
so that he made himself known through figures of speech adapted to
man's capacity.

22. See especially G. W. H. Lampe and K. J. Woollcombe, *Essays on Typology*
(London 1957).

23. Thus, if the Exodus is considered as a type of redemption by Christ, it
alerts the reader to various aspects of the redemption which he might
not otherwise consider, e.g. the slavery from which mankind is released,
the grand mythological and cosmic overtones of the death and resurrection of Christ, the opening of the way to reach the promised land, etc.

24. Keble shared the view of the Fathers, whose work he so much admired,
that theology is not separable from spiritual edification. To them the
object of theology is to know God experientially. Their expositions of
Scripture were intended to move the heart and the will as well as to
inform the mind, and there is no real knowledge of God without this.
Drawing on the work of Dilthey, Gadamer and Polanyi, Louth maintains
that there cannot be an objective knowledge of God, like scientific knowl-

edge in which the observer stands outside the object of study. The
knowledge of God is necessarily subjective, involving personal response.
The enriching of the understanding effected by the allegorical interpretation of Scripture is at the same time a quickening of the heart and will,
so that God is known in an act of loving. Keble is clear that epistemology
belongs to the realm of metaphysics, and lies outside the province of
theology as he understands it (Keble, Tract 89, p. 13).

14

A Tractarian Inheritance:
the religious life in a patristic perspective*

Benedicta Ward, SLG

> Let us now praise famous men and our fathers in their generation; their bodies are buried in peace and their name lives to all generations; people will declare their wisdom and the congregation proclaim their praise. (Eccles. 44:1, 14, 15)

Those 'famous men' Newman, Pusey and Keble are in a special sense 'our fathers' in the generation of the religious communities of the Anglican Church. 'Their name lives' most especially through those communities and above all in the city where they lived and became friends in that bond of *amicitia* which many have seen as the kindly face of God.[1] Their bodies are 'buried in peace' all, except Pusey, in other places, but Oxford remains especially the centre and heart of their shared vision, the 'Oxford Movement', as we call it. I would like to make some remarks about three aspects of this Oxford Movement which perhaps sound rather tangential and disparate but are in fact three parts of a single theme: first the link formed by Newman, Pusey and Keble with the monastic past of Christendom through their editions and translations of the Fathers of the Church; secondly their understanding and implementation of this monastic theme that they discovered there in re-establishing religious life in England; and thirdly their popularisation of this theme in their lighter works, poems, hymns, and that quintessential Victorian form of literature, the novel.

First; the Library of the Fathers. It is a commonplace to say that the Oxford Movement was based upon the theology of the undivided Church and its understanding of the Scriptures. This is a tradition within the Church of England which goes back to the sixteenth century, and in emphasising and exploring it the founders of the Oxford Movement were not innovators; they were re-discovering something at the heart of Anglicanism. There is inevitably an attraction for Anglicans to the Church of the first centuries and with it often goes an appreciation of the churches which still hold the Fathers as contemporaries, those 'ancient orients kirks' the eastern Orthodox churches. This was recognised among the Tractarians and bore especially rich fruit in the lively genius of J. M. Neale in his translations of eastern liturgical texts and in his amazing knowledge of eastern Orthodoxy. This deep and rich tradition of the theology of the undivided Church was however out of fashion in the rationalist atmosphere of nineteenth-century England. When Dean Gaisford conducted a visitor round the library at Christ Church, he dismissed the sombre volumes of the Fathers of the Church with a wave of the hand and the two words: 'sad rubbish'.² But from an early age Pusey had felt their attraction; as a present for attaining his degree he asked his father for a folio set (presumably the Mabillon edition) of the Fathers of the Church. Keble and Newman were equally aware of the Church Fathers, Newman in particular reading them at Oriel and using them as the basis for those writings which were to give him a permanent place among the theologians of Europe. These men were all scholars and classicists; they read Greek and Latin as easily as English, and wrote it too: Pusey's preface to his edition of Augustine's *Confessions* is in a Latin as clear and fine as Augustine's own. They were men who approached religion through reading – not only Pusey at Eton, Christ Church and as Hebrew Professor and editor of that amazing work, the list of Arabic manuscripts in Bodley; but Newman, student at Trinity and fellow of Oriel; and Keble, brilliant student at Corpus, also a fellow of Oriel, elected when he was only nineteen, and later Professor of Poetry at Oxford. It seems inevitable that so bookish a crew should turn to publication.

The Library of the Fathers, conceived by Newman, Pusey and Keble, was their most useful contribution to the spread of patristic studies in England. But it was not their only kind of publication. Before they turned to translations they put their hands to editions. The production of critical editions of ancient texts was in the air in the nineteenth century and it is necessary first to see the Tractarians in the wider world of academic scholarship before noticing how they went beyond this. The nineteenth century invented the scientific study of history as we know it, most of all by the careful collation of manuscripts in critical editions. This is the century which saw the flowering of the work of the Bollandists in Belgium with the *Acta Sanctorum* series in the able hands of Albert Poncelet, François van Ortroy and above all Hippolyte Delehaye. In Germany Georg Pertz and his most able pupil Jaffé continued the *Monumenta Germanica Historica*, that series of texts indispensable to medievalists still. In France, the Maurists had reached the end of their editions of patristic and medieval texts connected most of all with the names of Mabillon and d'Archery, which were to have a further popularity in their use, and even at times their misuse, by J. P. Migne in the massive series of *Patrologia Latina, Graeca et Orientalis*. The Alcuin Club, the Early English Text Society, the Camden Society and innumerable local antiquarian societies undertook in England the publication of records; above all, this was the moment when English public records were collected and published in the work of the Rolls Series, begun in

1822 when the House of Commons successfully petitioned George IV for the publication of the sources of English history. (Incidentally it is interesting to observe that while the government-sponsored project of the Rolls Series kept several historians in comfort for years, the editors of the Tractarian projects always needed to beg for money and were partly subsidised by the founders, partly by public subscription.) These vast and scholarly concerns certainly influenced Pusey, Newman and Keble in their presentation of Latin and Greek texts in critical editions. They were acquainted with the editions made by the Maurists, and there were personal connections with the Rolls Series in at least two ways: Henry Bickersteth, first Lord Langdale, was largely responsible for establishing the Public Records Office and was also notorious among Tractarians for his judgment in the celebrated case of *Gorham v. the Bishop of Exeter*. Joseph Stevenson, known for his work at the Records Office and for his catalogue of English historical writers, shared the doubts of Newman about the Anglican Church and in 1863 was received into the Catholic Church, a move which cost him his job; he retired to Birmingham to work for the Historical Manuscripts Commission and later became a Jesuit, completing his historical studies in the Vatican and at Farm Street.

The Tractarians edited the texts of Augustine, Chrysostom, Theodoret, and Cyril of Alexandria, the latter being the monumental work of Philip, the son of Dr Pusey, a task which took him to the libraries of Europe including those of Mount Athos. They are editions now largely superseded, but for their time they belong to the mainstream of European critical scholarship. In this, the Tractarians were no mere pedants. They wanted to present the works of the past as accurately as possible; to stand back from the texts and let them speak for themselves. Just as in prayer they learned the asceticism of standing back to allow God to speak without their interpretations and ideas, so in their scholarship they stood back, so that the writers of the past could be clearly heard. They might have remained only editors of texts; but they went further than their contemporaries. They presented also translations into English, in a great series of forty-eight volumes in the Library of the Fathers. It says a great deal for their insight and their energy that they conceived and carried out such a series, when they themselves were perfectly content for the texts to remain in the original languages and were even urging the retention of such languages in their university at the same time. It has been said that the central tradition of English scholarship lies not in the exploration of the past for its own sake but in 'the recurrent need to understand and stabilize the present by reviving the experience of the past;[3] it is to this stream of English scholarship that the Tractarians belong. They were realists, practical men, wanting to be in touch with the theology of the first centuries in order to 'understand and stabilize the present'. Realising that the revival of the Church ought not to be in the hands of a few dons but in the hands of the

people of God, and realising moreover that few of those would have
a first-rate reading knowledge of Latin and Greek much less Syriac,
they decided to make translations into English of the texts of the
early Fathers. They wanted to expand minds by contact with the
sources: 'It is a vulgar and commonplace prejudice' wrote Pusey,
'which would censure everything by its own habit of mind and
condemn as fanciful that to which it is unaccustomed.'[4] There was
a practical need to have translations; the editors were equally aware
of the need for the translations to be in no way beneath the new and
exacting standards of the day. The friends had severe critics; not
only the formidable Jowett at Balliol; but an earlier fellow of Oriel,
to whom they referred as 'poor Arnold', at Rugby; poor because he
did not believe as they did, but a fine Latinist and with an interest
in the Fathers of the Church. Through a friend, Arnold asked Pusey
for guidance about reading the Fathers and Pusey gave it hesitantly,
as one afraid to cast pearls before swine; Arnold must have put him
to shame with his generous comment on Pusey when he wrote, 'from
Pusey you will learn, I am sure, nothing virulent or proud or false,
but self-denial in its true form imbued with humility and loyalty'.[5]

Translation – one of the most difficult arts of mankind. Newman
and Pusey were aware of the pitfalls, indeed in one exchange they
present the continual problem of translation precisely: Newman, only
too well acquainted with the crabbed and pedantic style of Pusey's
English, feared for the style of his rendering of Latin; Pusey feared
rather more the freedom Newman might take with the text; he wrote,,
'the object of all translation must be to present the ideas of the author
as clearly as may be with as little sacrifice as may be of what is
peculiar to them – the greatest clearness with the greatest faithfulness.[6] So the translations were commissioned and eventually produced. Augustine, Cyril, Chrysostom, Athanasius, Gregory Nazianzen,
Ephraim the Syrian, all began to speak precise and rather pedantic
English. Each volume was produced with a most valuable preface,
many by Pusey himself. The idea of a translation series was very
much a part of the mood of the times, but ahead of its time in being
a translation series. Many translations have followed those early
volumes, they have been superseded and are out of print; but they
were the way in which the Tractarians sought to present the theology
of the undivided Church to Englishmen for their use, not just for
their pleasure.

What did the Tractarians themselves find in these texts which they
spent the greater part of their lives and incomes in presenting? First
they found the spiritual sense of the Scriptures, for the majority of
the texts they used were commentaries on the sacred page. Pusey
contrasted the commentaries of the Fathers on the Bible as 'ancient
and catholic truth' compared with 'modern private opinion.[7] 'The
Word', he wrote, 'is greater than the words and the Spirit greater
than the letter', echoing the phrase of Claudius of Turin's preface to

his Commentary on Leviticus: 'Blessed are the eyes which see divine spirit through the letter's veil.'[8] The mystical sense of the Scriptures absorbed the Tractarians; for them the Bible was indeed the sword of the Spirit, piercing the heart, and no mere collection of historical documents. Secondly they found in these texts, of course, the doctrine of the undivided Church. Thirdly they found there an essential concern for the poor, a concern which took root and flourished in the early Tractarian parishes such as St Saviour's, Leeds; and fourthly they found there that reverence for God expressed in forms of worship which sees the liturgy as the corporate prayer of the people of God with the hosts of heaven, a vision so magnificently expounded by J. M. Neale and so disastrously deformed by later ritualists.

But these were not the heart of the matter. What had aroused the Tractarians originally and continued to enrage them was not so much the apathy of Christians but their 'liberalism'. By this they meant that attitude to the Christianity which absorbs and is absorbed by the ideals and trends of the age instead of transfiguring those trends by the gospel of Christ; that attitude in which culture becomes an excuse for not obeying the commands of the gospel. The ideal of a Christianity which is a challenge to the world, which is in the margin of culture, a scandal and an offence, they found in the early Church, in the lives of the martyrs but also and perhaps especially in the accounts of the monks. What lies at the heart of the Oxford Movement as a direct inheritance from the early Church is the religion of the heart, the ideal of a life lived in conformity with the cross of Christ and this ideal is that which was central to early monasticism. Pusey, Newman and Keble were not unaware that almost every writer they admired, both in the early Church and in the Middle Ages, was a monk. All the Christian writings they proposed to their fellow Christians came from the milieu of monasticism. This central theme of monasticism remains still largely undiscovered, a secret to be explored and unpacked still further. There is more here than even the establishment of monastic communities for women, for men and the possibilities of hermit-life which have already appeared among us. But what in the context of the Tractarian Movement and the nineteenth century did this theme of monasticism mean?

First of all it meant opposition, criticism, incomprehension. The Tractarians were aware that the idea of vows, of celibacy, of a life apart from the well-known Christian ways, was not going to be well received in Victorian England. An instance of this peculiarly Protestant spirit is to be found in some sentences from an American publication. As Pusey had hoped, the Library of the Fathers translations were well received in America and soon the Americans were producing their own translations in the series of Ante Nicene, Nicene and Post Nicene Fathers. The volume of translations of Augustine's doctrinal treatises contains his *Praise of Virginity* and the sentence 'therefore go on saints of God, boys and girls, men and women, unmarried men and women . . . ye shall bring unto the marriage of the Lamb a new song which ye shall sing on your harps' is quoted but with the following austere reminder:

> We must admire [the fathers for] their power of self-denial . . . though we may dissent from their theory . . . The Reformation has abolished the system of monasticism and clerical celibacy, and substituted for it . . . the purity, chastity and beauty of family life, instituted by God in Paradise and sanctioned by our Saviour's presence at the wedding at Cana.[9]

The Tractarians were at pains to subdue any rumours that they wished to revive monastic life in England; the idea could only have brought the movement into disrepute; moreover it would have been distinctly contrary to their principle of reserve and restraint. So at the inception of Anglican monastic life, the idea proceeded against criticism, both inside and outside the Church. In this, the communities are most clearly seen as a protest, a comment from the outside, a challenge, to the Establishment. And in this also they are at one with the religious of the fourth century and in sharp contrast to the great churches of East and West in the Middle Ages and today, where monastic life is so integrated into the fabric of the church structures that its protest can rarely be heard. Rutilius Claudius Namatianus called the early monks 'squalid fugitives from the light' and referred to a friend who became one as a 'poor fool';[10] words that found an echo in many English minds when they encountered the first attempts in the Anglican Church at such a way of life.

The monastic life was, then, seen by the Tractarians first of all as a protest against the established liberalism of the age; but secondly, for the Tractarians themselves, monasticism was at the centre of their own lives. Keble might write:

> We need not bid, for cloistered cell,
> Our neighbour and our work farewell

but the same hymn embodies not only the 'little way' of St Thérèse of Lisieux, but the whole point of monasticism:

> The trivial round the common task,
> Will furnish all we ought to ask,
> Room to deny ourselves, a road
> To bring us daily nearer God'.[11]

Newman, a celibate priest, intent at first on founding a community at Littlemore, then involved in the Oratory at Birmingham, quite clearly found in primitive monasticism echoes of his own asceticism, as did the founder of the Oratory, St Philip Neri. Pusey saw the consecrated life of the priest as a total and monastic dedication and after the death of his wife undertook it as such. Moreover again and again these men proposed religious consecration for women quite specifically as a parallel to their own consecration through their ordination to the priesthood: for the women, they felt, there should be a similar possibility, and they presented it as the religious life.

Thirdly there were those within the Church of England who heard and understood the call of monasticism and those the Tractarians protected and encouraged. They found a way to present the total dedication of the sisters to an uncomprehending and hostile public through the grievous social needs of the day. To serve the sick and destitute without fear or care for self was comprehensible and within the understanding of Protestant England; indeed it went well with the philanthropy of the day. The idea, first proposed by Froude, was that religious life could be established under cover of certain pressing social needs.[12] The Park Village sisterhood, for instance, had for its works 'visiting the sick and poor in their own homes; visiting hospitals; workhouses and prisons; feeding, clothing and instructing destitute children, and (evocation of another age) giving shelter to distressed gentlewomen of good character, as well as assisting at the burial of the dead.'[13] Miss Sellon and her sisters made themselves acceptable through their work in a cholera epidemic; the sisters at Wantage, East Grinstead and Clewer, earned the same recognition for similar works.[14]

But it should be remembered that, as with the early monks, the works of mercy were not of the essence of the Anglican religious life. In all the Anglican communities, whether involved in active works or not, the priority was, and is, quite other. From the *outside*, in the deserts of fourth-century Egypt, it seemed that the withdrawal of the monks was justified because they offered the service of prayer for the world, 'These are they by whom the world is kept in being';[15] or by the care they had for the poor in the towns by their work and gifts of food; or by their support of those suffering for the faith. But the reality of both early monasticism and the Anglican communities, seen on the *inside* by their members, is quite other. The hard word of the desert was a call to repentance and the beginnings of monastic life in the Christian Church was in the discovery of the brokenness and hopeless scarring of human lives, which find their healing only and always in the life that comes from the cross of Christ. Abba Antony said, 'the greatest thing a man can do is to throw his faults before the Lord and expect temptation to his last breath'[16] 'if a man does not think in his heart that he is a sinner, God will not hear him';[17] and Abba Apollo prayed only: 'I as man have sinned, do thou as God forgive'.[18] Abba Pinufius said:

> our cross is the fear of the Lord. He who is crucified can no longer move his limbs and so should we become, attached, nailed to the cross, so that we can no longer follow our own will or desires . . . this fear creates in us compunction and leads us towards poverty and nakedness . . . it is a death which destroys our sin and gives

in return that purity of heart which is Christ; and that is perfect love.[19]

Another writer presented even more specifically the monk as crucified, standing with his arms held out and saying, 'so should the monk be, denuded of all the things of this world and crucified . . . in his thoughts the monk stands, his arms stretched out in the form of a cross to heaven calling upon God'.[20]

It is this discovery of compunction as the gateway to life that colours the sermons and letters of Pusey and it is there that the essential nature of Anglican religious life should be sought. In a well-known letter to Keble Pusey describes his own vivid apprehension of his sinfulness and he uses terms familiar to the monastic tradition from the beginning: 'I am seared all over and scarred with sin so that I am a monster to myself.'[21] Let me say, in parenthesis, that the phrases of this letter are so close as to be a paraphrase of another monastic writer in this tradition, Anselm of Canterbury, a translation of whose prayers and meditations (or rather whose supposed prayers and meditations) was published with an introduction by Pusey himself.[22] A later sermon suggests in calmer terms the way of the ascetic as a result of this conviction of sin:

> to empty ourselves of our self conceit, our notions of station, our costliness of dress, our jewellery, our luxuries, our self-love, even as He emptied himself of the glory He had with the Father, the brightness of his majesty, the worshipping hosts of heaven and made himself poor to make us rich[23] . . . He would give us all that He is; He asks in return the nothingness that we are.[24]

And elsewhere:

> it were a dream to think we could love the Passion of Christ and not engrave it on our lives . . . that we could be melted by his sorrows and not sorrow or suffer with him . . .[25]
>
> Our life from baptism to death should be a practice of the cross, a learning to be crucified, a crucifixion of our passions, appetite, desires, will, until one by one they be all nailed and we have no will but the will of our Father who is in heaven.[26]

The idea of a whole life of asceticism in union with the cross of Christ is the ideal of the desert; it is vividly there in the founder and inspirer of the first Anglican communities. Moreover Pusey, like the first monks, was quite practical about it: 'we are not formed to seek conviction', he wrote, 'but to have it'; and when consulted about the possibility of unceasing prayer, another great theme of the desert, he said merely, 'the one plain rule is to set about doing it'.[27] Did Pusey in fact know the writings of the Desert Fathers or is it only a case of parallelism, the same desert air which blows through later texts? There is indication that he had some acquaintance with the primary

sources of early monasticism, probably in Roswede's version of the
Vitae Patrum. There he would have found the story which he quotes
of a monk who was asked by the devil, 'Who are the sheep and who
are the goats?' and who replied, 'I am one of the goats, as for who
the sheep are, God alone knows.' Another story, told also in the *Life
of St Martin*, which he refers to, is familiar in this tradition of the
desert and occurs in many versions: the monk to whom the devil
appears dressed in majesty and claiming to be Christ, and who is
dispelled by the monk who refuses to see Christ glorified while on
earth.[28] A quotation from Athanasius, *Life of St Antony*, 'All who saw
him took delight in him', reveals his familiarity with this basic
monastic source, a familiarity confirmed by his reference to the *Life
of Antony the Great* in his edition of Augustine's *Confessions*.[29]

But what is most striking, beyond quotations, is the sense one has
in reading Pusey's works of the 'huge silence and great quiet'[30] of
Nitria, Scetis and the Cells, within the nineteenth-century pages. The
lifelong programme of conversion of life according to the gospel, the
identification with Christ crucified, lies at the centre of fourth-century
Egypt and the Anglican religious revival. Nor was Pusey, like the
monks, without a deep apprehension of the life of the Spirit which is
given to those who so embrace the cross, without which the language
of crucifixion and sorrow of heart can be simply self-pity and destruction. The proof that it is indeed the cross of Christ that is embraced
lies in the life of the monk with Christ in his resurrection: 'they who
so pray', he wrote, 'will find that their last prayer upon earth in the
name of Jesus will melt itself into the first halleluia of heaven'.[31] Most
movingly, both in his preface to the translation he made of the
forbidding Surin and in his own fierce sermon, 'Christianity without
the cross a corruption of the Gospel of Christ', he makes use of a
translation of the most tender of medieval monastic hymns, St
Bernard on the Name of Jesus: 'No tongue of man hath power to
tell/ No written words can prove/ But he who loveth knoweth well/
what Jesus is to love.'[32]

The Oxford apostles, like the desert monks, strike a sombre note
when they write of the inner life of repentance; but, like the monks,
they were not always grave. It was said of Abba Antony that one
day he was relaxing with some of the brothers and a hunter came
by and was shocked at such levity. So Antony told him to bend his
bow and shoot an arrow; and another; and another; until the hunter
protested that if he kept his bow always strung tight it would snap;
even so, said Antony, even so is the life of the monk.[33] So we find
the good Keble unable to accept the proposal of his new penitent
Pusey that he should not smile (an asceticism as familiar in the desert
as in the Rule of St Benedict), protesting that he should remember
the care he had for others, especially children.[34] Newman also could
relax, and coming one day to visit Mr Pusey for solemn conversation
instead took the young Puseys on his knees and told them about an

old woman who had a magic broomstick that went to the well to
fetch water for her; until she became tired of it and broke it in two;
and what did she have but two little broomsticks going to the well
to fetch water for her.[35] Pusey himself could relax with children and
not only with his own Lucy and Philip who shared so closely his
ideals. It is no surprise then to notice that these grave divines adopted
one of the popular literary styles of the day in order to popularise
the religious life, and wrote novels. Keble of course was the over-
whelmingly popular poet of the group; Newman, like Wiseman, produced his novel of the early Church, *Callista*, to Wiseman's *Fabiola*.
Others followed them – Shorthouse had popularised Little Gidding
in his novel *John Inglesant*; John Mason Neale was to write and publish
many short stories and novels, popularising the early Church and
monasticism. Apart from the most famous, *Ayton Priory*, there is for
instance *The Quai of the Discori*, a novel about Arius, who looks
remarkably like a nineteenth-century heretic, with his daughter
Helladia, dying of that interesting scourge of the nineteenth century,
tuberculosis. To her bedside Neale brings, in fact, Antony the Great
and his words echo the tradition of the desert: 'My child,' he says,
'I am a sinner who dwells in the desert.'[36] In another novel, *The
Lazar House of Leros*, an amazing book, centred around that strange
figure the seventeenth-century Patriach of Constantinople, Cyril
Lucaris is who had Calvinist sympathies. Sophia, the heroine,
becomes a nun and undertakes work which would have appealed to
many an Anglican sister of mercy – nursing those with leprosy.
Significantly she does not die of this, but as a martyr, that other kind
of witness to total consecration to God, which has always given to
monasticism its chief image.[37] From Dr Pusey we have, alas, no
novel. But once on holiday on Hayling Island with Philip and Lucy
he became the centre of a group of children: 'We were very merry
at times,' wrote one of the adults later, 'little children were more at
home with him than the rest of the world'. To them he told at least
one story and his choice is perhaps typical of his life and prayer:

> one day one of the boys asked him to tell them a story. He agreed,
> and taking down a beautiful print of the Good Shepherd, gathered
> us all around him and drew out the story of the lost sheep and the
> Good Shepherd in such language as the little ones could well
> understand and with many a word of help for the elder children
> around whose little troubles he knew a good deal about.[38]

The lives and writings of Pusey, Newman and Keble became a
new spring of life within the Church of England. Today the external
expressions of their work have largely disappeared or changed
radically; but the secret of love, prayer and sacrifice hidden in the
heart of the movement survives and still carries with it their conviction of the power of God in the lives of men. Perhaps, if we called
for rebels like the Tractarians, they would place the sign of the cross

again over the secularisation of the world. There is already within the Church of England a silent rebellion of the heart, which follows and deepens the teaching of the first Oxford rebels and makes its own a prayer from the Evangelical tradition of the Church of England: 'O Lord, revive Thy Church; and begin with me'.

1. e.g. Aelred of Rievaulx, *On Spiritual Friendship*, ed. A. Hoste and C. H. Talbot (Corpus Christianorum 1981), Bk 1.69, p. 301, *'Deus amicitia est'*.
2. H. P. Liddon, *Life of E. B. Pusey*, 4 vols (London 1894), I, ch. 18, p. 434 (hereinafter 'Liddon').
3. R. W. Southern, Presidential Address, *RHS, Aspects of the European Tradition of Historical Writing*, IV, 'The Sense of the Past', iv.p.263, in *TRHS*, 5th ser., 23 (1973).
4. Liddon I, p. 419.
5. ibid. p. 410.
6. ibid. p. 423.
7. Quoted by G. Rowell, in *The Vision Glorious* (Oxford 1983), p. 78 (hereinafter 'Rowell').
8. Claudius of Turin, *P.L.*, civ. Col. 617.
9. Philip Schaff, in Preface to *Nicene and Post-Nicene Fathers*, III (New York 1887), p. iv.
10. Claudius Rutilius Namatianus, *De Reditu Suo* ed. J. Vessereau (1933), Book 1, 439–452, p. 23.
11. J. Keble, *The Christian Year* (London 1827).
12. R. H. Froude, *Remains* (London 1838), I, p. 322.
13. Quoted by A. M. Allchin: *The Silent Rebellion: Anglican religious communities 1845–1900* (London 1958), p. 62. This invaluable book remains the key to an understanding of religious life in the Church of England.
14. ibid. esp. ch. 3–8.
15. *Lives of the Desert Fathers*, ed. N. Russell and B. Ward (Oxford 1979), Introduction, p. 50.
16. *Sayings of the Desert Fathers* tr. B. Ward (Oxford 1974), Antony, 4, p. 2.
17. ibid. Moses, 3, p. 141.
18. ibid. Apollo, 2, p. 31.
19. Cassian, *Institutes*, Book IV, xxxiii.
20. B. Ward, tr., *The Wisdom of the Desert Fathers* (The Apophthegmata Patrum, Anonymous Series) (Oxford 1975), p. 3, No. 11.
21. Liddon, III, p. 96.
22. *Prayers and Meditations to the Holy Trinity and our Lord Jesus Christ, by St Anselm of Canterbury* (London 1856). Preface by E. B. Pusey.
23. E. B. Pusey, *Sermons during the Season from Advent to Whitsuntide* (London 1848²), p. 59, quoted, Rowell, p. 82.
24. ibid. p. 355, quoted, Rowell, p. 83.
25. id., Leeds Sermons (London 1847²) p. 176, quoted, Rowell, p. 85.
26. id., *Parochial Sermons* (London 1878, rev. edn), III, p. 50, quoted, Rowell, p. 84.
27. ibid. p. 211, quoted, Rowell, p. 86.
28. Quoted by E. B. Pusey in his preface to *Foundations of the Spiritual Life* by Jean Joseph Surin (London 1844).

29. E. B. Pusey, ed., St Augustine, *Confessions*, Bibliotheca Patrum (Oxford 1838), I, pp. 134–5.
30. *Lives of the Desert Fathers*, p. 149.
31. E. B. Pusey, *The Miracles of Prayer* (London 1866), pp. 28–30, quoted, Rowell, p. 87.
32. id., preface to Surin.
33. *Sayings of the Desert Fathers*, Antony 13, p. 3.
34. Liddon, III, p. 108.
35. ibid. I, pp. 407–8.
36. J. M. Neale, *The Quai of the Discori* (London 1847), p. 83.
37. id., *The Lazar House of Leros* (London 1849), p. 95.
38. Liddon, III, p. 187.

15

The Understanding of Unity in Tractarian Theology and Spirituality*

A. M. Allchin

Our relationship to the Oxford Movement is something which has altered radically during the last thirty years. Our own situation has changed so much that we can sometimes see the past in new ways. Perhaps I may explain these statements autobiographically. Thirty years ago, when I was working on a thesis on Tractarian history, the Oxford Movement would at times still seem very close. My supervisor was the late Dr Claude Jenkins, Regius Professor of Ecclesiastical History, a man of prodigious, if sometimes disorganised learning. He loved to recall how as a boy in Oxford he had seen Newman on one of his last visits to the university. 'The most beautiful face I have ever seen,' he would repeat with emphasis. The house in the corner of Tom Quad was always spoken of as 'Dr Pusey's house, Dr Danby's as it is now', as if Pusey had left it a few months before. Processing into cathedral he would never walk over Dr Pusey's grave, he always walked around it. Like Pusey he would kneel down in the pulpit before delivering his sermon. On one memorable occasion at the Pusey House, he began an after-dinner speech with the words, 'I cannot think why I have been asked to speak on this occasion, for I have to admit that I never actually knew Dr Pusey personally.' But it was not only through Dr Jenkins that the Oxford Movement seemed close. In some old-fashioned clergy houses, in the guest houses of some religious communities, time seemed to have stood still. There could still be seen the last relics of what had been a great and vital movement, a movement whose direct influence could still be faintly felt.

Now after thirty years the world and the Church have changed beyond all recognition. The last vestiges of the Oxford Movement have been swept away. No one at Cowley can any longer give you memories of Father Founder. Some of the original Oxford sisterhoods are no more. The Oxford Movement, in that sense, has vanished for ever. And yet at this very time we seem in a curious way to have come closer to the original leaders of the movement than we were a generation ago. As we have got further from them in time we have come to be able to see them in a new and larger perspective for we

* © 1986 A. M. Allchin.

see more of the ways in which their influence has spread. As we have lost sight of the details, we seem to be able to see more of the outlines of the movement.

Let me expand this generalization.

(a) We live in a time which is heavy with the sense of catastrophe and apocalypse. It was this sense which the Oxford leaders had in ways which may at times seem to us exaggerated, but which may also seem to us to be prophetic. Newman in Tract 1 spoke of bishops being ready to be martyrs. In our time many bishops, Catholic, Orthodox and also Anglican, have followed Christ in that way. Like Kierkegaard in Denmark, the Oxford men sensed that the old Christendom was coming to an end. We are living in the midst of that end. It is often the youngest of their expositors who see their relevance most clearly.

(b) But while in the world at large, and also within the Church, we live through the experience of the break-up of inherited patterns of thought and action, within the Church we have also received unlooked for confirmations, assurances of the inherent vitality and unity of the Christian tradition. Through the breakdown of the old, a new pattern comes to birth. One of the most important examples of this has come from the presence in our western Christian world, in Paris, Oxford, New York, of the living witness of eastern Orthodoxy, a witness which has been virtually absent from western Christendom for more than nine centuries. This presence of Orthodoxy in our midst has a particular significance for Anglicans, since our tradition has since the Reformation shown a constant if hesitant tendency to turn towards the East to find its own deepest roots and direction. Reading the chapters on Keble, Newman and Pusey, in a survey like Geoffrey Rowell's *The Vision Glorious*, one may well ask whether the primary clue to understanding the basic intuitions of the Oxford Movement does not lie here; in seeing it as a sudden epiphany within the Christian West, of the prayer, the vision, the theology of the Greek Fathers. In a remarkable way, since their direct contacts with eastern Orthodoxy were minimal, they succeeded in penetrating into its ethos. The doctrine of *theosis* is the key to understanding their whole vision of Christian faith and life. Without understanding that, we shall grasp little of the inspiration behind what happened in Oxford 150 years ago. It is small wonder that so much of the teaching of the movement has not yet been heard or understood. It needs to be read against an eastern Christian background. It looks towards a fuller understanding of unity. We have yet to catch up with its prophetic vision.

(c) But there is another event in the history of the Church in the last thirty years which has altered for ever our evaluation of the Oxford Movement, and that is the Second Vatican Council and all that has followed from it. Suddenly and apparently unexpectedly, though in reality there had been much hidden preparation, the

apostolic see of Rome has turned to face the divided Christian families
of East and West in a new spirit of love and recognition. The old
claim to universality has been re-interpreted inclusively and no longer
exclusively. The Tractarian vision of an underlying unity which holds
together churches outwardly separated (what has been called the
branch theory) has been newly affirmed in ways they could scarcely
have foreseen. For the bishop of Old Rome and the bishop of New
Rome to embrace one another as brothers, and to recognise one
another's churches as sister churches is a confirmation of the deepest
Tractarian convictions about the continuing unity of East and West
despite nine centuries of separation. For the Pope to stand with the
Archbishop of Canterbury and the Moderator of the Free Church
Federal Council at the high altar of Canterbury Cathedral, and to
affirm with them our common baptismal faith, is a fulfilment of their
prayers and hopes which goes beyond what they could have
imagined. By their insistent affirmation of the oneness and catholicity
of their Church, while remaining out of communion with Constantinople and Rome, the Tractarians put a great question mark against
the finality of the separations both of the eleventh and the sixteenth
centuries. They refused to think that God the Holy Spirit had ceased
to act on both sides of the schisms. Now that the interrupted dialogue
between Rome and the Reformation is everywhere being taken up
anew, we can see the unexpected fulfilment of prayers which they
were among the first to frame.

Let us be specific and come to the heart of the matter, to that
great, and from the Anglican point of view, catastrophic event which
brought the first phase of the movement to its conclusion, Newman's
conversion. How should we see that event? As one which hardened
the barriers between Canterbury and Rome? Anglicans have often
seen it in that way. Or can we think of it as an event which casts
down the barriers between them? Let us listen to Pusey on this
subject, writing in the *English Churchman* less than a week after the
fateful event. That Pusey could be severe and demanding, especially
with himself, no one could deny. He was a man who knew much
grief, but it was a grief which made for joy, the *charopoion penthos* of
the Fathers, not a self-regarding grief which leads to death. It is such
a man who could write of Newman's going in terms such as these:

Yet, since God is with us still, he can bring us even through this
loss. We ought not indeed to disguise the greatness of it. It is the
intensest loss we could have had. They who have won him know
his value. It may be a comfort to us that they do . . . With us, he
was laid aside. Our Church has not known how to employ him.
And since this was so, it seemed as if a sharp sword were lying in
its scabbard, or hung up in the sanctuary because there was no
one to wield it. Here was one marked out as a great instrument of
God, fitted through his whole training, of which, through a friend-

ship of twenty-two years, I have seen at least some glimpses, to carry out some great design for the restoration of the Church; and now after he had begun that work among ourselves, in retirement – his work taken out of his hands, and not directly acting upon our Church. I do not mean, of course, that he felt this, or that it influenced him. I speak of it only as a fact. He is gone unconscious (as all great instruments of God are) what he himself is. He has gone as a simple act of duty with no view for himself, placing himself entirely in God's hands. And such are they whom God employs. He seems then to me not so much gone from us, as transplanted into another part of the Vineyard, where the full energies of his powerful mind can be employed, which here they were not. And who knows what in the mysterious purposes of God's good Providence may be the effect of such a person among them? You too have felt that it is what is unholy on both sides which keeps us apart. It is not what is true in the Roman system, against which the strong feeling of ordinary religious persons among us is directed, but against what is unholy in her practice. It is not anything in our Church which keeps them from acknowledging us, but heresy existing more or less within us. As each, by God's grace, grows in holiness, each Church will recognize, more and more, the Presence of God's Holy Spirit in the other; and what now hinders the union of the Western Church will fall off. As the contest with unbelief increases, the Churches which have received and transmitted the substance of the Faith as deposited in our common Creeds must be on the same side with it. One can see great ends to be brought about by this present sorrow; and the more so, because he, the chosen instrument of them, sees them not for himself. It is perhaps the greatest event which has happened since the Communion of the Churches has been interrupted, that such a one so formed in our Church, and the work of God's Spirit as dwelling within her, should be transplanted to theirs. If anything could open their eyes to what is good in us, or soften in us any wrong prejudices against them, it would be the presence of such an one, nurtured and grown to such ripeness in our Church, and now removed to theirs. If we have by our misdeeds (personal or other) 'sold our brother', God, we may trust, willeth thereby to 'preserve life.'[1]

Reading this passage in the 1950s it seemed quixotic, generous, but somewhat unreal. Could anyone, at that time, think that Newman's conversion had brought the two churches closer together? Was it not simply an outstanding example of an individual conversion, which had left the churches just where they were, or even hardened the division between them? Before Vatican II it would have been difficult to see in Pusey's letter more than the expression of a particularly warm-hearted friendship. Even Liddon, so little inclined to be critical of the master, felt ill at ease with it. 'The heart has a logic of its own, which is often, in point of courage and generosity, more than a match for that of the bare understanding.'[2]

Looking at these lines now, after Vatican II, knowing as we do the great but often hidden influence of Newman's thought on the theology which found expression in that council, witnessing as we have done the revolution in the relationships between the churches which the council has brought about, we can see in Pusey's words a genuine substance of prophetic insight.

These words were written at a time of great anxiety and difficulty for Pusey. One of the consequences of his move which Newman can hardly have envisaged was the acute problem which it created for those he left behind in the Church of England. Thrust into the position of leadership in a movement whose outstanding spokesman had just abandoned it, Keble and Pusey found themselves bearing a burden of publicity and unpopularity which neither of them can have relished. And at this very moment, mid-October 1845, Pusey was preparing for the consecration of St Saviour's Church in Leeds, a new church in an industrial slum which he had built with his own money. He had planned to mark the consecration with a week-long series of sermons on the basic principles of the Catholic faith. There were to be nineteen sermons in all, ten of which were to be the work of Pusey. The others were to be contributed by friends, Keble, Manning, Charles Marriott, Isaac Williams among them. In the end scarcely any of the friends were able to come, though some sent the texts of their sermons. These Pusey read on their behalf. Seventeen of the nineteen sermons were preached by him.

Pusey's own sermons in this series are among the most striking and profound of all his utterances. If we wished to consider Pusey as a mystical theologian, there are few better sources to which we could turn. But here we are concerned with Pusey's thoughts about unity, his attitude towards divisions in the Church, in these weeks so close to Newman's final departure. We turn primarily to a sermon entitled 'Progress our Perfection', on the text Philippians 3:15–16, 'Let us therefore, as many as be perfect, be thus minded; and if in anything ye be otherwise minded, God shall reveal even this to you. Nevertheless whereto we have already attained, let us walk by the same rule, let us mind the same thing.'

The theme of the sermon is that in this world perfection consists in recognising our imperfection, in being always ready to press on. St Augustine, St John Chrysostom, St Bernard, are all quoted to support St Paul in this intention. And then as we come to the question of the unity of Christians among themselves, we come, perhaps surprisingly, to an allusion to one of Newman's best known hymns.

Yes, my brethren, wherever we are in the Christian course, as we have all one End, God; one Faith, in the one Object of Faith, the

Ever-blessed, Co-equal, Co-eternal Trinity, as that Faith has been
revealed to us and fenced against every error in our Creeds; one
Hope, to see him; one Food of Life, himself in his sacraments; one
Spirit who is the life of all the members of the one body, the life
of all alike, although his gifts be manifold; so also for saints or
penitents, there is one only way to Heaven, to walk on in him who
is the Way, to hold fast that ye have and press onward. This is
the remedy of all doubts in faith and practice. 'One step,' it has
been well said, 'enough for me.' Today is thine by the gift of God;
tomorrow yet is his. Fear not whither you may be led; see only
that you be now 'led by the Spirit of God', led, not going before,
not holding back, not standing still, but 'led'. It is the very part
of faith, to go forth, as Abraham went, not knowing whither he
went . . . Hold fast what thou hast; act up to what thou believest;
walk on in his strength; halt not; and what thou yet lackest, he
has said, 'He will reveal it unto thee'.[3]

These precepts which are true of personal life are true also in
relation to our whole apprehension of the Christian faith, and to our
attempts, both personal and corporate, to go beyond our divisions.

Thus alone, my brethren, may we hope that in doctrine, our sad
manifold divisions will cease. Thus they must cease; for, he has
said, 'God will reveal it unto thee.' Not by disputing, not by
teaching alone, not by learning, not by reading Holy Scripture
only, shalt thou know the truth; but by gaining, through God's
grace, a childlike mind; by cleansing the eye of the soul, by
obedience . . . In those who love him and keep his commandments,
should he himself dwell by his Spirit, the life of their life, the Spirit
of their spirit; and so should they know things by a higher sense,
not of reasoning, or influence, but in his own clear light, whose
Spirit liveth in their hearts by love . . .
    And this might, as I said, bring us back from our manifold
divisions to the one Truth. Where there are so many discordant
voices, all cannot be right. How then shall we discover the one
voice of our one Shepherd, which his sheep know and follow him?
He has taught us, Hold fast that ye have; walk ye on by the light
of it; and what ye see not now, ye shall see; what ye see dimly
shall be clear . . . Would that we, living in a Church founded by
God, could all so live, day by day, in the devotions, creeds, hymns
of praise, preserved to us in her, as to imbibe their spirit in
ourselves. This would be no uncertain voice to us, did we learn it
in the presence and the house of God. Words have a different
meaning when tossed to and fro in argument, and when prayed in
the communion of saints, the voice of the one Dove, moaning to
its Lord. The full heart, then, stints not the meaning of the words;
thinks not how little they may mean but how much; a ray of light
falls on them from above; we stand not without them as judges,

but within them as worshippers; he who has taught the Church
her prayers is present in our souls; and with his blessed unction
from above, comfort, life and fire of love, anoints both them and
us. Disputing divides, devotion knits in one; for in it we pray to
One, through One, by One.[4]

It is a remarkable passage which foreshadows much of what has
been discovered about spiritual ecumenism in the last hundred years.
The way towards unity is to be found through entering more deeply
into the spirit of the liturgy, by letting the one Holy Spirit pray in
us and through us. In prayer words reveal their fullness of meaning,
their *mira profunditas*, their many-levelled quality. We stand within
the words as worshippers, not outside them as judges, and in so
doing the Holy Spirit descends on us and on them, and opens our
hearts and our minds to the true catholicity of their meaning.
Through the words we are able to see into the reconciling mystery
of God. The hardness and shallowness which controversial usage has
given to the concepts of theology and the words of faith, is healed
and removed by their renewed use in prayer and worship; for there
we look at those words in all their poetic meaning and mystery. We
do not use them as weapons with which to attack others. When we
do that we always lose the sense of their true value. Rather we use
them for our own healing and the healing of others. We allow the
eyes of our mind to be cleansed by God's grace. We allow the
Church's thinking to be rooted in its praying.

Pusey continues:

Our strifes everywhere are not about what we hold, but about
what any do not hold. It has been said at times, 'let us drop our
differences and hold fast what we have in common'. Good were it
and true if it be not thereby meant, that any should part with any
truth he holds. We need not, should not, part with any truth; but
mere denials are not truths.

If only, Pusey says, we would hold on to what is positive and affirm-
ative in our faith, we should find that it is not opposed to the
affirmation of others.

Men deny plain, blessed truths, because they think them opposed
to other truths, which they are not; and which, would they only
hold the truths they have, God would make plain unto them.
Wouldest thou arrive at the whole truth of God; part with nothing
which the grace of God has worked into thine inward life; deny
nothing which the Church of God has not denied; whatsoever thou
hast attained, seek by that grace therein to grow; and pray that
he perfect whatsoever be lacking to thy faith; and he from whom
thou hast what thou hast, will give thee what as yet thou hast not;
he himself has promised that 'he will reveal it unto you'.[5]

Pusey here enunciates a number of basic principles for ecumenical work. Hold fast what you have, work on from there. Look at what other people affirm, where they are usually in the right, not at what they deny, where they are usually in the wrong; recognise a reconciling principle of catholicity, that truths which appear to be opposed to one another in fact may be seen to be complementary. It is remarkable how close Pusey here comes to the position of F. D. Maurice, set out in his great work. *The Kingdom of Christ*, first published in 1838. In that book Maurice has sketched out a set of ecumenical convictions, a basic ecumenical methodology which has been used by Anglicans ever since. He too affirms that people are generally right in what they affirm and wrong in what they deny. In point after point of Christian doctrine Maurice seeks to show how the positive principles of Lutherans, Quakers, Calvinists, Anglicans, can all, when rightly understood, be seen to co-inhere in a Catholic faith larger and more inclusive than any of their partial one-sided statements.

Maurice, it is true, approaches the question in a more philosophical way than Pusey. Lying behind his convictions on this matter, there is not only his painful personal experience of Christian disunity within his own family circle, but Coleridge's formulation of the question in *Biographia Literaria*, a formulation which itself draws directly on the work of Leibniz more than a century earlier: 'We have imprisoned our own conceptions by the lines which we have drawn in order to exclude the conceptions of others. *J'ai trouvé que la plupart des sectes ont raison dans une bonne partie de ce qu'elles avancent, mais non pas tant en ce qu'elles nient.*' And this affirmation is itself based on one of the fundamental axioms of Leibniz's thought. '*Nicht leicht etwas zu verachten*' – not to despise anything easily. '*Je ne meprise rien facilement*,' he writes in another place, and again, '*Itaque nihil puto contemnendum*.'[6] This sense of respect for the inherent mystery of things chimes in well, when transposed into a more explicitly religious key, with the Tractarian emphasis on the necessity for reverence and wonder in our approach to the things of God. It reinforces Pusey's intuition about the way in which any belief which has been proved in life is not to be lightly cast aside. When we see how close Pusey and Maurice come to one another in this vital question it becomes all the more tragic that in later life they should have become locked together in fruitless and bitter controversy, in which neither truly honoured the vision which they had earlier enunciated.

We can see more in detail how Pusey worked out these convictions in the preface to his translation of Surin's work, *The Foundations of the Spiritual Life*, published in the previous year. Pusey begins by asserting the inner identity of what is Evangelical with what is Catholic. Catholic teaching, he says, 'assumes as its basis the same two truths, which have been strongly, though of late somewhat nakedly, enforced among ourselves as the instrument of conversion to God', that is, a sense of our corruption and nothingness on the one side, the proclamation of the love of God in the cross, on the other.

> For these, if expanded duly on all sides, must needs contain the whole of our reception of the Gospel. The fervent words of a saint's devotion. 'Who art Thou, and who am I?' are a summary of the Gospel, since they comprise him who is our end, as he is, and ourselves in relation to him. The conviction of our own nothingness and of God's infinity, our sinfulness and his holiness, our own boundless misery and his boundless mercy, is the condition for prayer, the preparation for Sacraments, the ground of penitence, the element of faith, hope and love. Of course, this must not be understood negatively (as too often it is) to the exclusion or disparagement of any truth not distinctly expressed in it (this were at once heretical), but as entering into all; not as a distinct confession of faith, but as the outline of it, and the life of all our practice.[7]

For Pusey, as for Newman, at the heart of Catholic faith and life there lies the basic Evangelical affirmation of the personal encounter between God and each human soul, the encounter between the sinfulness of man and the forgiving love of God made known in Christ. Without the realisation of this inwardness, this essential central point, the whole Catholic system can become dead and lifeless. The outward objective structure needs the subjective, inner principle. The inner experience needs for its development the given, outward framework. Thus Pusey goes on to say that he hopes that Surin will help:

> those who have an earnest perception of certain limited fundamental truths, to see the truths about which they are anxious, to be the very foundation of Catholic teachings . . . it is proposed to them, not to unlearn anything they have learnt of positive truth, but to act upon it, carry it out, expand it; to receive, it may be, the other truths in addition but to part with nothing which has been a portion of their own spiritual existence . . . Heresy itself consists in the denial of truth; it is simple poison, and must therefore destroy and not nourish. If there be anything in connexion with it which nourishes and preserves life, then it is not heresy, but faith, however mingled with misbelief.[8]

Here again we have theological affirmations with many implications. Heresy is seen as essentially negative and destructive. Where there is life in God, there must be truth, even if mingled with error. Partial truths held vigorously, practically, are preferable to more complete formulations of truth, when they are held in an abstract lifeless way. We see here evidence of Pusey's wide reading in the literature of pietism in the seventeenth and eighteenth century in Germany, no less than of his knowledge of the growth of evangelicalism in England. He recognises the strength and value of that movement. 'It was a vivid and energetic, however partial, preaching of the Cross, which by the providence of God broke in upon an age of torpor and easy ways in religion . . .' The Church system as taught in the eighteenth century had itself become imperfect and partial, not so much through the lack of particular items of belief, as through the abstract dry way in which it had been enforced.

> Both of the systems which were in conflict in the last century were partial, and could not meet together because they were so. Neither was extensive enough to embrace the other. Each had its strong points and its weak ones; each had its own texts; until at last people came tranquilly to divide Holy Scripture between them, leaving as the other's property what they could not master as their own.[9]

This is a very interesting formulation. It is a prime characteristic of narrow, partial systems that they seek to master, to appropriate as their own a part of the whole faith, some elements of the witness of Scripture. What is Catholic, according to the wholeness of faith, involves our being mastered, our being called to enter into a mystery of faith larger than our understanding of it. Pusey at once goes on:

> The true Catholic system, of course, is co-extensive with Holy Scripture. It must embrace all which a partial system cannot grasp. It can reconcile the doctrine of predestination with sacramental grace, the necessity of the entire conversion of sinners with baptismal regeneration, deep repentance with Christian joy, the acceptableness of good works with the imperfection of the Christian's best acts. It can combine forms of prayer with the freest and highest mental devotion, spiritual Communion with the intensest devotion for the sacramental, inspired understanding of Holy Scripture with implicit submission to the Church, the superiority of the teaching of the Holy Spirit with deference for divine learning.[10]

It would be interesting to analyse in detail this rather surprising list of polar opposites and to trace them back to points of controversy current at the time. But what is evident, taking them in general, is that Pusey's vision of catholicity is of a reality which holds together and reconciles theology and spirituality, the initiative of God and the response of man, the inner experience of prayer and faith and the outer framework of sacrament and tradition. Catholicity for him involves the bringing together of many elements of Christian faith and life which have become opposed to one another in the last four centuries of western Christendom. His vision still has much to say to us. Indeed it may have more to say to us now than it did at the time when Pusey first announced it. Here again he seems in the middle years of his life to have had a prophetic gift, which for one reason or another he could not fully sustain in the latter part of his life. The demands made on him by the uncongenial role of a party

leader, the sometimes unthinking way in which he let himself be
drawn into controversy and his apparent inability to discriminate
great matters from small when once involved in controversy, all these
things seem to have prevented him from living out fully the insights
of the 1840s. But this fact should not blind us to the remarkable
character of the vision of the Church's unity and catholicity which
he had during those years. It was a vision truly ecumenical in its
content, reconciling Evangelical and Catholic, the commitment of
prayer and devotion with the proportion and balance of faith, holding
together the freedom of the inner life of each member of the Church
with the given, corporate structures of sacrament and liturgy. The
rediscovery of the Greek and Latin Fathers as living masters of prayer
and faith had made possible a vision of the fullness of the mystery
of Christ, which has had surprising consequences for the bringing
together of the separated traditions of the Reformation and Rome.

What is still more unexpected is that this ecumenical vision has
consequences beyond the borders of Christendom. Here we are
entering upon a field where Pusey might well have been unwilling
to follow us. But the conviction that while doctrine divides, devotion
unites, the insight that when we pray a text we stand within it and
perceive its fullness of meaning, rather than standing outside it as a
critic or judge, the conviction that where there is life and holiness
there must also be truth to sustain it, all these are convictions which
have been and are of vital importance in the growing dialogue
between Christians and men of other faiths. As we can see from the
example of men like Thomas Merton, Jules Monchanin or William
Johnston, it is the way which passes through prayer to doctrine,
through spirituality to theology, which is most rewarding in this field.
And though in his own day Pusey could scarcely have seen the
question in the way in which it now unfolds, it is remarkable that in
the introduction to the first volume of his parochial sermons,
published in 1848, he not only speaks of the reconciliation of Catholic
and Evangelical but also shows himself aware of the growing attrac-
tions of Indian philosophy and religion, which were even then
apparent in Germany and the United States of America. Once again
there is a prophetic note to his writing. He seems almost to have
foreseen developments much more characteristic of our own generation than of his.

We said at the beginning that changes in our own situation had
made it possible to see the Oxford Movement in a new perspective.
We must go further and say that what, thirty years ago, had seemed
to be a closed episode in the past rapidly receding into the distance,
appears now to be a movement of new insights and new beginnings
which we are only now coming to appreciate more fully.

1. H. P. Liddon, *Life of Edward Bouverie Pusey*, II, pp. 460–1.

2. ibid. p. 465.
3. E. B. Pusey, *Sermons preached in St Saviour's Church, Leeds, 1845*, pp. 320–1.
4. ibid. pp. 321–4.
5. ibid. p. 324.
6. See the discussion of this point in Thomas McFarland, *Coleridge and the Pantheist Tradition* (Oxford 1969), pp. 135–8.
7. J. Surin, The *Foundations of the Spiritual Life, drawn from the Book of the Imitation of Christ* (1874 edn), pp. iii–iv.
8. ibid. p. iv.
9. ibid. pp. v–vii.
10. ibid. p. vii.